MATH-MAGIC

Book 3

Textbook in Mathematics for Class III

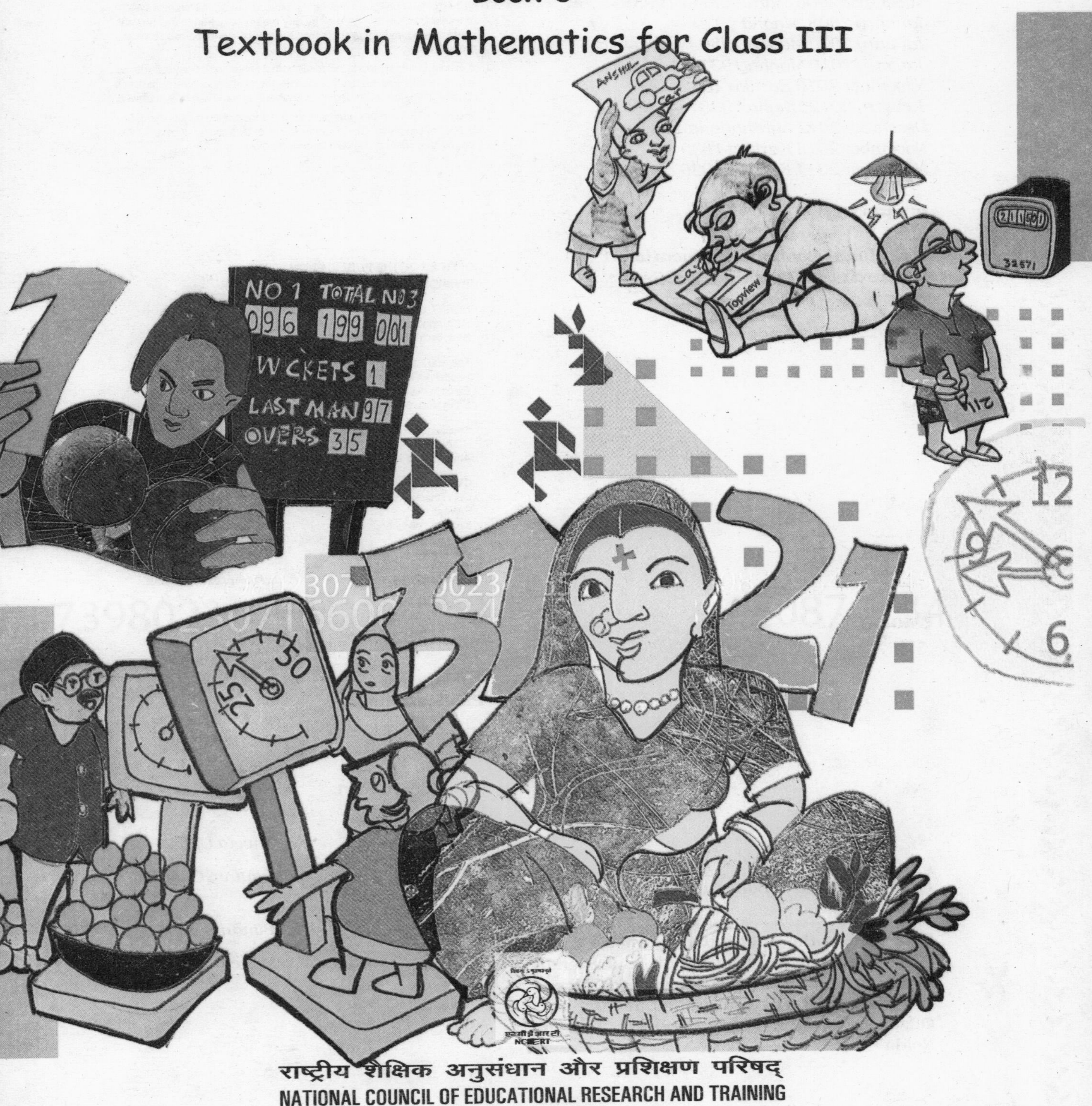

राष्ट्रीय शैक्षिक अनुसंधान और प्रशिक्षण परिषद्

NATIONAL COUNCIL OF EDUCATIONAL RESEARCH AND TRAINING

First Edition
February 2006 Phalguna 1927

Reprinted
November 2006 Agrahayana 1928
January 2008 Magha 1929
January 2009 Magha 1930
January 2010 Magha 1931
November 2010 Kartika 1932
January 2012 Magha 1933
December 2012 Agrahayana 1934
November 2013 Kartika 1935
November 2014 Kartika 1936

PD 400T IJ

₹ 50.00

Printed on 80 GSM paper with NCERT watermark

Published at the Publication Division by the Secretary, National Council of Educational Research and Training Sri Aurobindo Marg, New Delhi 110 016 and printed at Supreme Offset Press, 133, Udyog Kendra-I, Greater Noida

ISBN 81-7450-510-5

OFFICES OF THE PUBLICATION DIVISION, NCERT

NCERT Campus
Sri Aurobindo Marg
New Delhi 110 016 **Phone : 011-26562708**

108, 100 Feet Road
Hosdakere Halli Extension
Banashankari III Stage
Bangaluru 560 085 **Phone : 080-26725740**

Navjivan Trust Building
P.O.Navjivan
Ahmedabad 380 014 **Phone : 079-27541446**

CWC Campus
Opp. Dhankal Bus Stop
Panihati
Kolkata 700 114 **Phone : 033-25530454**

CWC Complex
Maligaon
Guwahati 781 021 **Phone : 0361-2674869**

Publication Team

Head, Publication Division	:	*N.K. Gupta*
Chief Production Officer	:	*Kalyan Banerjee*
Chief Editor	:	*Shveta Uppal*
Chief Business Manager	:	*Gautam Ganguly*
Editor	:	*Bijnan Sutar*
Production Assistant	:	*Mukesh Gaur*

Foreword

The National Curriculum Framework (NCF), 2005, recommends that children's life at school must be linked to their life outside the school. This principle marks a departure from the legacy of bookish learning which continues to shape our system and causes a gap between the school, home and community. The syllabi and textbooks developed on the basis of NCF 2005 signify an attempt to implement this basic idea. They also attempt to discourage rote learning and the maintenance of sharp boundaries between different subject areas. We hope these measures will take us significantly further in the direction of a child-centred system of education outlined in the National Policy on Education (1986).

The success of this effort depends on the steps that school principals and teachers will take to encourage children to reflect on their own learning and to pursue imaginative activities and questions. We must recognise that given space, time and freedom, children generate new knowledge by engaging with the information passed on to them by adults. Treating the prescribed textbook as the sole basis of the examination is one of the key reasons why other resources and sites of learning are ignored. Inculcating creativity and initiative is possible if we perceive and treat children as participants in learning, not as receivers of a fixed body of knowledge.

These aims imply considerable change in school routines and mode of functioning. Flexibility in the daily time-table is as necessary as rigour in implementing the annual calendar so that the required number of teaching days are actually devoted to teaching. The methods used for teaching and evaluation will also determine how effective this textbook proves for making children's life at school a happy experience, rather than a source of stress or boredom. Syllabus designers have tried to address the problem of curricular burden by restructuring and reorienting knowledge at different stages with greater consideration for child psychology and the time available for teaching. The textbook attempts to enhance this endeavour by giving higher priority and space to opportunities for contemplation and wondering, discussion in small groups, and activities requiring hands-on experience.

National Council of Educational Research and Training (NCERT) appreciates the hard work done by the Textbook Development Committee responsible for this book. We wish to thank the Chairperson of the Advisory Committee, Professor Anita Rampal and the Chief Advisor for this book, Professor Amitabha Mukherjee for guiding the work of this committee. Several teachers contributed to the development of this textbook; we are grateful to their principals for making this possible. We are indebted to the institutions and organisations which have generously permitted us to draw upon their resources, material and personnel. We are especially grateful to the members of the National Monitoring Committee, appointed by the Department of Secondary and Higher Education, Ministry of Human Resource Development under the Chairpersonship of Professor Mrinal Miri and Professor G.P. Deshpande, for their valuable time and contribution. As an organisation committed to the systemic reform and continuous improvement in the quality of its products, NCERT welcomes comments and suggestions which will enable us to undertake further revision and refinement.

Director
National Council of Educational
Research and Training

New Delhi
20 December 2005

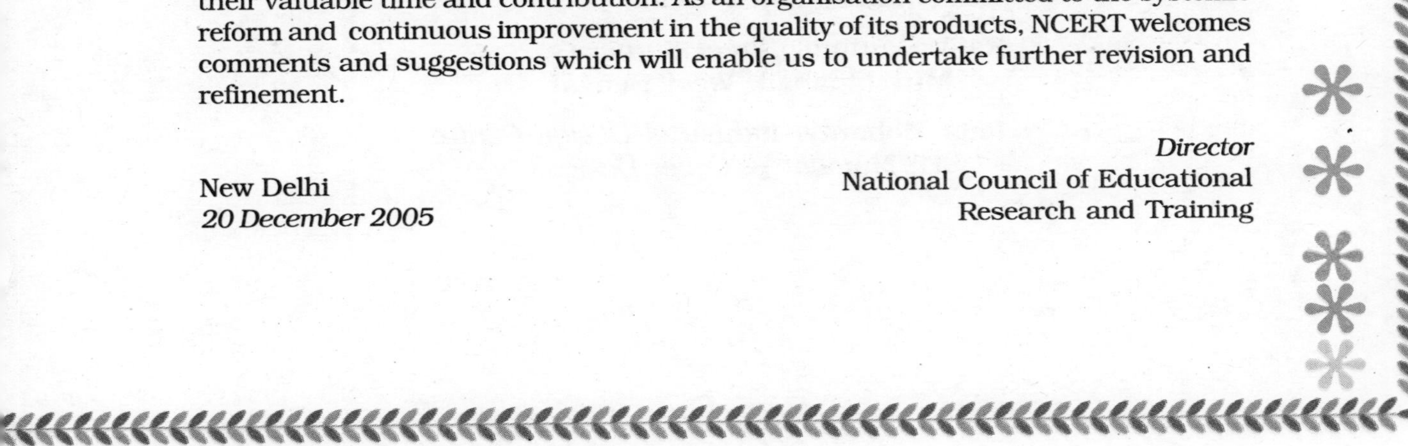

Textbook Development Committee

CHAIRPERSON, ADVISORY COMMITTEE FOR TEXTBOOKS AT THE PRIMARY LEVEL

Anita Rampal, *Professor,* Department of Education, Delhi University, Delhi

CHIEF ADVISOR

Amitabha Mukherjee, *Director*, Centre for Science Education and Communication (CSEC), Delhi University, Delhi

MEMBERS

Anita Rampal, *Professor,* Department of Education, Delhi University, Delhi

Asha Kala, *Lecturer*, DEE, Institute of Home Economics, New Delhi

Asmita Varma, *Primary Teacher*, Navyug School, Lodhi Road, New Delhi

Bhavna, *Lecturer*, DEE, Gargi College, New Delhi

Dharam Parkash, *Reader*, CIET, NCERT

Preeti Chaddha, *Primary Teacher*, Basic School, CIE, Delhi University, Delhi

Suneeta Mishra, *Primary Teacher*, Nagar Palika School, Bapudham, New Delhi

MEMBER-COORDINATOR

Surja Kumari, *Professor,* Department of Elementary Education, NCERT

Illustrations and Design Team

Srivi Kalyan, Chennai

Anita Varma, Delhi

Taposhi Ghoshal, New Delhi

Vandana Bist, New Delhi

Rajiv Gautam, *Street Survivors,* Murshidabad, West Bengal

Raja Mohanty, *Industrial Design Centre IIT, Mumbai — Cover Design*

Acknowledgements

National Council of Educational Research and Training (NCERT) thanks the following persons and institutions for their contribution towards this textbook. Special thanks are due to the Centre for Science Education and Communication (CSEC), Delhi University, for providing academic support and hosting all the textbook development workshops. The teams were fully supported by the staff and put in tremendous effort through long working hours even on holidays.

The Council acknowledges the advisory support of Rohit Dhankar, *Director,* Digantar, Jaipur and the contributions of K. Subramaniam, Homi Bhabha Centre for Science Education, Mumbai and Indu Dogra, *Primary Teacher*, M.C.D. Model School, Seva Nagar, New Delhi. This book has drawn upon ideas from existing materials, such as, *Numeracy Counts!* (National Literacy Resource Centre, Mussoorie), *Mathematics For All* (Homi Babha Centre for Science Education, Mumbai) and *Mathematics: A Textbook for Class III* (SCERT, Delhi).

The Council also gratefully acknowledges the contributions of Sandeep Mishra and Shashi Vij for their voluntary technical support and of Sadiq Saeed and Subodh Kumar, *DTP Operators* and Inderjeet Jairath, *Proof Reader* in shaping this book.

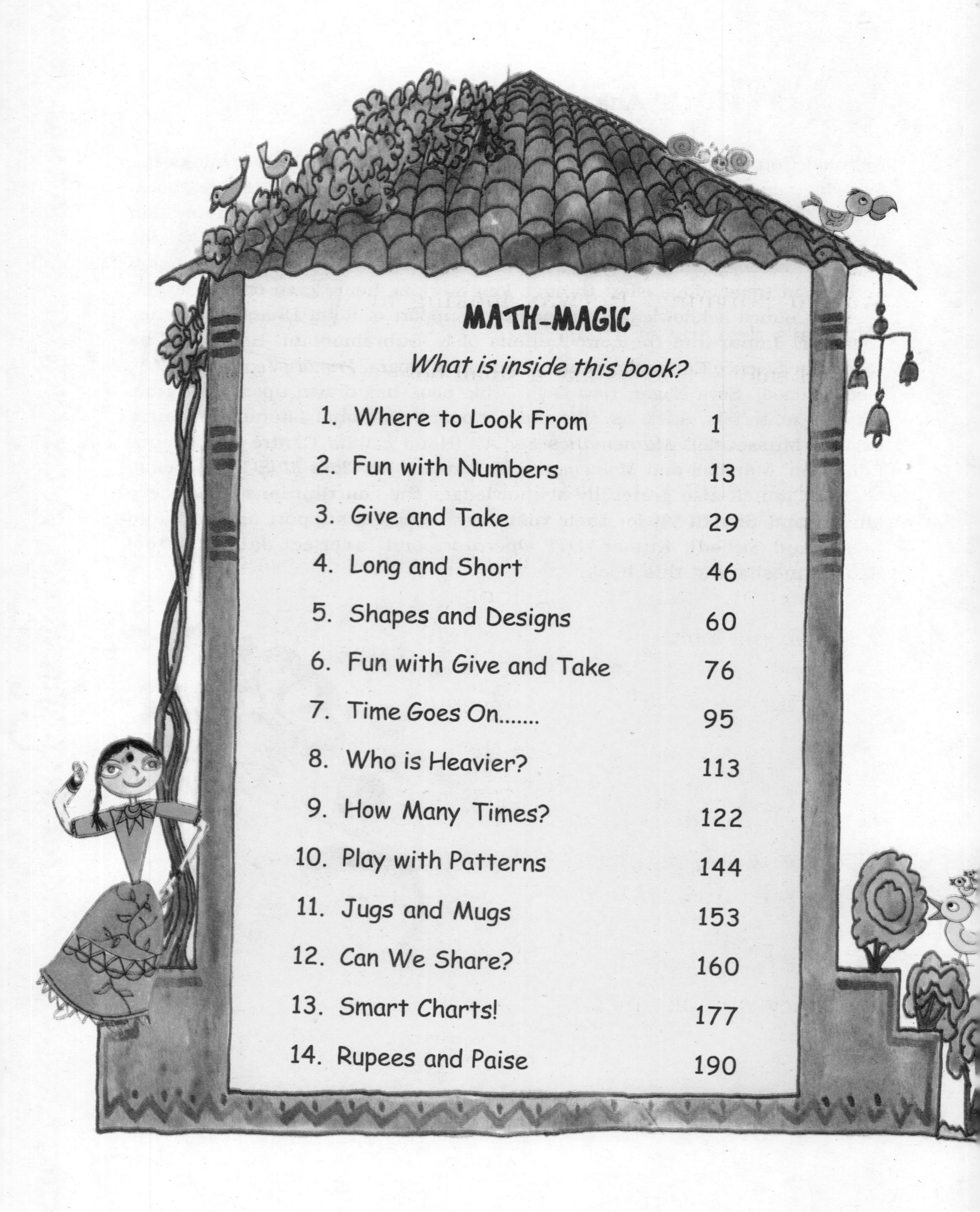

MATH-MAGIC

What is inside this book?

1. Where to Look From 1
2. Fun with Numbers 13
3. Give and Take 29
4. Long and Short 46
5. Shapes and Designs 60
6. Fun with Give and Take 76
7. Time Goes On....... 95
8. Who is Heavier? 113
9. How Many Times? 122
10. Play with Patterns 144
11. Jugs and Mugs 153
12. Can We Share? 160
13. Smart Charts! 177
14. Rupees and Paise 190

Where to Look From

Our teacher told us to draw a picture of a car. We all drew the car differently. Next day, when we showed our pictures to each other, we were very excited. But Anshul started laughing. He was looking at Dheeraj's drawing of a car.

Anshul said — it looks like a small box kept in a bigger one. Then Anshul showed his drawing to Dheeraj.

Both of them drew the picture of the same car. But the drawings look different.

Dheeraj said he had looked at the car from the terrace. Do you think his funny drawing is right?

✡ Have you looked at things from different sides?
Do they look the same or different?

✡ Look at the pictures drawn here. How does the table look from the side? Which picture is from the top?

Some pictures are drawn below. Imagine how these things will look if seen from the top.

Will they look like this?

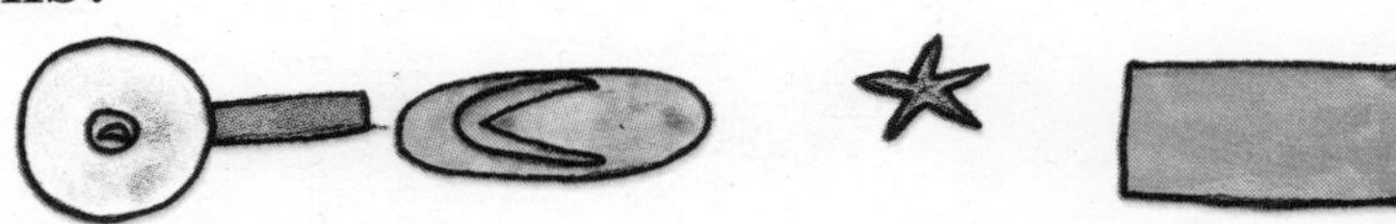

Practice Time

A. A cat is peeping into a classroom. Can you help her find out where the teacher is?

B. Here are some pictures. Find out from where you have to look to see the things this way.

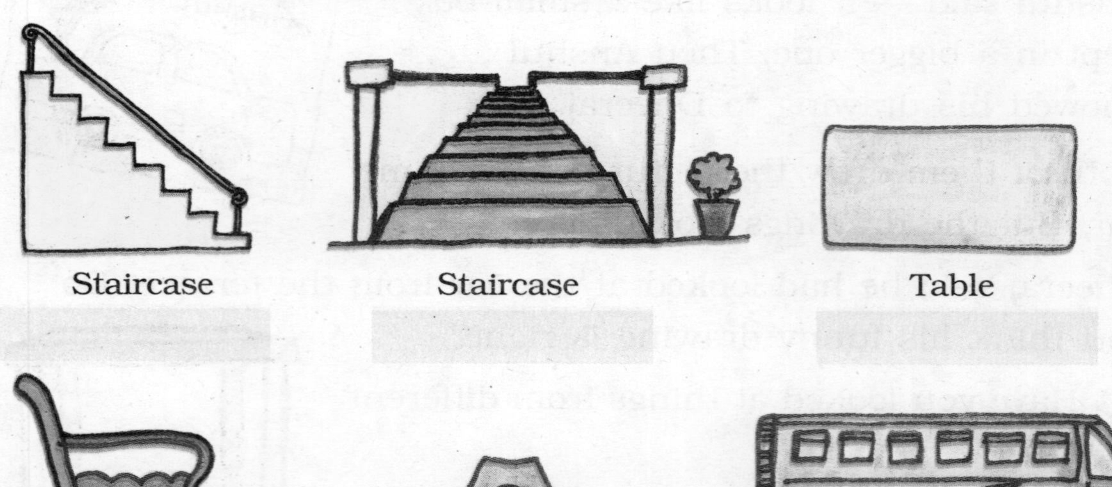

Staircase Staircase Table

Chair Pencil Bus

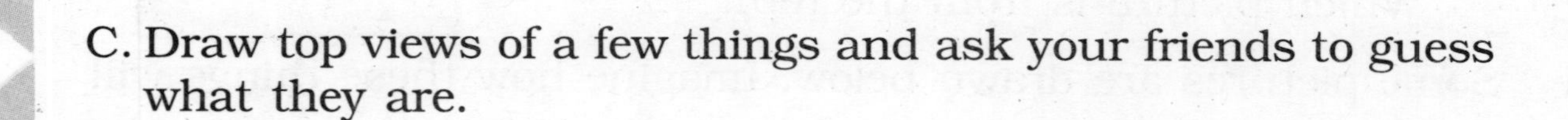

C. Draw top views of a few things and ask your friends to guess what they are.

Rangoli

You can also try and use the dots given below to make patterns. Two examples have been drawn here.

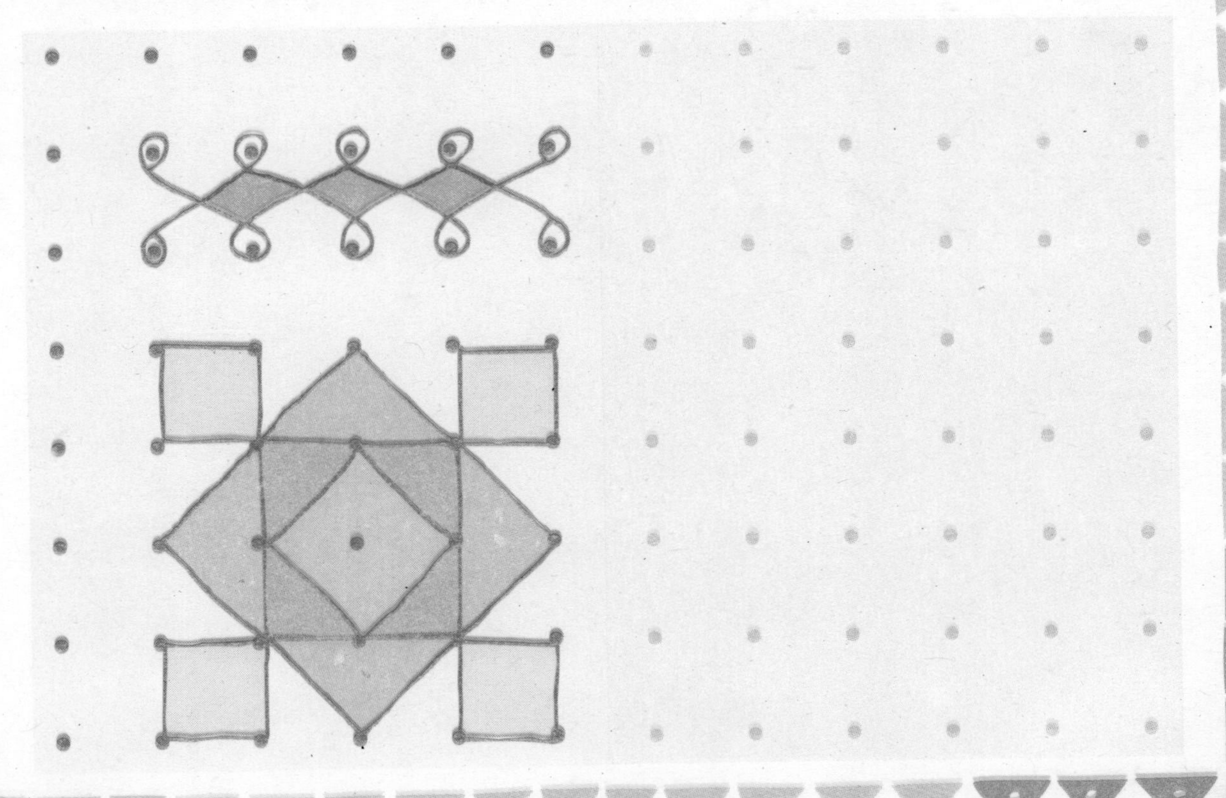

Make Other Patterns Yourself

1. Copy these shapes on the dot grid. Note that some lines in the shapes are straight and some are not.

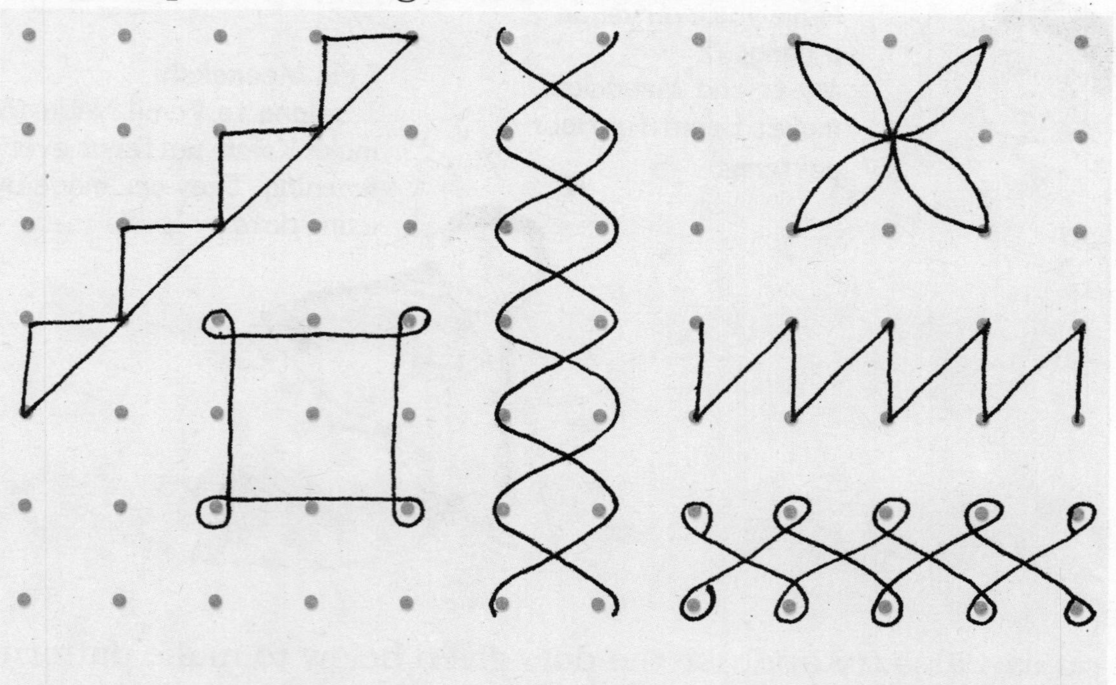

2. Use the dot grid given below to draw your own designs and shapes.

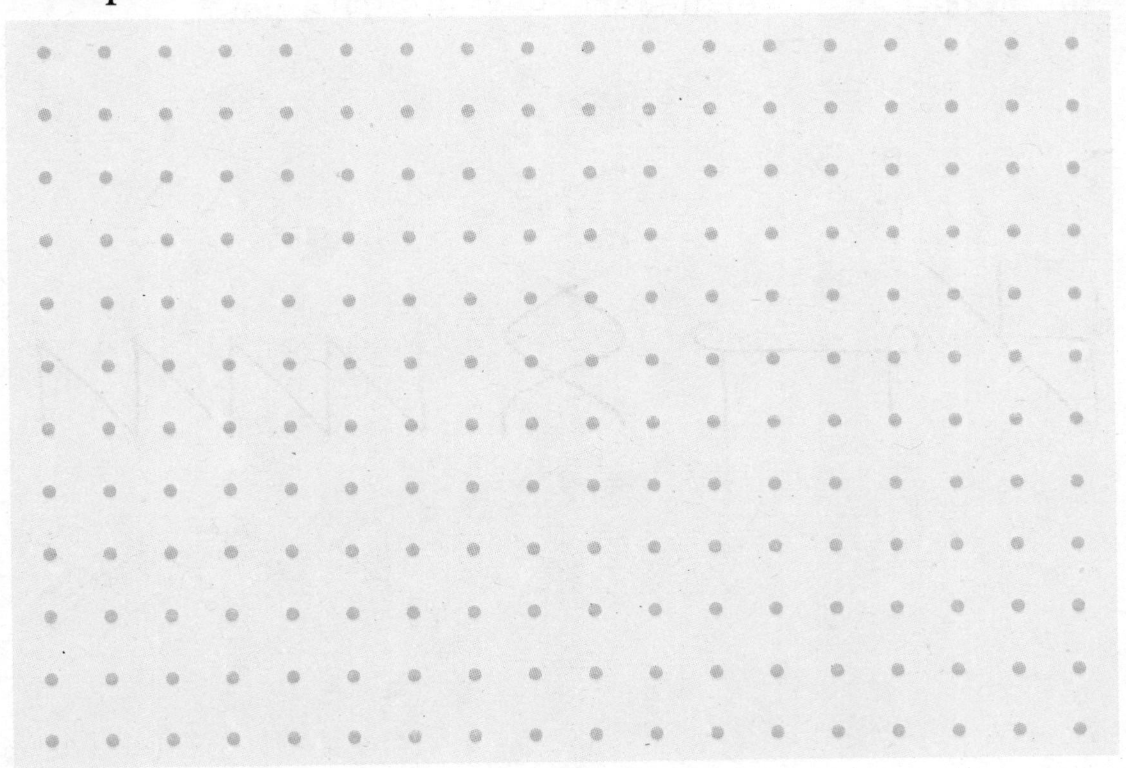

3. Complete these figures to make squares and rectangles.

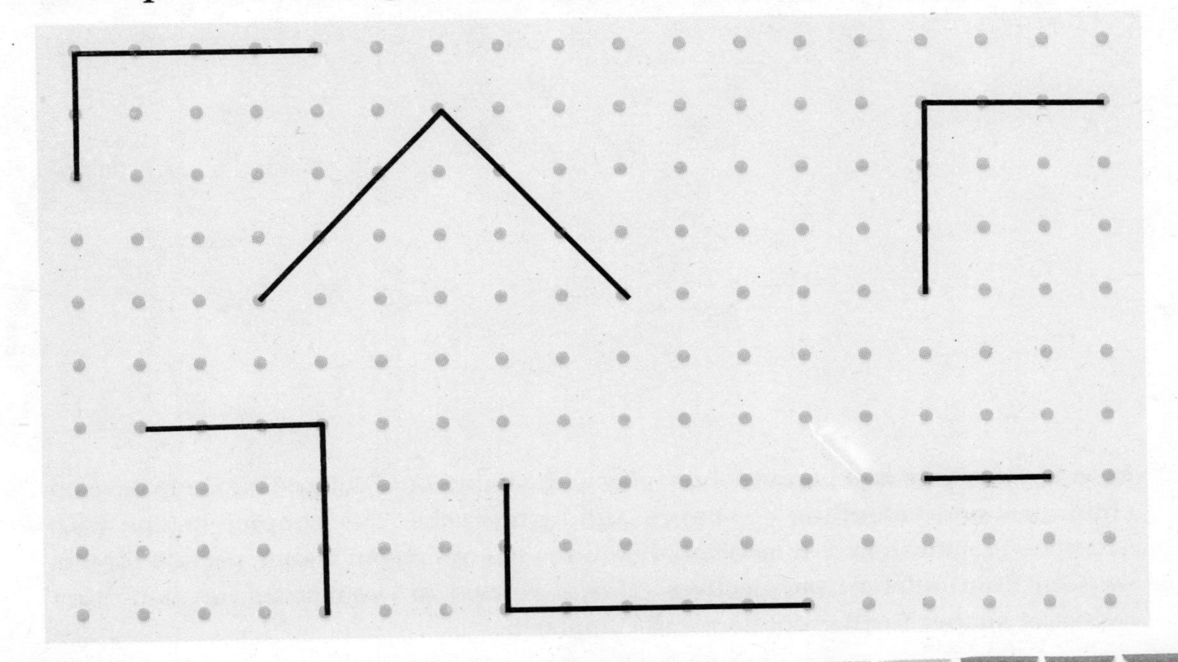

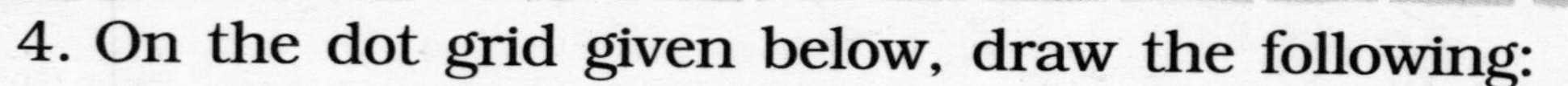

4. On the dot grid given below, draw the following:

a) a kite
b) a leaf
c) a flower
d) a boat
e) a star
f) a pot

Note for teachers and parents: Free play with shapes on a dot grid can help develop children's understanding of shapes and symmetries. The chapter begins with activities to show how 2-dimensional pictures can represent 3-dimensional objects as seen from different perspectives. This is related to symmetries, an important aspect of shapes further developed in Chapter 5.

Tit for Tat

One day Amina met a painter.

After a while the painter showed her the picture.

Amina gave him a hundred-rupee note.

The painter had made many such pictures in which he drew only one half of the things. Draw the other half of these pictures and find out what these things are. Try doing it with a mirror.

Can we repeat the painter's trick, while drawing pictures of the following?

If you ask the painter to draw things which cannot be divided into two similar mirror halves, then he cannot play the trick. Draw three more such things which do not have similar mirror halves.

Mirror Halves

Look at the pictures given below. Does the dotted line divide each picture into two similar mirror halves?

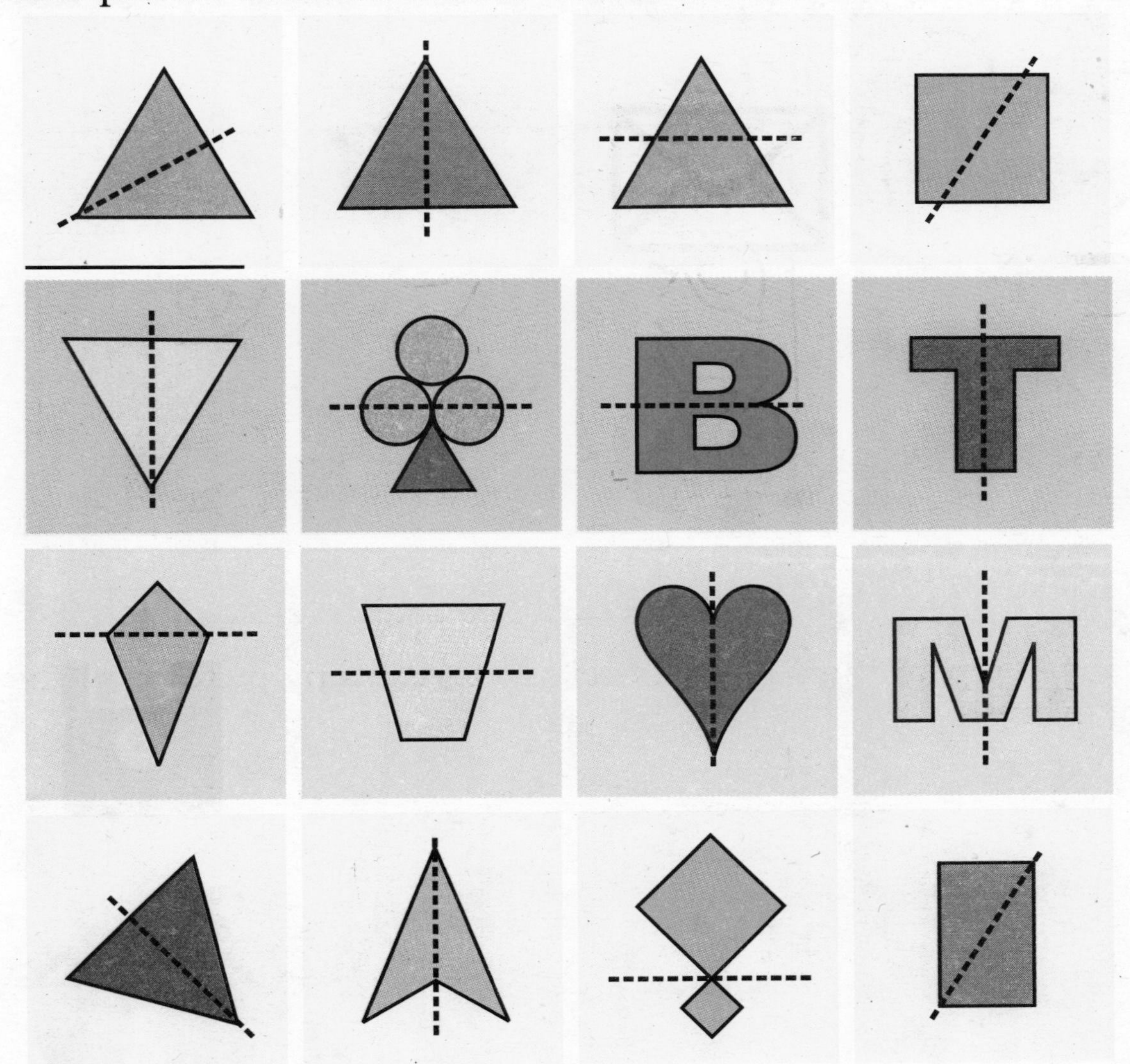

Give some more examples.

In two rectangles above, the dotted line cuts each into identical halves, but note that they are not mirror halves?

Using a dotted line, can you divide the following pictures into two similar halves?

Using such letters we can also make words which have similar halves.

Making A Mask

Now, I can teach you how to make the mask of a cat...

Take a piece of paper.

1. Fold it along the middle.

2. On one side draw the figure.

3. Cut it out using a pair of scissors.

4. Now open the fold and make the eyes, nose etc.

5. Colour it and tie a rubber band on its back.

Your mask is ready.

You can make more such masks by taking help from the following pictures.

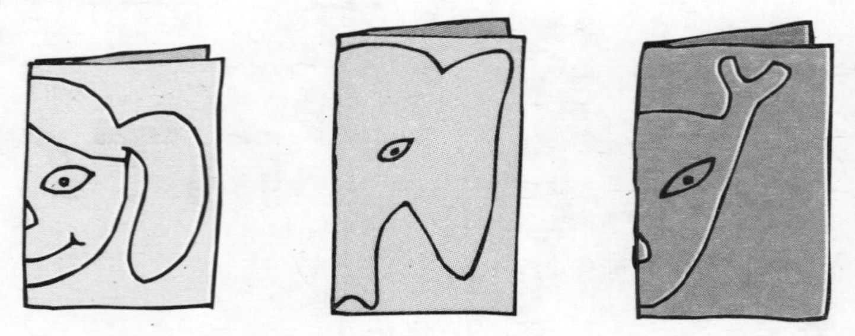

2 Fun with Numbers

Radhika, Gauri, Vicky, Indra and Sunil were collecting *Imli* (tamarind) seeds.

- _______ collected the most seeds.
- Sunil will collect _______ more seeds to be equal to Vicky.
- If Radhika gets 6 more seeds, she will have _______.
- How many children have more than 40 seeds?_______
- _______ needs 3 more seeds to have 50.
- Sunil has 2 seeds less than 40 and _______ has 2 seeds more than 40.

Dot Game

Guess the number of dots in the circle. Now count and check your guess. Play this game with your friends by making circles. See who can guess best.

Children need interesting exercises to help them with visual estimation of numbers – of things arranged randomly and in symmetrical groups. Teachers could use other instances, such as bundles of leaves sold in the market, the school assembly, designs on mats, etc. to make them guess and estimate different numbers. In this book an ant has been used to show the child that a guess or estimate has to be made.

Dhoni's Century

One-day match between India and South Africa in Guwahati......., India batting first......

Fill in the blanks:

Dhoni scored 96 + _____ = _______ runs.

How many runs do these players need to complete a century?

	Runs scored	*Runs needed to complete a century*
Player 1	93	______
Player 2	97	______
Player 3	89	______
Player 4	99	______

Numbers are understood not by reciting them in order but by making associations in familiar contexts. Here the idea of a "century" of runs is used. Teachers could add other examples from children's lives to think about 3-digit numbers. Encourage them to speak about large numbers even if they cannot read or write them.

Fill in the Blanks:

99-112		**195-206**	
Number (in figures)	*Number (in words)*	*Number (in figures)*	*Number (in words)*
99	Ninety-nine	195	One hundred ninety-five
100	One hundred	196	One hundred ninety-six
101	One hundred one	197	One hundred ninety-seven
102	______________	198	One hundred ninety-eight
103	One hundred three	___	One hundred ninety-nine
104	One hundred four	200	Two hundred
____	One hundred five	201	Two hundred one
106	One hundred six	___	______________
107	______________	203	Two hundred three
____	One hundred eight	___	Two hundred four
109	One hundred nine	205	Two hundred five
110	One hundred ten	206	______________
111	One hundred eleven		
____	One hundred twelve		

Oh! 206! Guess how many more to make a triple century?

Top Ten Scores in the Cricket World Cup

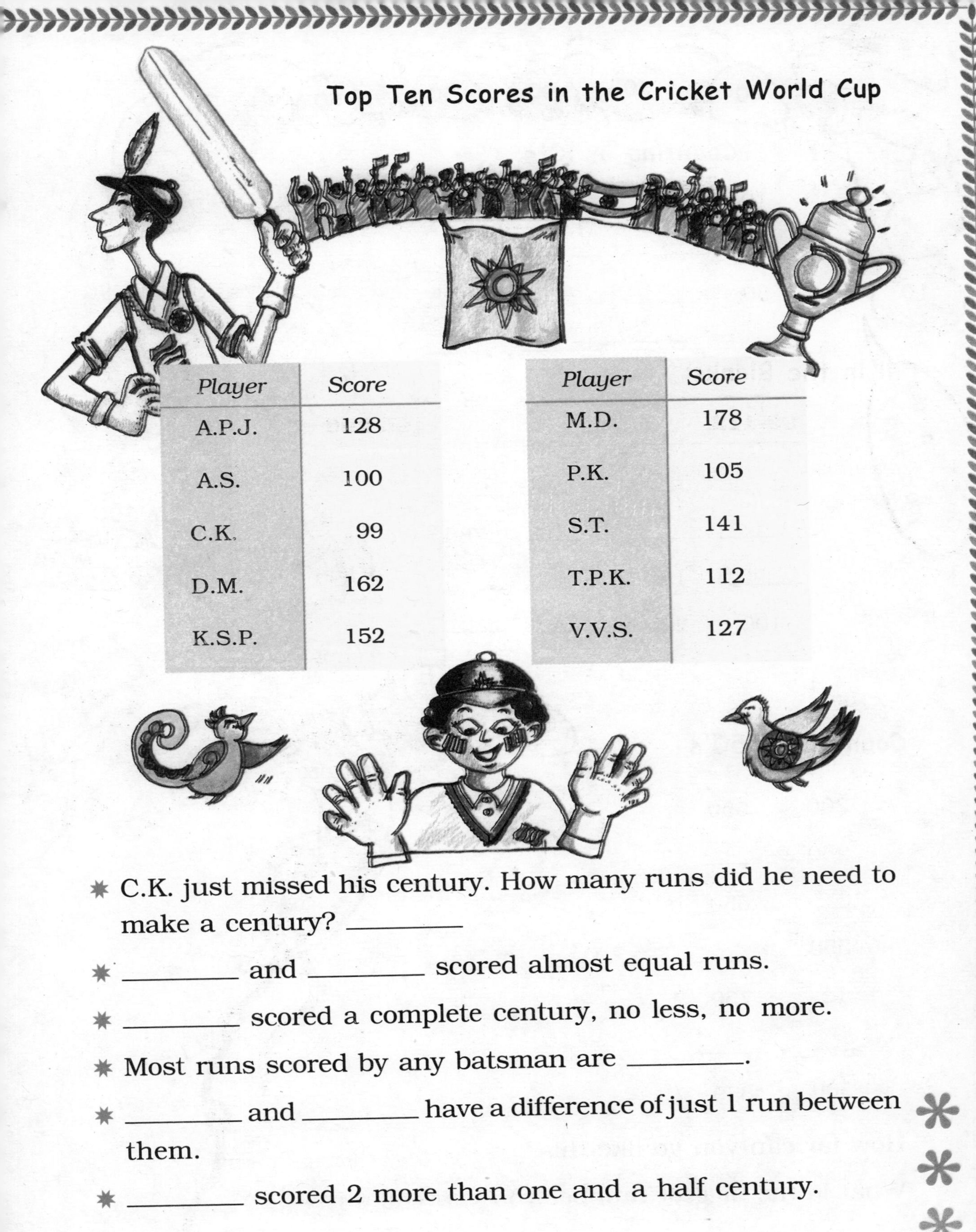

Player	Score
A.P.J.	128
A.S.	100
C.K.	99
D.M.	162
K.S.P.	152

Player	Score
M.D.	178
P.K.	105
S.T.	141
T.P.K.	112
V.V.S.	127

- C.K. just missed his century. How many runs did he need to make a century? ________
- ________ and ________ scored almost equal runs.
- ________ scored a complete century, no less, no more.
- Most runs scored by any batsman are ________.
- ________ and ________ have a difference of just 1 run between them.
- ________ scored 2 more than one and a half century.

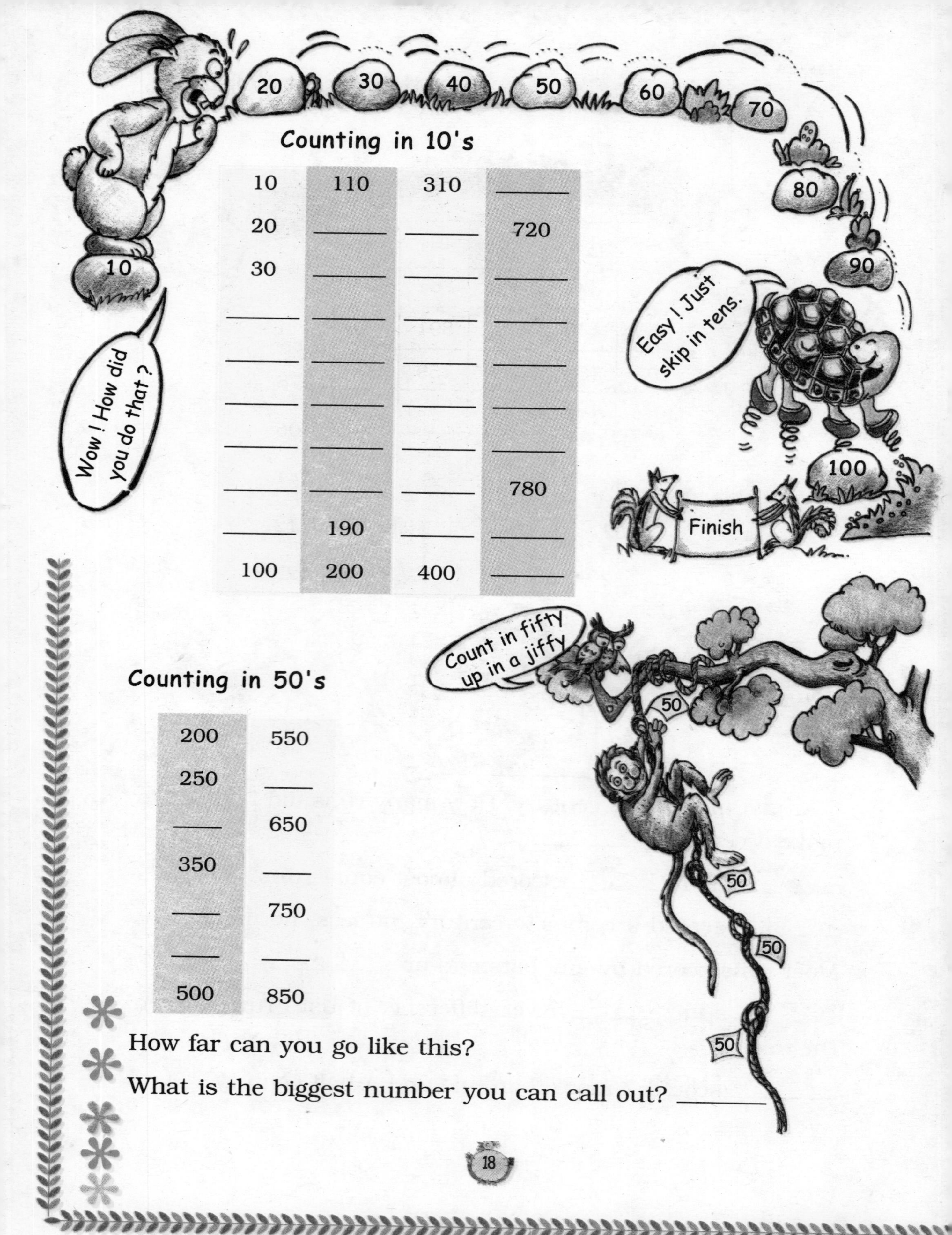

Counting in 10's

10	110	310	______
20	______	______	720
30	______	______	______
______	______	______	______
______	______	______	______
______	______	______	______
______	______	______	______
______	______	______	780
______	190	______	______
100	200	400	______

Counting in 50's

200	550
250	____
____	650
350	____
____	750
____	____
500	850

* How far can you go like this?
* What is the biggest number you can call out? ________

Colour the Numbers

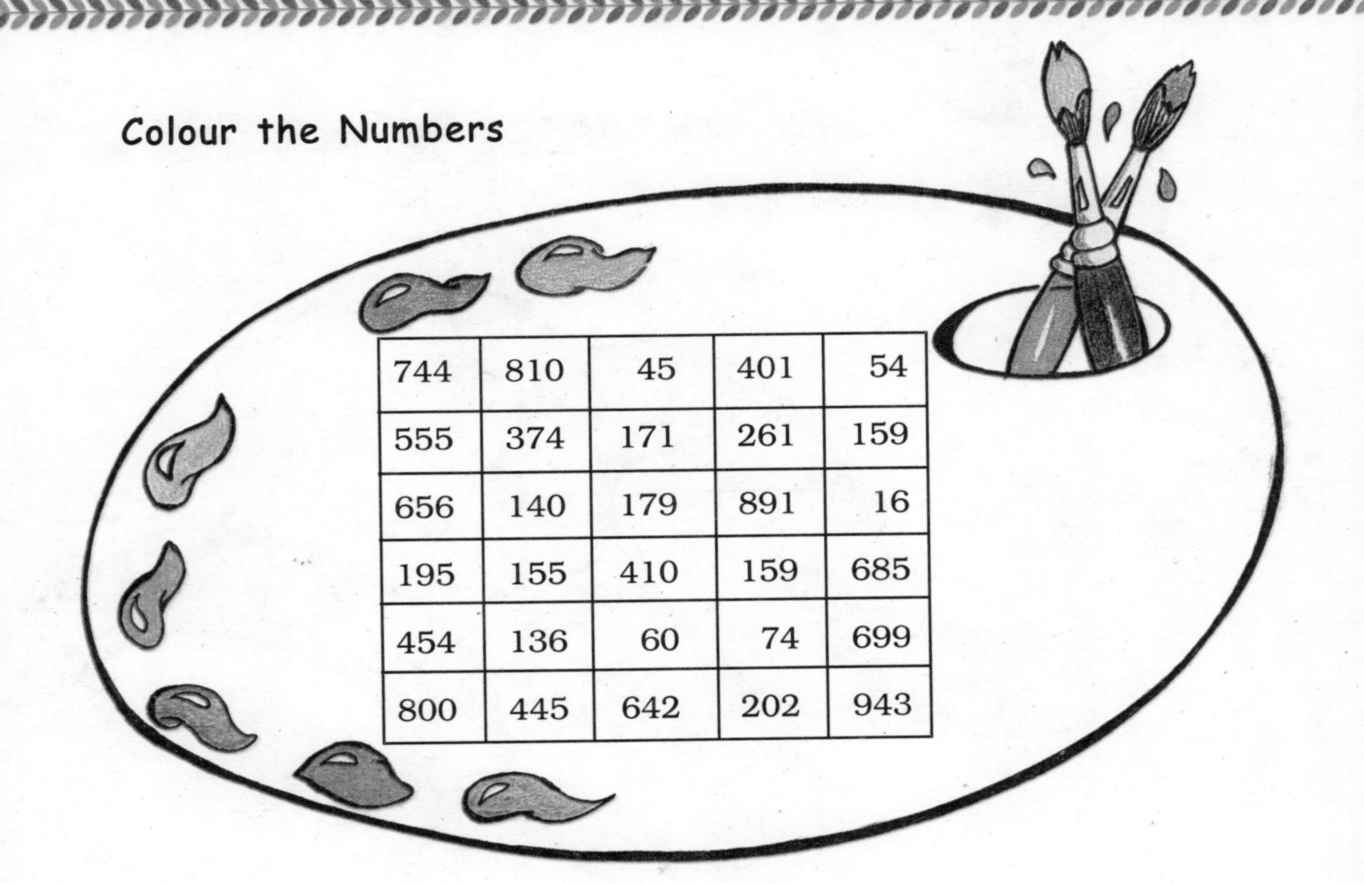

744	810	45	401	54
555	374	171	261	159
656	140	179	891	16
195	155	410	159	685
454	136	60	74	699
800	445	642	202	943

Find these numbers in the above chart. Colour them.

Green	*Red*	*Yellow*
One hundred forty	Fifty-four	Four hundred forty-five
Two hundred two	Sixty	Sixteen
Two hundred sixty-one	One hundred ninety-five	One hundred fifty-nine
Eight hundred	Five hundred fifty-five	Six hundred eighty-five
300 + 70 + 4	600 + 40 + 2	600 + 90 + 9
600 + 50 + 6	100 + 70 + 9	70 + 4
5 + 50 + 100	800 + 10	1 + 90 + 80

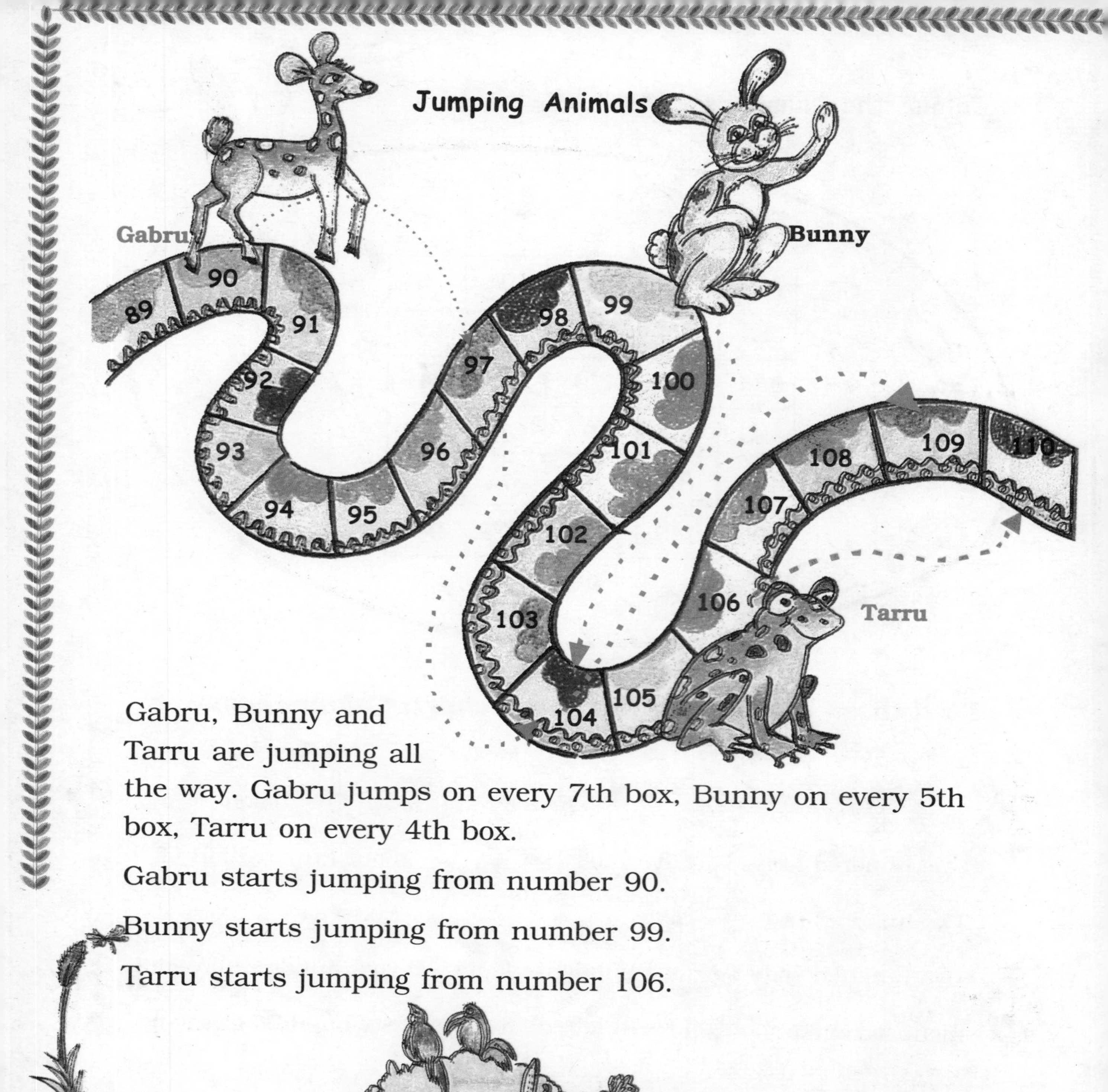

Gabru, Bunny and Tarru are jumping all the way. Gabru jumps on every 7th box, Bunny on every 5th box, Tarru on every 4th box.

Gabru starts jumping from number 90.

Bunny starts jumping from number 99.

Tarru starts jumping from number 106.

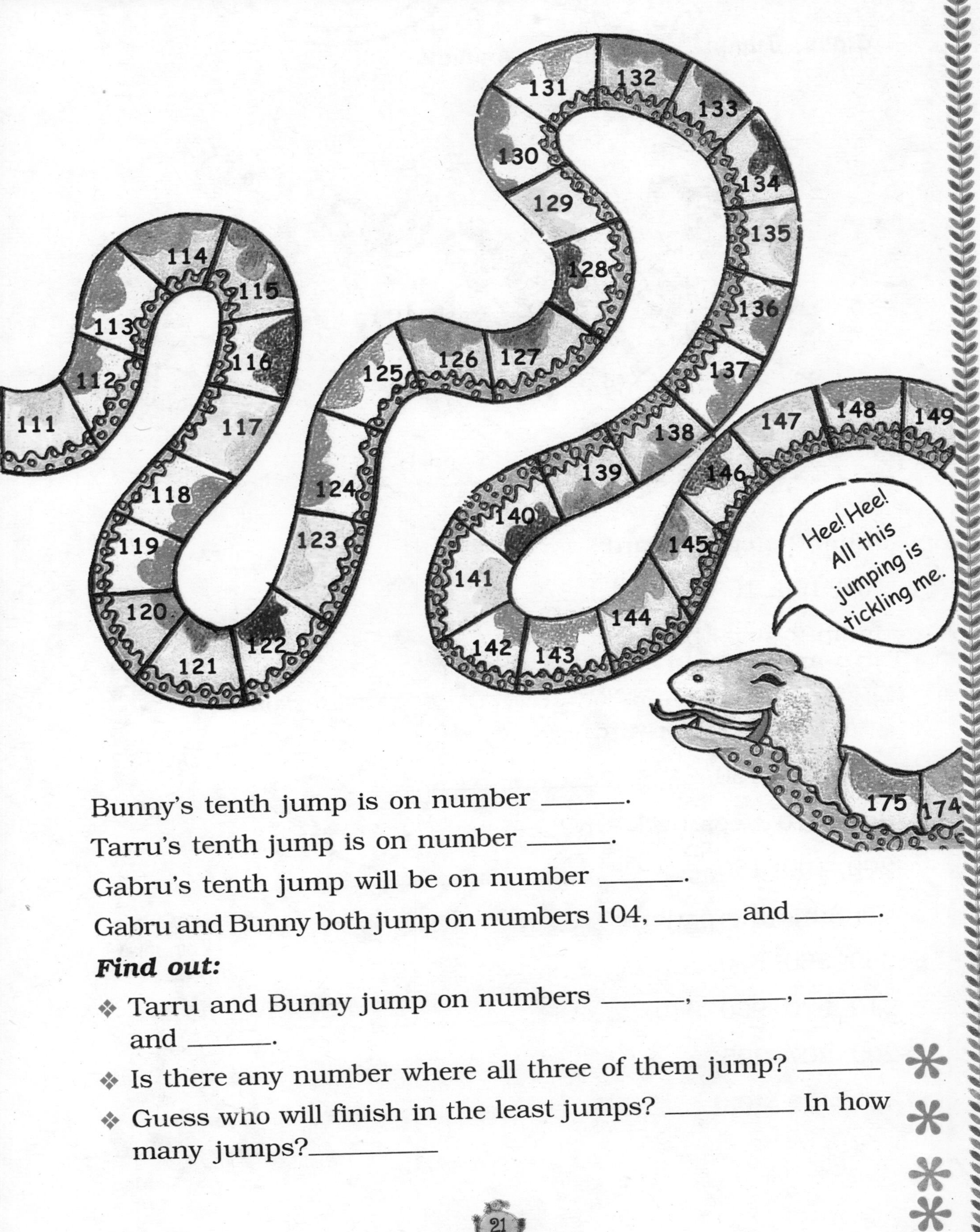

Bunny's tenth jump is on number ______.

Tarru's tenth jump is on number ______.

Gabru's tenth jump will be on number ______.

Gabru and Bunny both jump on numbers 104, ______ and ______.

Find out:

- Tarru and Bunny jump on numbers ______, ______, ______ and ______.
- Is there any number where all three of them jump? ______
- Guess who will finish in the least jumps? ________ In how many jumps?________

Class, Jump!

Jump 2 steps forward:

104, 106, 108, ______, ______, ______, ______.

Jump 2 steps backward:

262, 260, 258, ______, ______, ______, ______.

Jump 10 steps forward:

110, 120, 130, ______, ______, ______, ______.

Jump 10 steps backward:

200, 190, 180, ______, ______, ______, ______.

Continue the pattern:

550, 560, 570, ______, ______, ______, ______.

910, 920, 930, 940, ______, ______, ______, ______.

209, 207, 205, ______, ______, ______, ______.

401, 402, 403, ______, ______, ______, ______.

Join in!

JUMPING SCHOOL

Lazy Crazy Shop

This is the jungle shop. Lazy Crazy gives things only in packets of tens, hundreds and loose items.

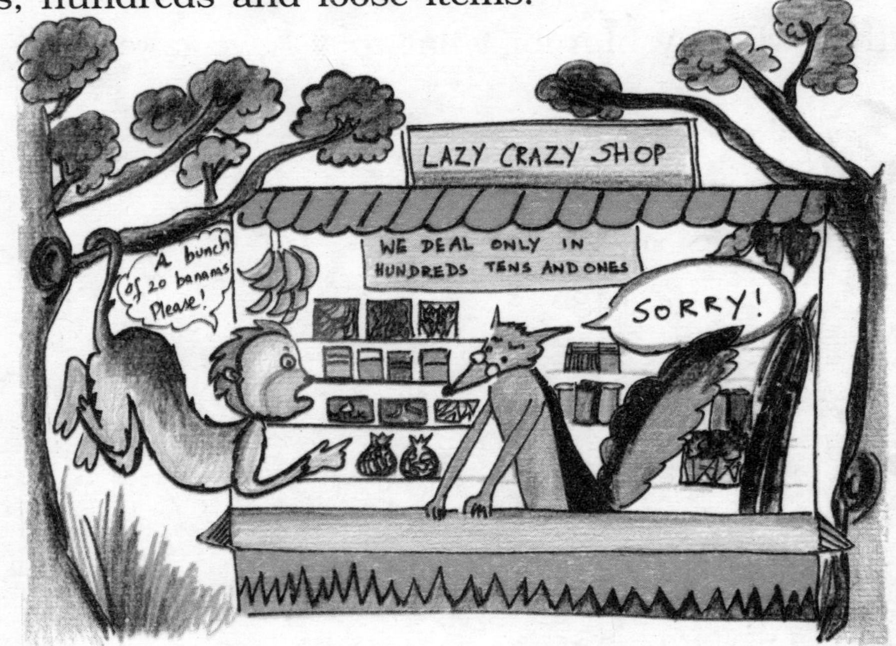

Find out how many packets of tens, hundreds and loose items each animal will take. Fill in the blanks.

	Packets of 100	*Packets of 10*	*Loose items*
143	100	10 10 10 10	
210	___	___	___
242	___	___	___
552	___	___	___

Lazy Crazy also has a crazy way of taking money. He takes only in 100 notes, 10 notes and coins. Now find out how they will pay him for what they have taken.

Rs 420

Rs 143

Rs 242

Rs 55

Who am I? Match with the number.

a) I come between 40 and 50 and there is a 5 in my name.	96
b) I have 9 in my name and am very close to 90.	150
c) If you hit a 4 after me, you score a century.	45
d) I am equal to ten notes of 10.	89
e) I am century + half century	87
f) I am exactly in between 77 and 97.	100

In this chapter several stories and exercises are used to help children understand the decimal number system. The term 'place value', which often confuses children, has not been used at all. Teachers could also find out about other locally used number systems, if any, especially while working in tribal communities.

How Many are these?

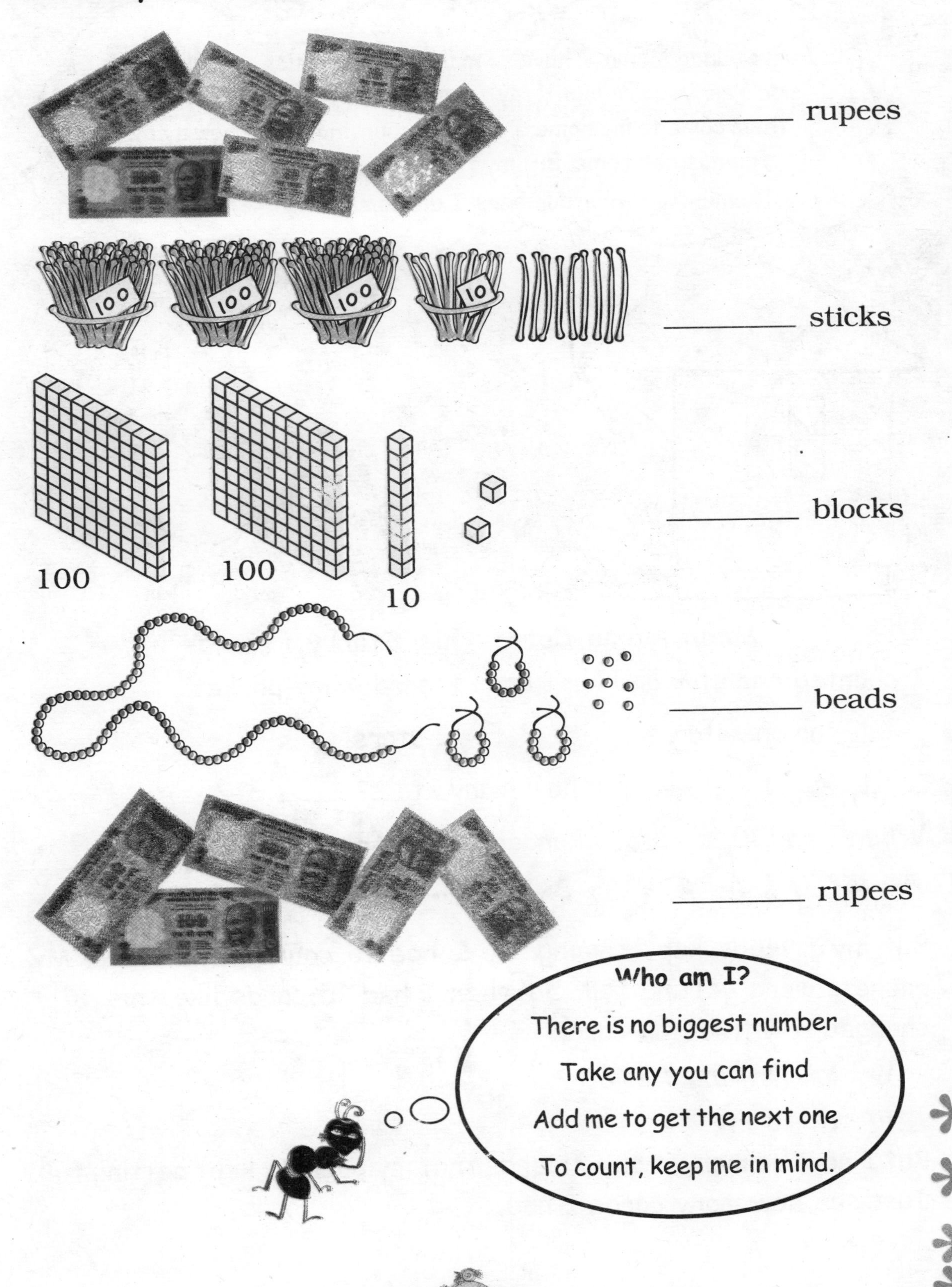

Moon Mama Counts his Starry Friends

I counted one star and kept one 1 card in my pocket.

1 for one star. 1 1 for 2 stars.

1 1 1 1 1 for how many stars? ____

When I had 10 cards, I changed it with this card 10.

1 1 1 1 1 1 1 1 1 1 ⟶ 10

But my friends kept coming. So I had to count more stars. My pockets were getting full. So when I had 10 cards like this 10 I changed it with a 100 card.

10 10 10 10 10
10 10 10 10 10 ⟶ 100

But I have so many, many, friends that my pockets kept getting full. Just see how many cards I had.

Which cards will I have in my pocket if I have counted up to...

a. 19 ⟶ 

b. 21 ⟶

c. 95 ⟶

d. 201 ⟶ 

e. 260 ⟶

f. 300 ⟶

g. 306 ⟶

h. 344 ⟶

i. 350 ⟶

j. 400 ⟶

When I had 10 10 cards in my pocket, I knew I had counted 20 stars. Now you tell me the number of stars counted in each case. Write the answer in the blank space.

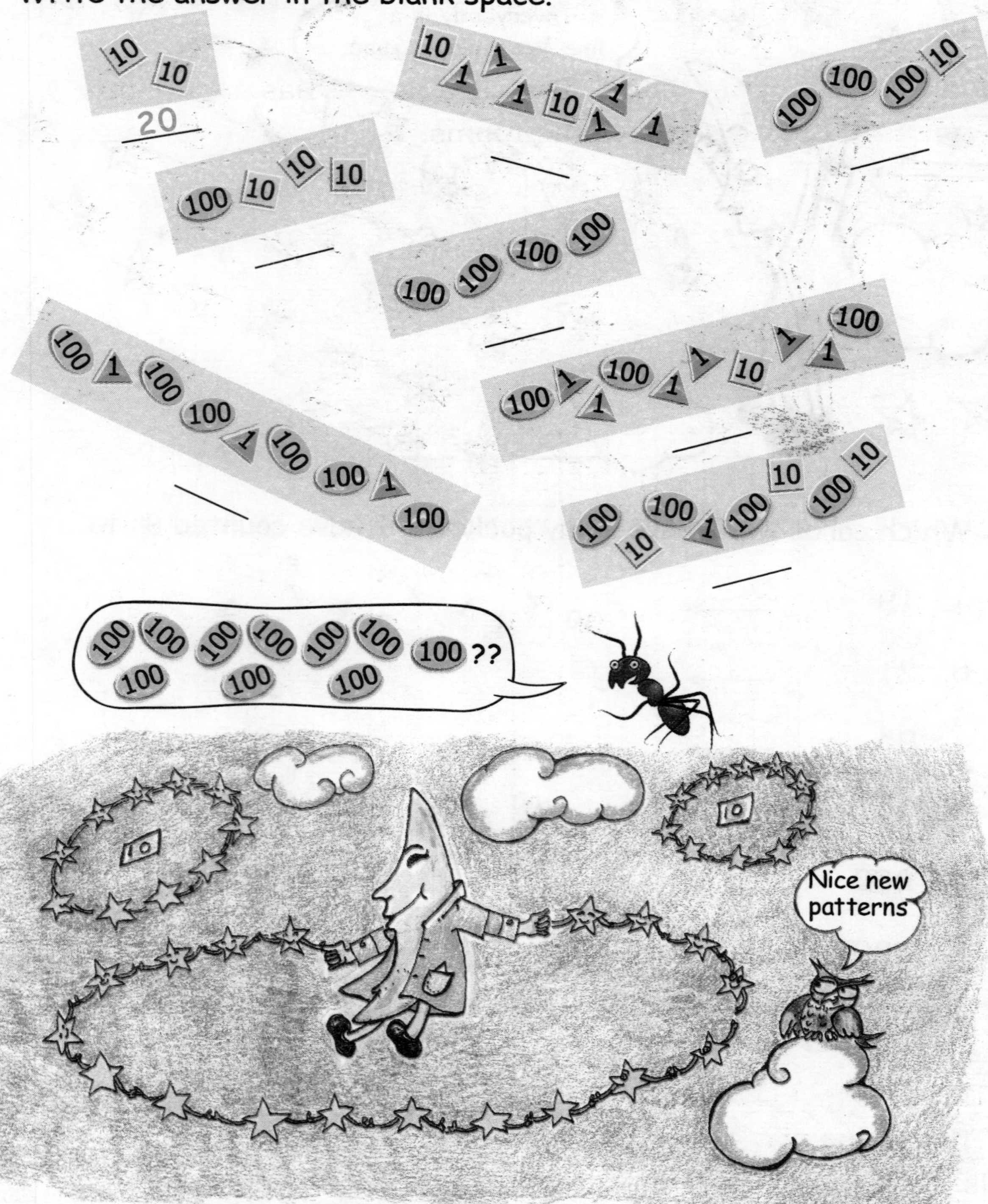

Guess how many starry friends I have in all... !!!

Give and Take

I am Kittu. This is my home. Isn't it huge? It has 100 rooms. Help me in painting some of the rooms.

91	92	93	94	95	96	97	98	99	100
81	82	83	84	85	86	87	88	89	90
71	72	73	74	75	76	77	78	79	80
61	62	63	64	65	66	67	68	69	70
51	52	53	54	55	56	57	58	59	60
41	42	43	44	45	46	47	48	49	50
31	32	33	34	35	36	37	38	39	40
21	22	23	24	25	26	27	28	29	30
11	12	13	14	15	16	17	18	19	20
1	2	3	4	5	6	7	8	9	10

✡ I start from room 2. I add 10 to 2 to reach room 12 and paint it. To add 10 to 2, we can go all the way to the right to 10. Then up to 11, and one step right to 12.
This is one way to go from 2 to 12.
Is there a shortcut? Of course! Follow me.
We can jump up one row.
A jump from 2 to 12 is like taking ______ steps.

✡ Now try one jump up from 14.

14 + 10 = 24

Colour this room.

24
14
4

✡ How will I go from 22 to 41? Jump from 22 to 42.

Then one step left. We can write it like this.

22 + 20 = 42

42 – 1 = 41

How many steps did I go in all? __________

You could also go this way:

From 22 take one step left to 21.

Then two jumps up to 41.

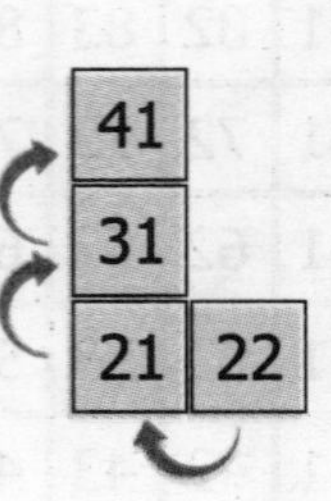

22 – 1 = 21

21 + 20 = 41

Try these on Kittu's home:

a) 10 less than 34 is __________.

b) 53 – 20 = __________

c) 11 more than 31 is __________.

d) 11 less than 66 is __________.

e) 62 + 13 = __________

f) 23 less than 89 is __________.

g) 10 and 40 more is __________.

The 10×10 number grid is a useful aid for adding and subtracting two-digit numbers. Children should be encouraged to try these operations mentally using the grid as often as possible.

h) 9 added to 28 gives ________.

i) The sum of 9 and 44 is ________.

j) Reducing 98 by 34 gives ________.

k) 4 and 37 more is ________.

l) Take 35 away from 83. We get ________.

Find My Food

Hey! I have something more interesting for you.
Ma told me, there are things to eat in some rooms.
Help me find those room numbers. Mark them in my home.
See what you get!

91	92	93	94	95	96	97	98	99	100
81	82	83	84	85	86	87	88	89	90
71	72	73	74	75	76	77	78	79	80
61	62	63	64	65	66	67	68	69	70
51	52	53	54	55	56	57	58	59	60
41	42	43	44	45	46	47	48	49	50
31	32	33	34	35	36	37	38	39	40
21	22	23	24	25	26	27	28	29	30
11	12	13	14	15	16	17	18	19	20
1	2	3	4	5	6	7	8	9	10

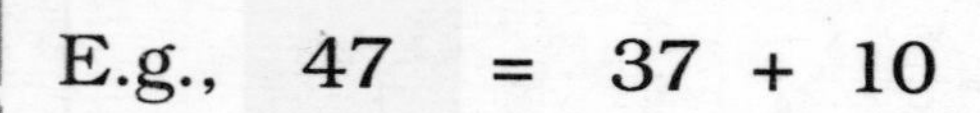

E.g., 47 = 37 + 10

37 + 9 = ____

65 – 30 = ____

____ = 46 + 21

____ = 87 – 30

66 – ____ = 11

36 = ____ + 9

45 + ____ = 99

40 + ____ = 76

____ + 26 = 75

98 = ____ + 50

____ – 21 = 35

57 – ____ = 20

Adding Made Easy

Anisha bought apples for 37 rupees. Raja bought bananas for 21 rupees. The woman selling fruits said:

37 is 30 and 7

21 is 20 and 1

So 37 and 21 make 58.

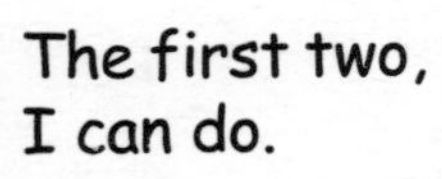

✡ Let us also try. Look at this sum.

26 + 43

20 + 6 + 40 + 3

20 + 40 + 6 + 3

60 + 9

69

The answer is 69.

We break 26 into 20 + 6 and 43 into 40 + 3.

Then it's easy: we add 20 + 40 and 3 + 6 !

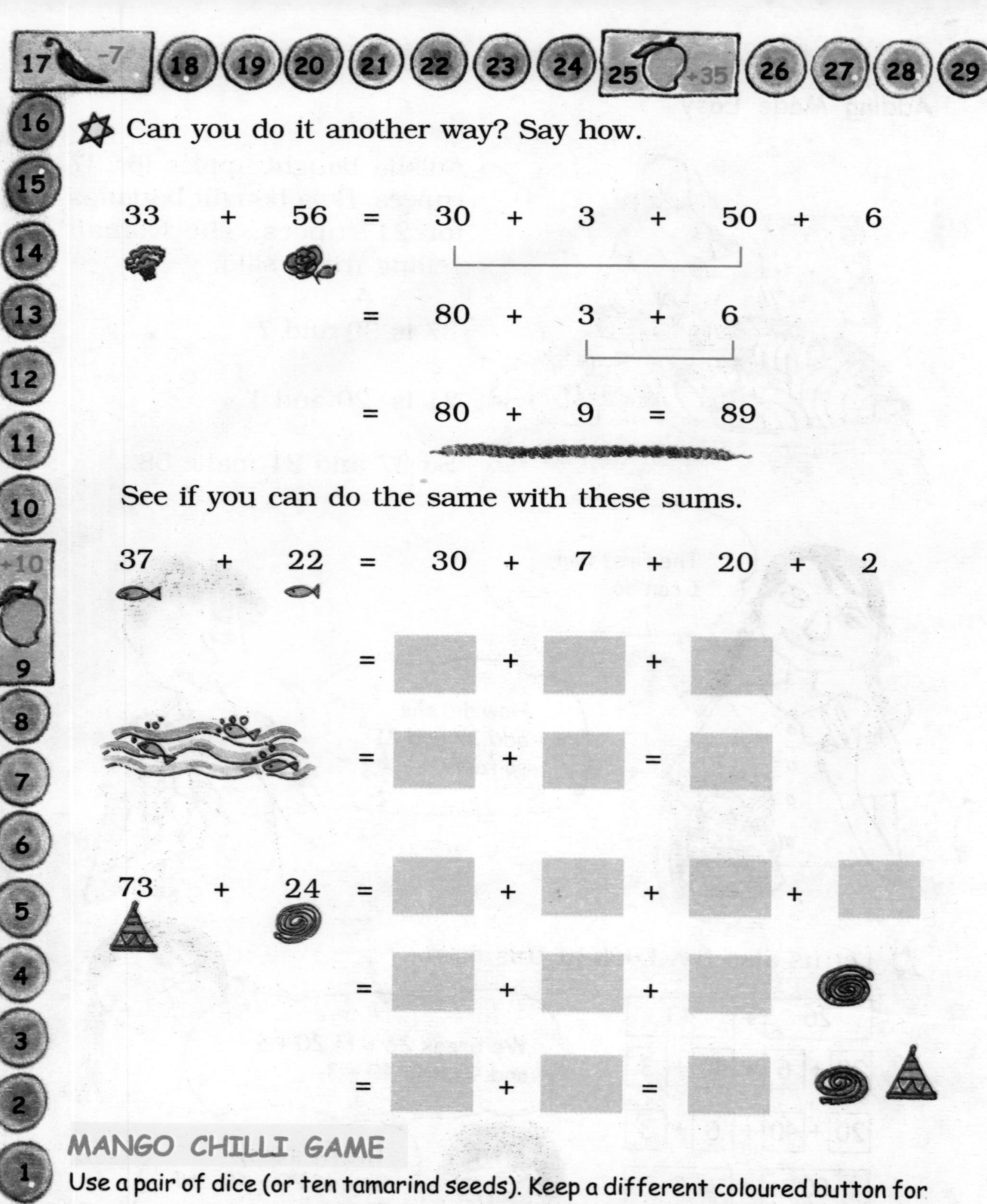

Can you do it another way? Say how.

33	+	56	=	30	+	3	+	50	+	6
			=	80	+	3	+	6		
			=	80	+	9	=	89		

See if you can do the same with these sums.

37	+	22	=	30	+	7	+	20	+	2
			=	☐	+	☐	+	☐		
			=	☐	+	☐	=	☐		

73	+	24	=	☐	+	☐	+	☐	+	☐
			=	☐	+	☐	+	☐		
			=	☐	+	☐	=	☐		

MANGO CHILLI GAME

Use a pair of dice (or ten tamarind seeds). Keep a different coloured button for each player. If you reach a mango you go forward (+). If you step on a chilli you have to go back (-). See who reaches back home first !

Now work out the steps in your mind.
Write the answers directly in the boxes.

33 + 42 = ____ ____ = 33 + 27 55 + 25 = ____

19 + 61 = ____ ____ = 34 + 63 67 + 25 = ____

____ = 48 + 42 ____ = 53 + 64 72 + 56 = ____

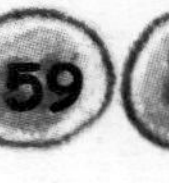

Let Me Tell You a Story..........

Once a baby lion lost his way in the jungle. He started crying and called out for his mother. An old deer took pity on him. He took him to his place. But the other deer got really scared. So did their other friends — rabbits, squirrels and birds. A lion among us! Oh, no! He will eat up our babies. The old deer said — don't worry. I will warn him about this. In the morning the baby lion thanked every one and started to leave. But a rabbit said — wait, he cannot go like this! Let us count to see if he has done any mischief. We should be 240 in all. Let's count.

Tillu counted rabbits and deer.
There were 27 and 48

The old deer counted birds and squirrels.
There were 124 and 38

In the chapter Fun with Numbers, children would have made token cards. The same token cards should be used for exercises in addition before children do written sums.

✡ Let's add and find out how many deer and rabbits were there...

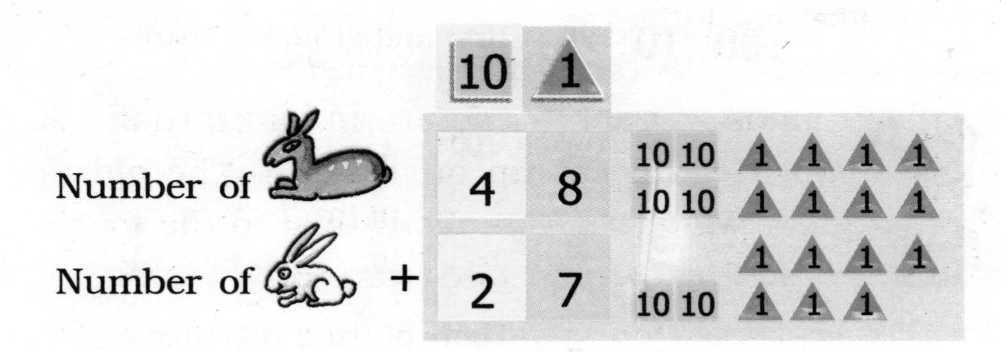

	10	1
	1 4	8
+	2	7
		5

10

10 10 1 1 1 1
10 10 1 1 1 1
1 1 1 1
10 10 1 1 1

Putting all the 1 s together,
we get fifteen 1 s
Ten 1 s make one 10 and
we are left with five 1 s

	10	1
	1 4	8
+	2	7
	7	5

10

10 10
10 10
1 1
10 10 1 1 1

Now putting together all the 10 s,
we get seven 10 s

So total number of and = 75

✡ Similarly we add the number of birds and number of squirrels.

	100	10	1
		1	
Number of (bird)	1	2	4
Number of (squirrel) +		3	8
	1	6	2

Putting all the 1s together first and grouping them

100 | 10 | 10 10 | 10 10 | 10 | 1 1 1 1 | 1 1 1 1 | 1 1 1 1

Then putting together the 10 s and lastly the 100 s we get

100 | 10 10 10 | 10 10 10 | 1 1

So together birds and squirrels were 162, and deer and rabbits were 75.

The old deer said — we were 240 in number, now how many are we in all?

To find out, do the addition in the box below:

	100	10	1
Number of (birds) and (squirrels)			
Number of (deer) and (rabbits) +			

How Many Bulbs?

1. A factory made 270 bulbs on the first day.
   On the second day it made 123 bulbs.

How many bulbs did the factory make altogether?

First day - 270 bulbs

Second day - 123 bulbs

270 + 123
Is the sum more than 350
or less than 350?

I think..
270 and 100 is 370?
The sum is more than 350.

How many altogether?

Solution:

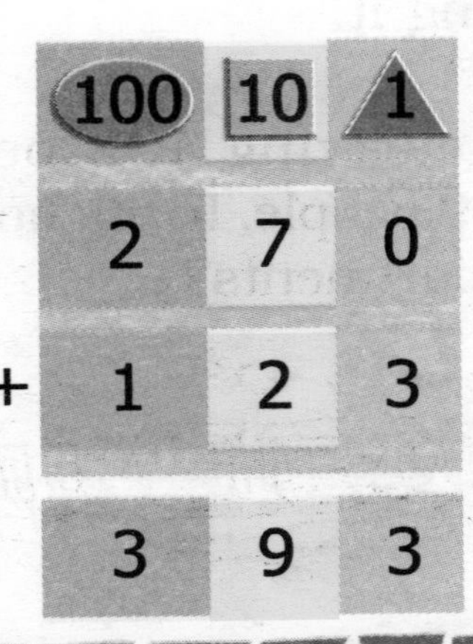

		100	10	1
Bulbs made on first day		2	7	0
Bulbs made on second day	+	1	2	3
Sum		3	9	3

2. A shopkeeper Rafi had 153 candles. Paras gave him 237 more candles. How many candles does Rafi have now?

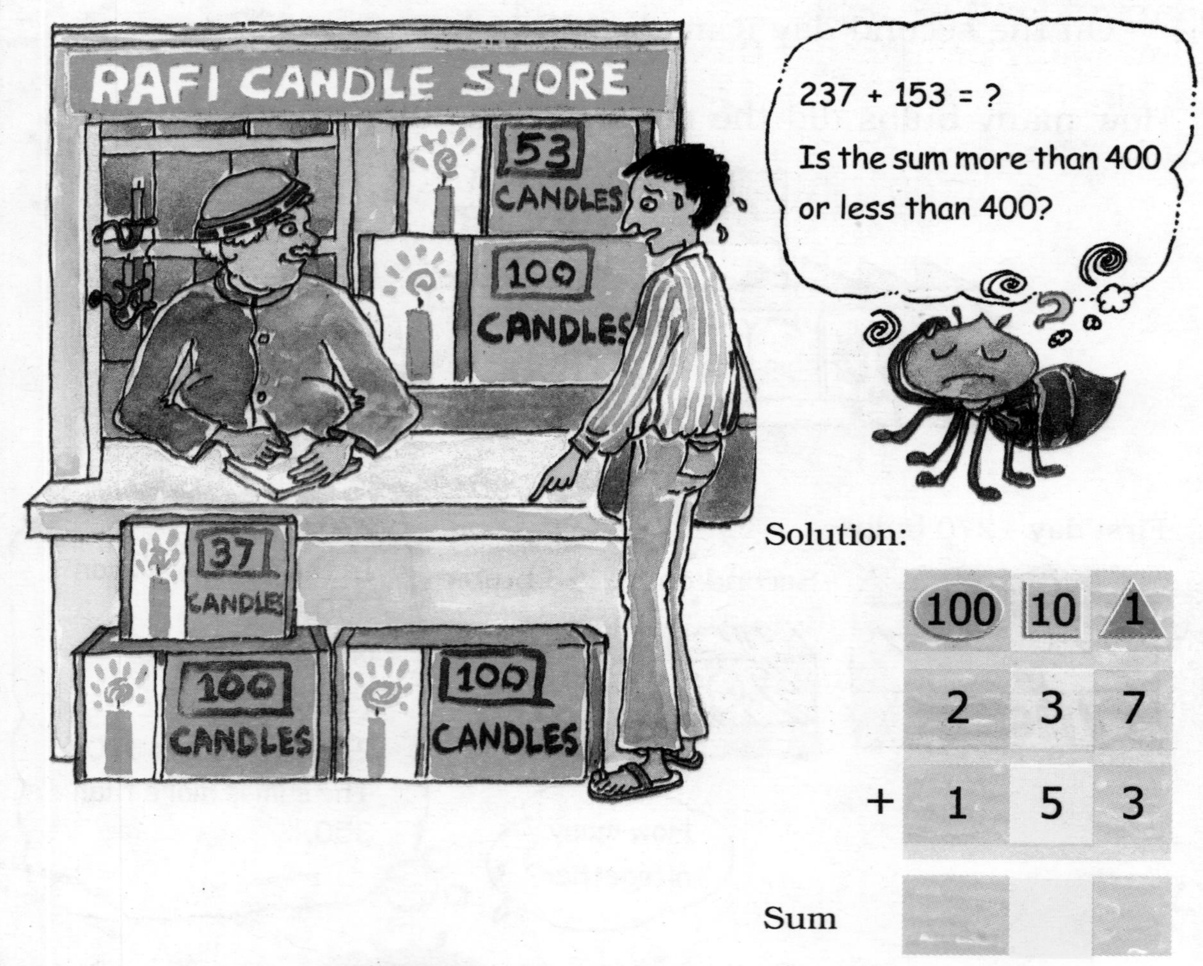

Solution:

	100	10	1
	2	3	7
+	1	5	3
Sum			

Work out the following story problems in the same way.

Read each problem and say it in your words.

Guess the answer before writing it.

A. A train compartment is carrying 132 people. Another compartment is carrying 129 people. In all, how many people are there in both the compartments?

B. Shanu found 138 pebbles.
Karim found 44 pebbles.
How many pebbles did they find in all?

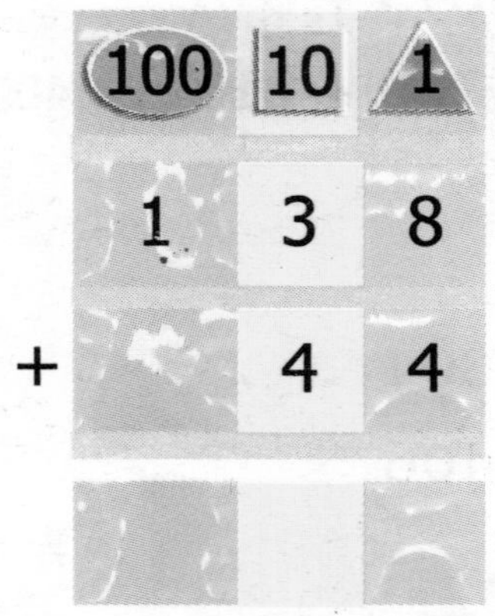

100	10	1
1	3	8
+	4	4

C. A teacher kept a note of which fruits students like in her school. This is what she found:

Students	Oranges	Mangoes	Total
Girls	136	240	
Boys	128	243	
Total			

Find out:

(a) How many students in the school like oranges?

(b) How many students in the school like mangoes?

(c) Altogether, how many students are there in the school?

(d) Is the number of girls more than 350 or less than 350?

Practice Time

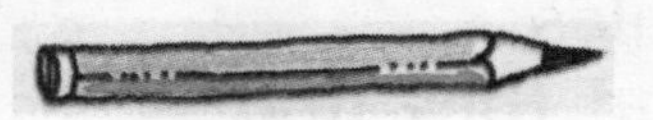

A. (i) 345 + 52

(ii) 492 + 29

(iii) 245 + 93

(iv) 643 + 345

(v) 750 + 219

B.

319	304	363
+ 323	+ 406	+ 456

427	684
+ 248	+ 232

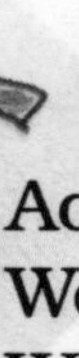

Puzzle

Addition is my best friend
We never have a fight
When I am done
Call out to him
And check if I am right

MIND TRAIN GAME :

Two friends play this game. You look at each train. Some people come in (+) and some leave (–). How many are there in all? Solve in your MIND! Discuss your answer. The friend who gets the right answer first wins some points. List down your points. Add to find who wins the most!

WIN 5 POINTS

WIN 5 POINTS → 19 - 5 + 6 - 15 + 7 - 3 + 6 - 10 + 4 + 20 + 1 - 7 + 5 - 4 ? WIN 5 POINTS

Work out four different ways to write the numbers.

If you add all the numbers in the first box, you will always get 59.

59	78	83
50 + 9	+	+
30 + 29	+	+ 43
19 + 40	30 +	+
59 + 0	+	+

99	102	168
+	+	+
+ 39	+	+
+	+	+ 68
+	+ 50	+

Can You Solve this Puzzle?

Write the numbers 1, 2, 3, 4, 5, 6 in the circles, so that the sum of the numbers on each side of the figure is 12.

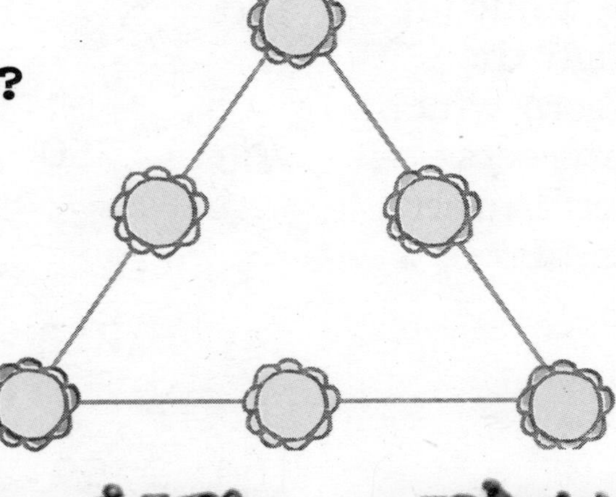

+ 9 + 12 + 9 - 20 ←

Find Mithoo's Bag

Do all the sums mentally:

a) 75 + 20 = 95

b) 90 + 60 = 150

c) 25 + 30 + 3 =

d) 9 + 40 + 31 =

e) 500 + 200 =

f) 400 + 350 =

g) 670 + 120 =

h) 380 + 210 =

i) 205 + 650 =

j) 128 + 600 =

k) 150 + 69 =

l) 37 + 46 + 3 =

Find Mithoo's bag and check your answers.

Draw a line through the numbers which are answers written in the boxes above.

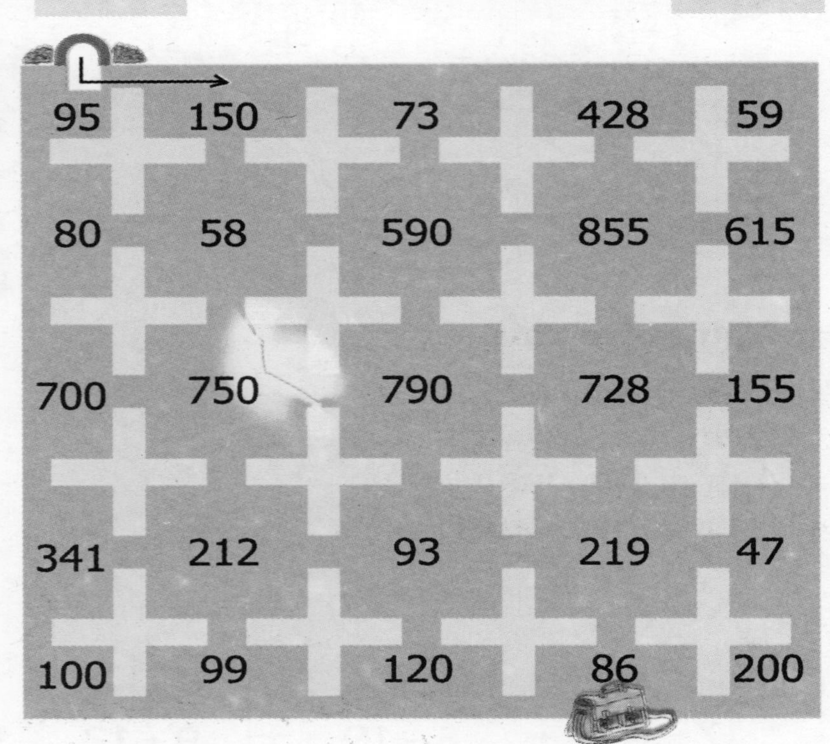

Card Game

One day Bubbly and Gopu were playing. Bubbly gave three number cards to Gopu. He arranged the cards in two ways.

150	–	30	=	120

Bubbly arranged them this way:

120	+	30	=	150
30	+	120	=	150

Isn't it interesting?

You can also play it. Here are the cards for you. Work out the combination. Place the cards in the right boxes.

a)

b)

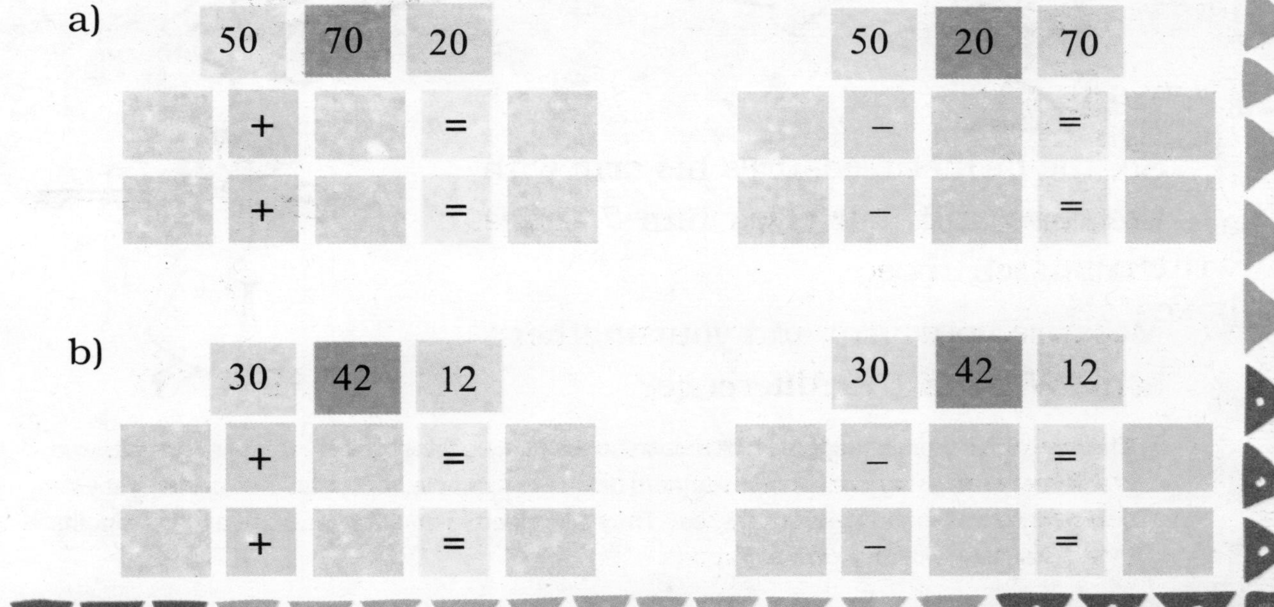

4 Long and Short

Lali is selling things at her father's shop. A farmer comes to buy rope.

So, the farmer measures his arm with the rope and Lali gives him 7 times that much rope.

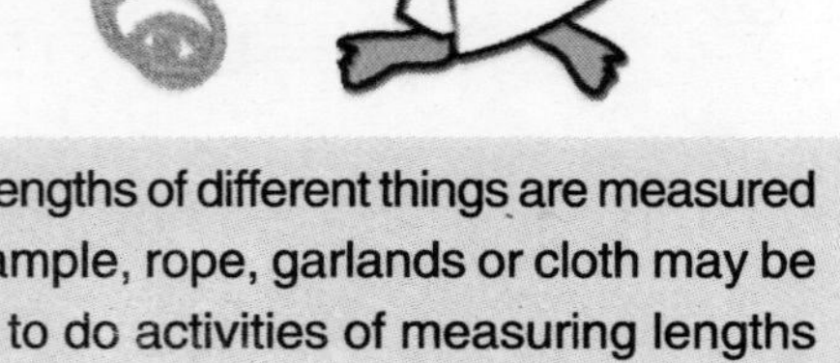

Measure your arm and your mother's arm. What is the difference?

Children should be encouraged to look around and see how lengths of different things are measured in different ways using local or non-standard units. For example, rope, garlands or cloth may be sold by the cubit, handspan, fingers, etc. They also need to do activities of measuring lengths (and distances) with their own body parts.

How Many?

* In how many steps will Dorji cross the road?

* How many cups can be placed in a line on this table?

* How many pots can be placed to reach the tree branch?

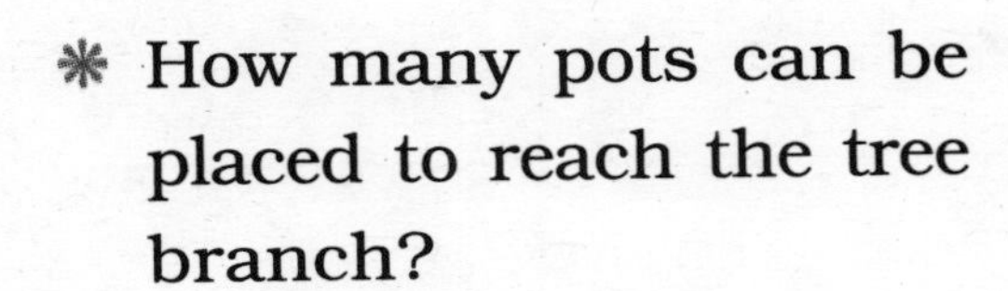

* How many shirts can be hung on this wire?

How Much is a Centimetre (cm)?

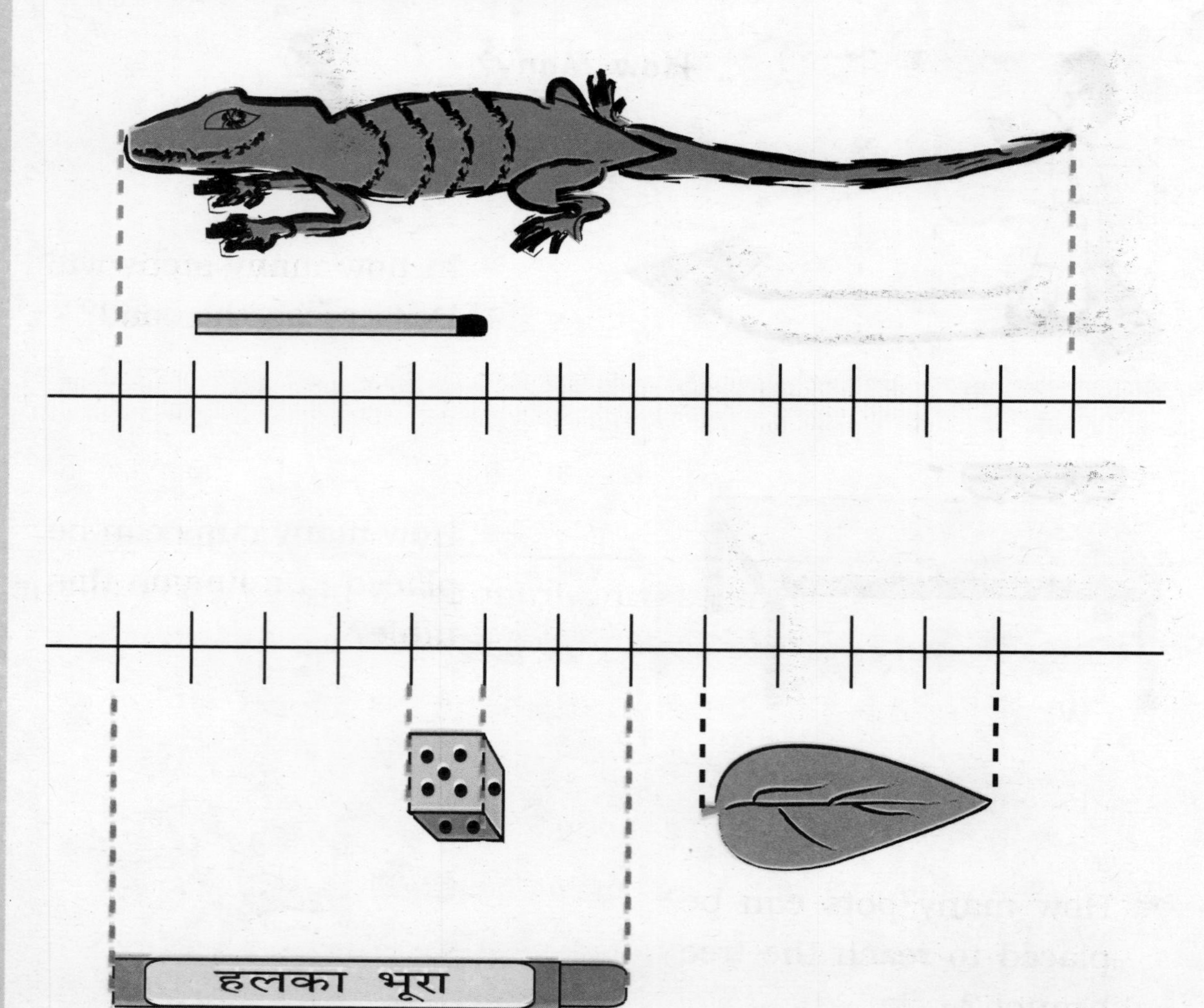

The matchstick is 4 centimetres long.

The die is 1 centimetre from every side.

The lizard is 13 centimetres long.

The leaf is ______ centimetres long.

The wax colour is ______ centimetres long.

Now, look at a scale that you find in a geometry box. How many centimetres does it have? ______

The small scale that you mostly use in school is like this one.

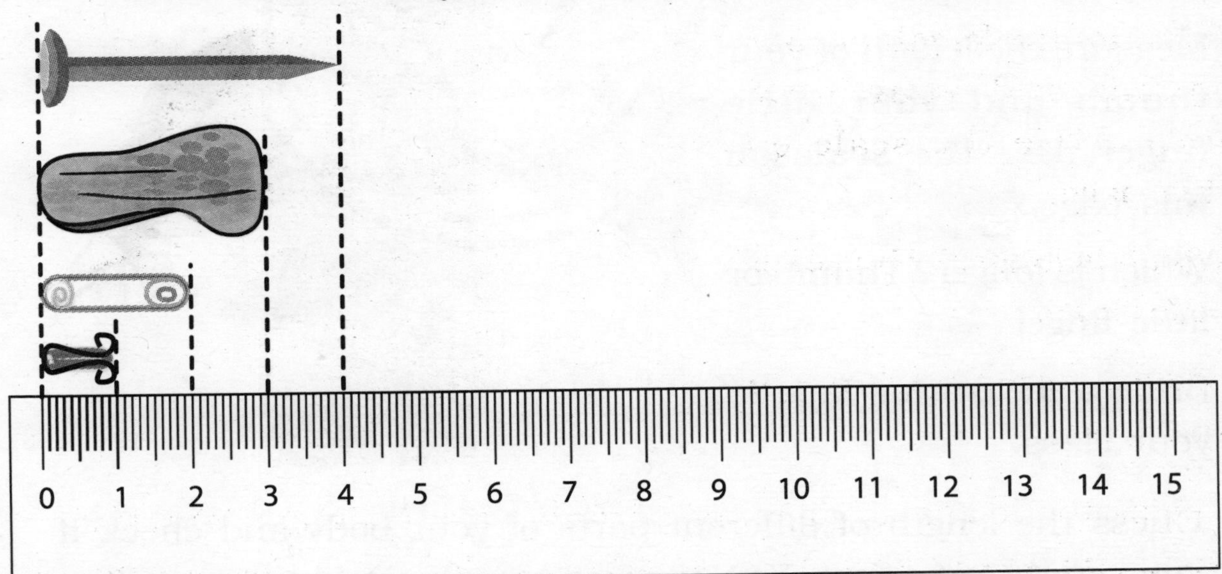

Is it easier to start measuring from the 0 mark? Look at the things drawn near the scale and find out their lengths.

* What are the little lines on the scale used for?
* Look for things that are
  * About 10 centimetres long
  * Between 10 and 20 centimetres long
  * Less than 1 cm long.
* Draw some of them here.

How Big is My Hand?

Measure the length of your thumb and your little finger. Use the scale on this page.

Which is longer? Thumb or little finger?

Bring a measuring-tape to your class.

Guess the length of different parts of your body and check if your guess is correct. You can use a scale, string, measuring-tape etc.

Think – How will you know the number of centimetres if you measure with a rope, shoe-string, thread etc.?

	*My measurement*	*My friend's measurement*
Nose	_____ centimetres	_____ centimetres
Around the wrist	_____ centimetres	_____ centimetres
Around the head	_____ centimetres	_____ centimetres
Ear	_____ centimetres	_____ centimetres
Hand (tip of middle finger to wrist)	_____ centimetres	_____ centimetres

Compare your measurement with your friends'.

- Who has the biggest head and who has the smallest head? __________, __________
- Who has the longest hand (from middle finger to wrist)? __________
- Which is longer? Your ear or your nose? __________
- Is any of your nails more than 1 centimetre long? __________

Gibli and the Grains

Ant Gibli has to reach the grains. She is looking for the shortest road. Can you tell her which is the shortest?

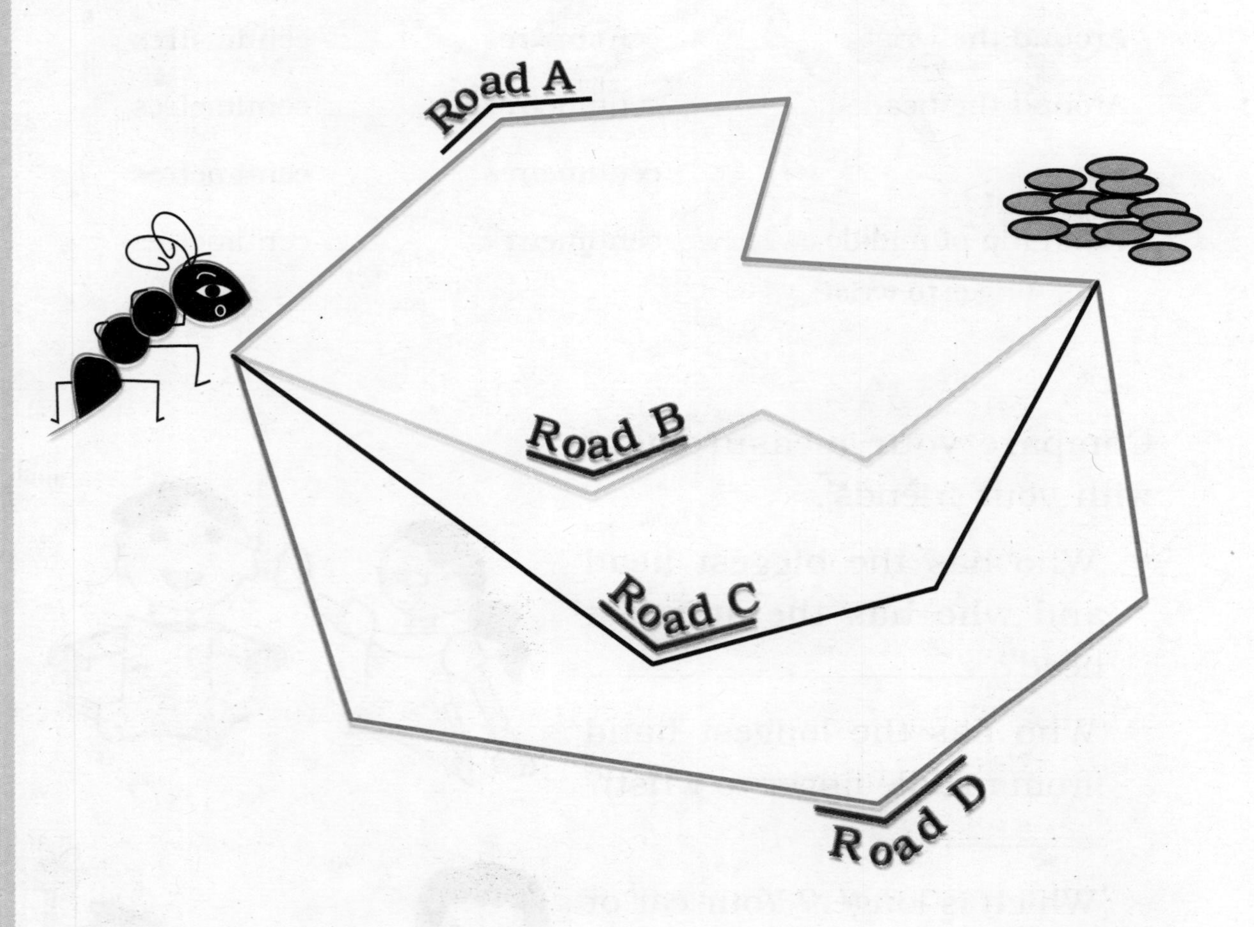

Can you draw a road shorter than these? What is the length of that road? _______________

It is more important for children to be able to get an estimate of a metre as related to known things, such as, their own heights, rather than do tedious exercises of converting metres to centimetres, etc. Children at this stage may not be able to perceive of bigger units such as a kilometre. They must be encouraged to speak of a kilometre in the context of a story or narrative. The Map of Agra is an exercise with a narrative involving children, with familiar images (icons) to help the initial understanding of mapping in 2 dimensions.

How Long is a Metre?

Let Us Make a Metre-rope

You must have seen shopkeepers measuring cloth with a metre rod.

- Use a metre rod and a rope.
- Make a knot at one end of the rope.
- Keep the metre rod with the rope.
- Mark 1 metre on the rope and make a knot there.
- Now the length between the two knots is 1 metre. This is your metre-rope.

If you don't get a metre rod use a measuring-tape and mark 100 centimetres on the rope. 100 centimetres are equal to a metre, so you get the metre-rope.

Guess and Check

Activity 1

- Find some things that look 1 metre long.
- Use your metre-rope to find which of these things are more or less than 1 metre.

Name of the thing	*More than 1 metre*	*Less than 1 metre*
Length of table	–	–
Width of table	–	–
Width of door	–	–
Length of door	–	–
	–	–
	–	–
	–	–

Activity 2

Some Class III children have marked a 1 metre height on the wall of their class.

You can also mark 1 metre on your class wall.

Now make a chart of the heights of your friends.

To measure the centimetres, you can use your small scale.

Name	*Taller/Shorter/Equal to 1 metre*	*How many centimetres more or less than a metre*
Shambhu	Taller	4 centimetres
______	______	______
______	______	______
______	______	______
______	______	______

Centimetres or Metres?

Which of these will be in centimetres and which will be in metres?

- Width of a computer screen
- Length of a Pagdi worn by Sikhs

- Height of a 1-year old child
- Length of a banana

- Waist of an elephant
- Height of a sugarcane
- Depth of a well
- Height of your mother
- Distance from classroom to school gate
- Length of your father's arm.

Trip to Agra

Marie and Baichung are going with their family to Agra. They get down at Agra Cantt. Railway Station and take a rickshaw to Taj Mahal. After 3 hours, they start for Agra Fort, again in a rickshaw. In the afternoon they take a bus to go to Fatehpur Sikri.

MAP OF AGRA

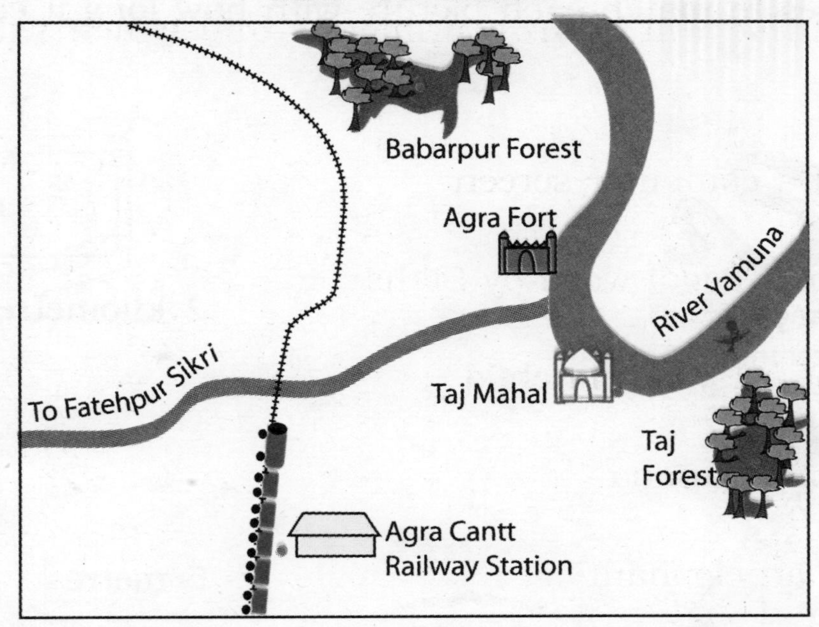

Now look at the distances between these places (for kilometres we write km).

- Agra Cantt. Railway Station to Taj Mahal – 5 km
- Taj Mahal to Agra Fort – 2 km
- Agra Fort to Fatehpur Sikri – 40 km

Now find from the map

- Which is farther from Agra Cantt. Railway Station — Taj Mahal or Fatehpur Sikri?

  ++++++++++++++++++ shows the railway line.

Which of these is nearer to the railway line:

- Babarpur forest or Taj forest?
- Agra Fort or Taj Mahal?

Which is closer to the river Yamuna:

- Taj Mahal or the Railway Station?

Match the Correct Length

Draw lines to match each picture with how long it can be.

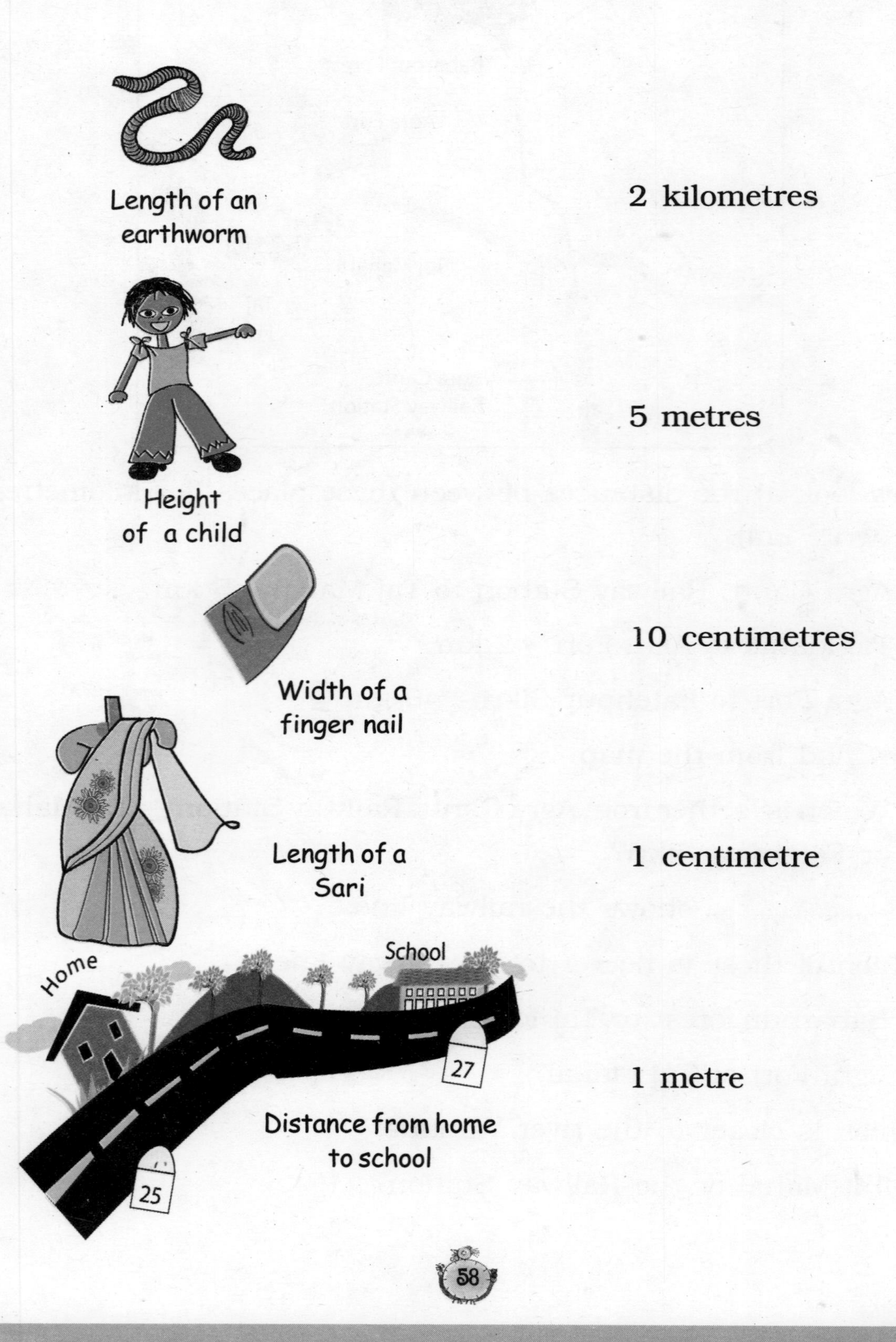

2 kilometres

5 metres

10 centimetres

1 centimetre

1 metre

The Long Tail Competition

The animals in this picture had a competition. The animal who had the longest tail won a prize. Now who do you think won the first prize and who won the second....? Just guess the length of the longest tail.

Shapes and Designs

Make a Clapper

1

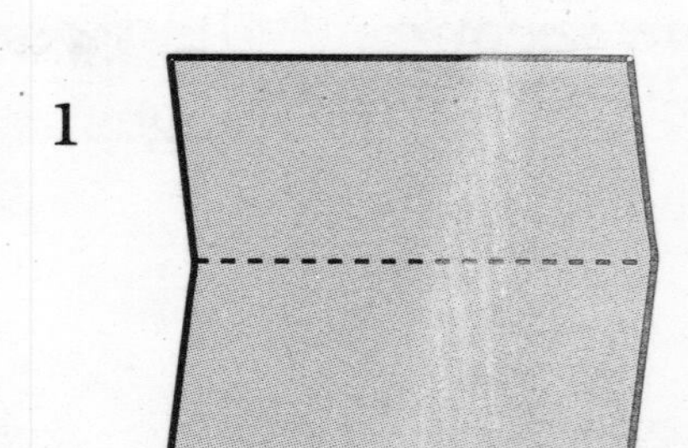

2

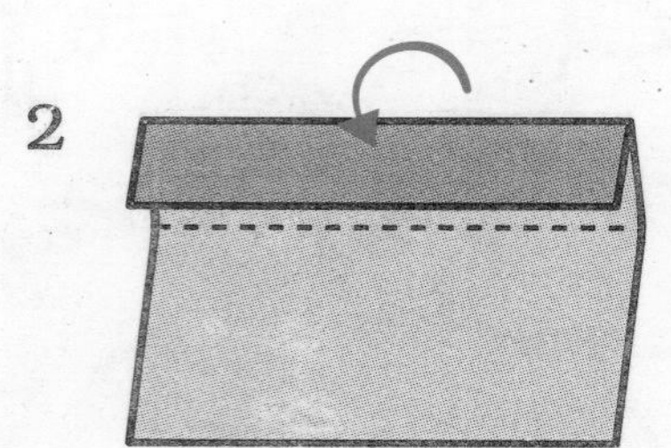

3

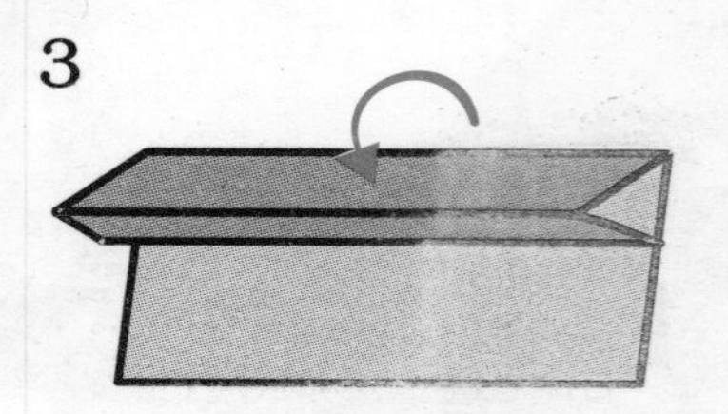

4

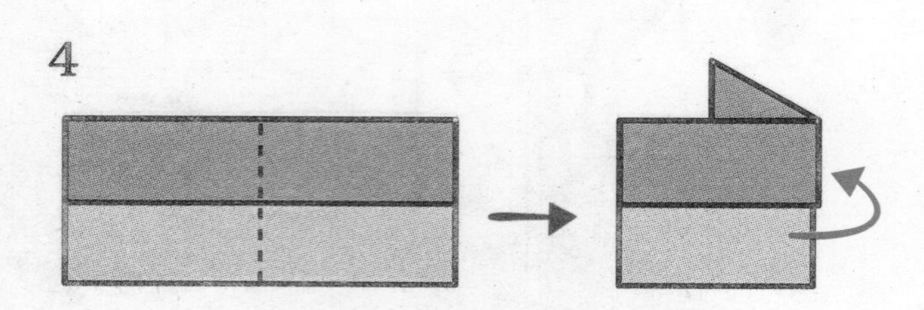

5

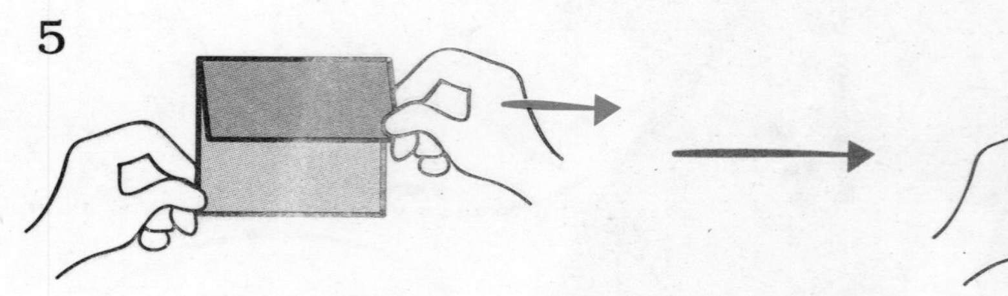

6

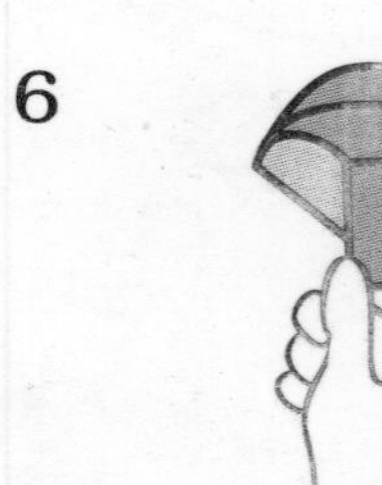

Have Fun with Shapes

Colour the clown following the directions given below :

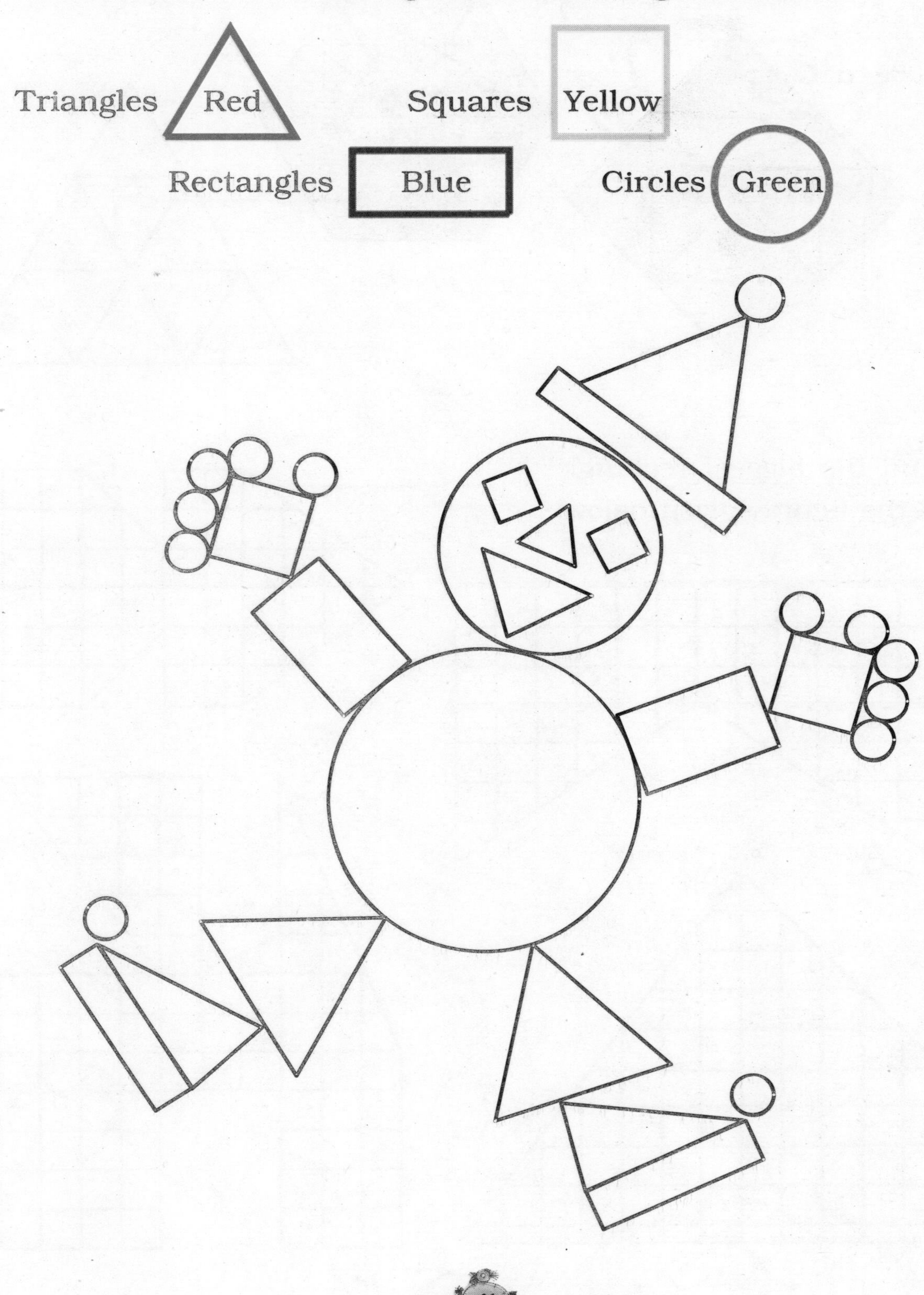

How many triangles are there in the following figures?

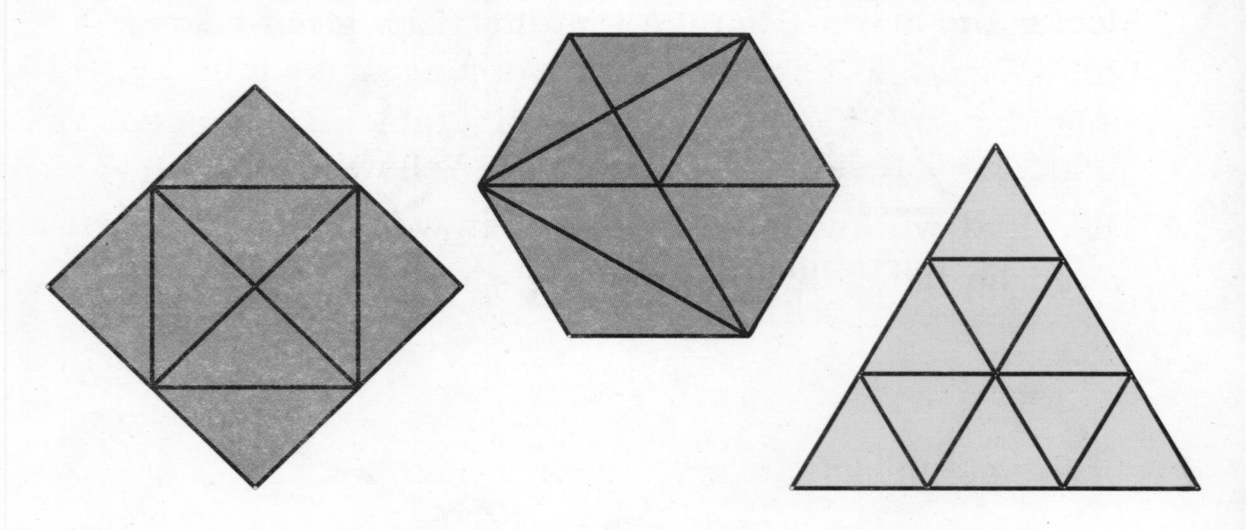

Find the biggest rectangle in the figures given below.

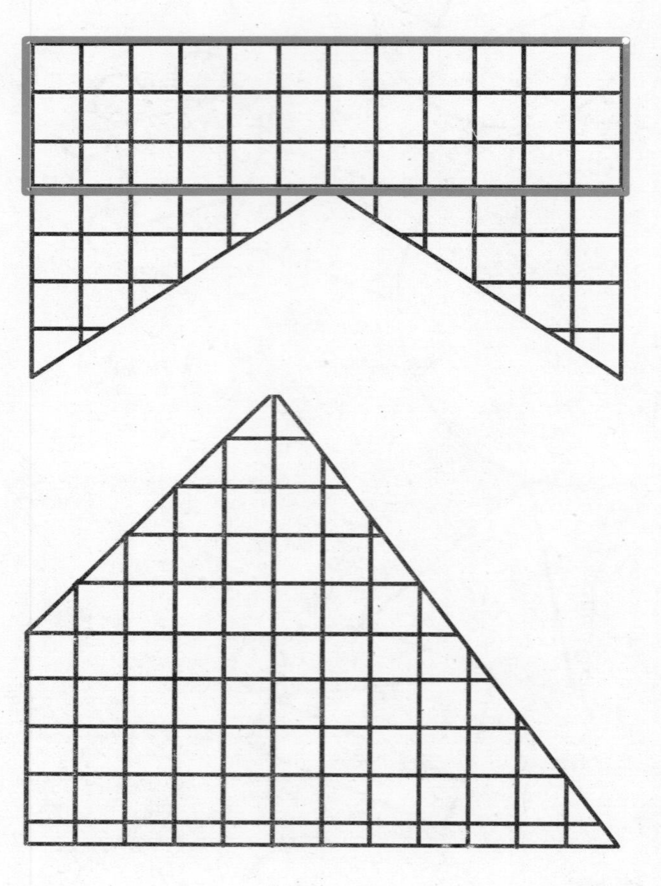

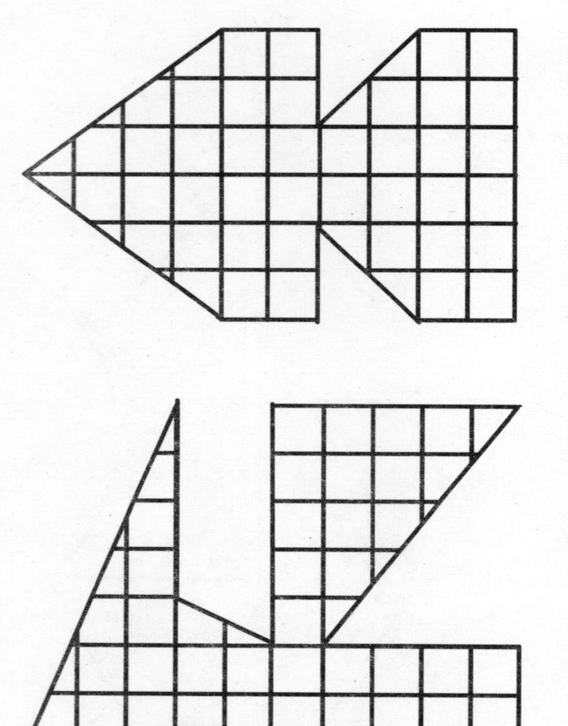

Edges and Corners

Meeta and her 5 friends were playing a game. Tinku was blindfolded and asked to keep clapping as long as he wished while the others would move round a table. The moment Tinku stopped clapping, everybody would stop wherever they were. The child who was not at a corner would be out. Then she would be blindfolded.

a) Looking at the picture given above, can you tell who is out?

b) Where is Guddu standing?

c) Can this game be played around a round table? Why?

Many things around us have **straight** edges. For example:

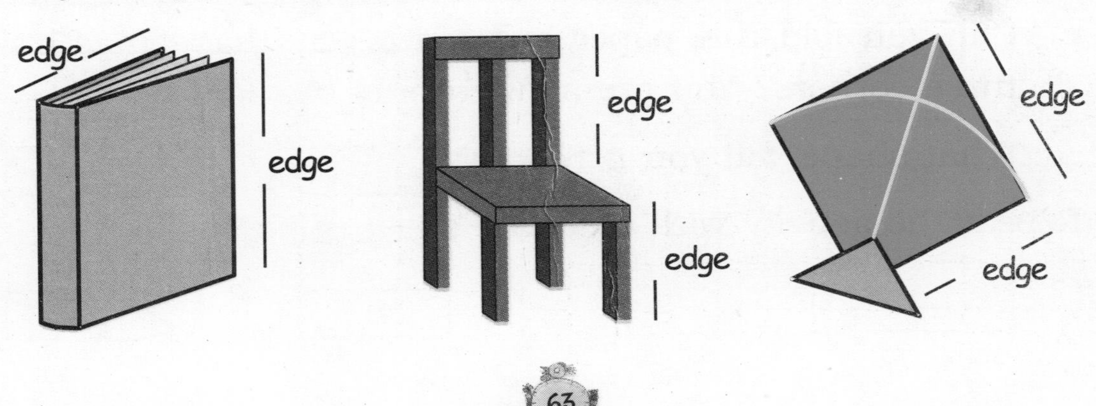

Other things have **curved** edges. For example:

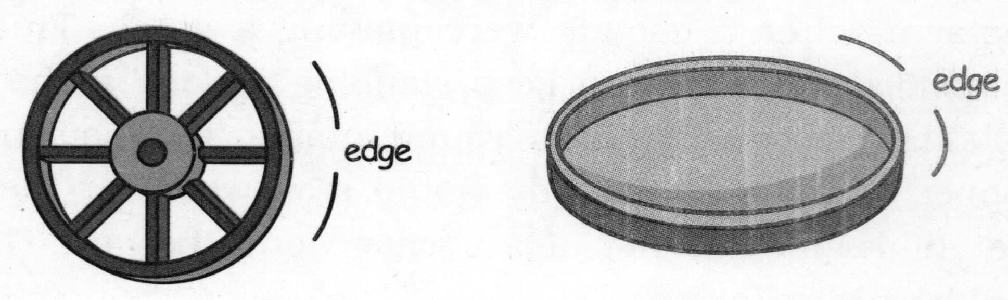

a) Look around you and identify things with straight and curved edges.

b) Do the things with straight edges have corners?

c) Do the things with curved edges have corners?

d) Try to find things which have both straight and curved edges.

Activity Time

1. Take a rectangular sheet of paper.
2. Count its corners.
3. Now fold one of its corners.

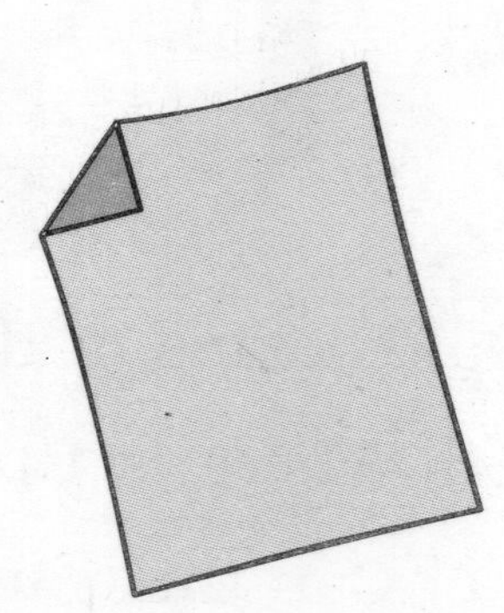

   a) How many corners does it have now?

   b) How many corners will you get by folding

      i) 2 corners

      ii) 3 corners

      iii) 4 corners

   c) Can you fold this paper in such a way that it has only three corners? You are allowed only two folds.

      What shape will you get?

4. Repeat the activity with a square sheet of paper.

5. Can you fold all the corners of the square sheet in such a way that the number of corners remains unchanged?

Look at the following table and tick (✓) the names of things that have corners. Also count the number of edges and corners in each of them.

Name of thing	*Whether it has corners*	*Number of edges*	*Number of corners*
Die	Yes		8
Ball			
Eraser			
Egg			
Sheet of paper			

In the following figures, tick (✓) those which have corners.

Do these figures have curved lines?

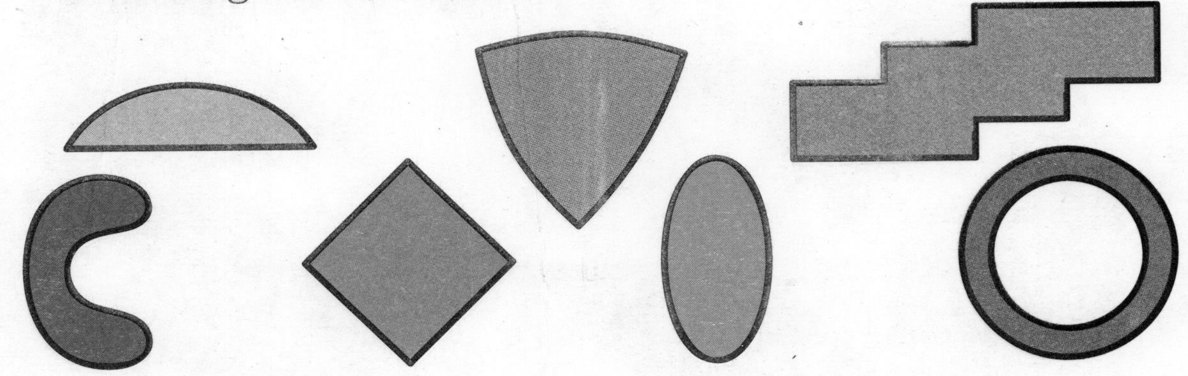

Using only straight lines, can you draw a figure which has no corners?

Tangram

The tangram is an old Chinese puzzle. From the pieces of the tangram, we can make many shapes of animals, people and things.

At the back of the book you will find a square like the one in this figure. Cut it out carefully and cut the pieces. This set of five pieces is called the 5-piece tangram.

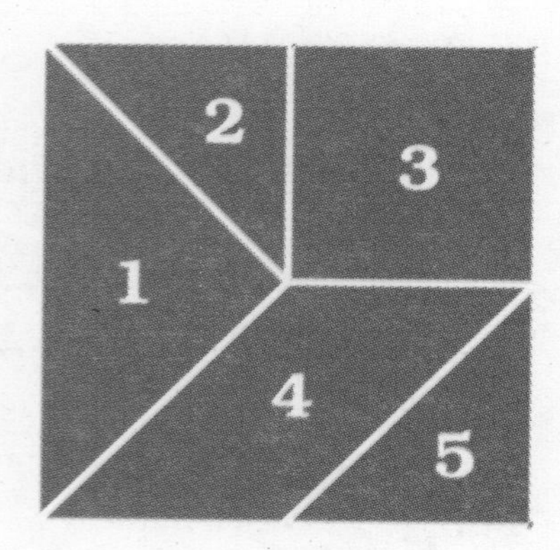

Use these five pieces to make the following figures:

1. How many triangles do you have in your set? Are all of them equal in size? Find out.
2. Use the two small triangles in the tangram set to get the following shapes:

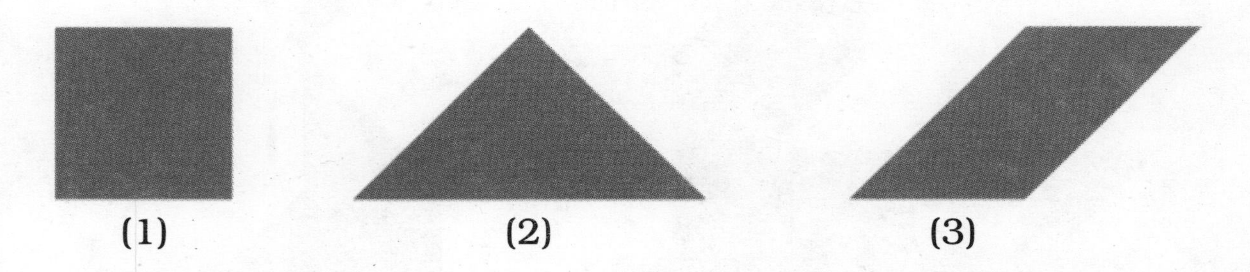

3. Which two pieces of the tangram set are exactly same? Find out.
4. Take pieces 4 and 5 from the set and find out on which side of the triangle you can join the other piece.
5. Find matching sides among the following pairs of pieces.

a) Pieces 1 and 2

b) Pieces 2 and 4 (See figure on page 66)

c) Pieces 1 and 5

d) Pieces 2 and 5

The 7-piece tangram

Here is the picture of a seven–piece tangram.

You can cut out these pieces and put them together in different ways to make some very interesting shapes.

Try making these shapes.

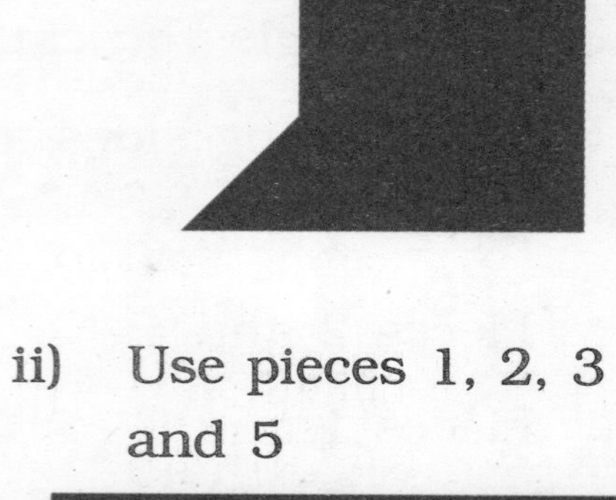

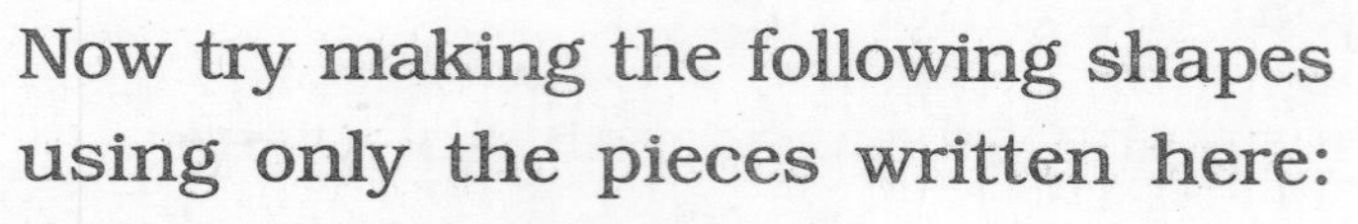

Now try making the following shapes using only the pieces written here:

i) Use only triangles

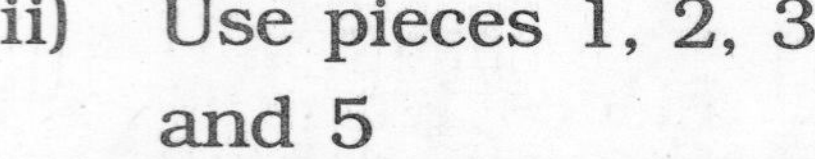

ii) Use pieces 1, 2, 3 and 5

iii) Use only two triangles

iv) Use pieces 1, 2, 3, 4 and 5

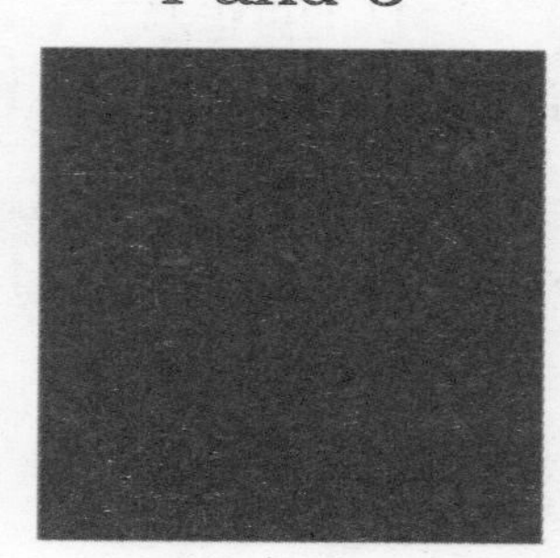

Weaving Patterns

Golu and Binu went to the market with their aunt. They saw many rugs (durries).

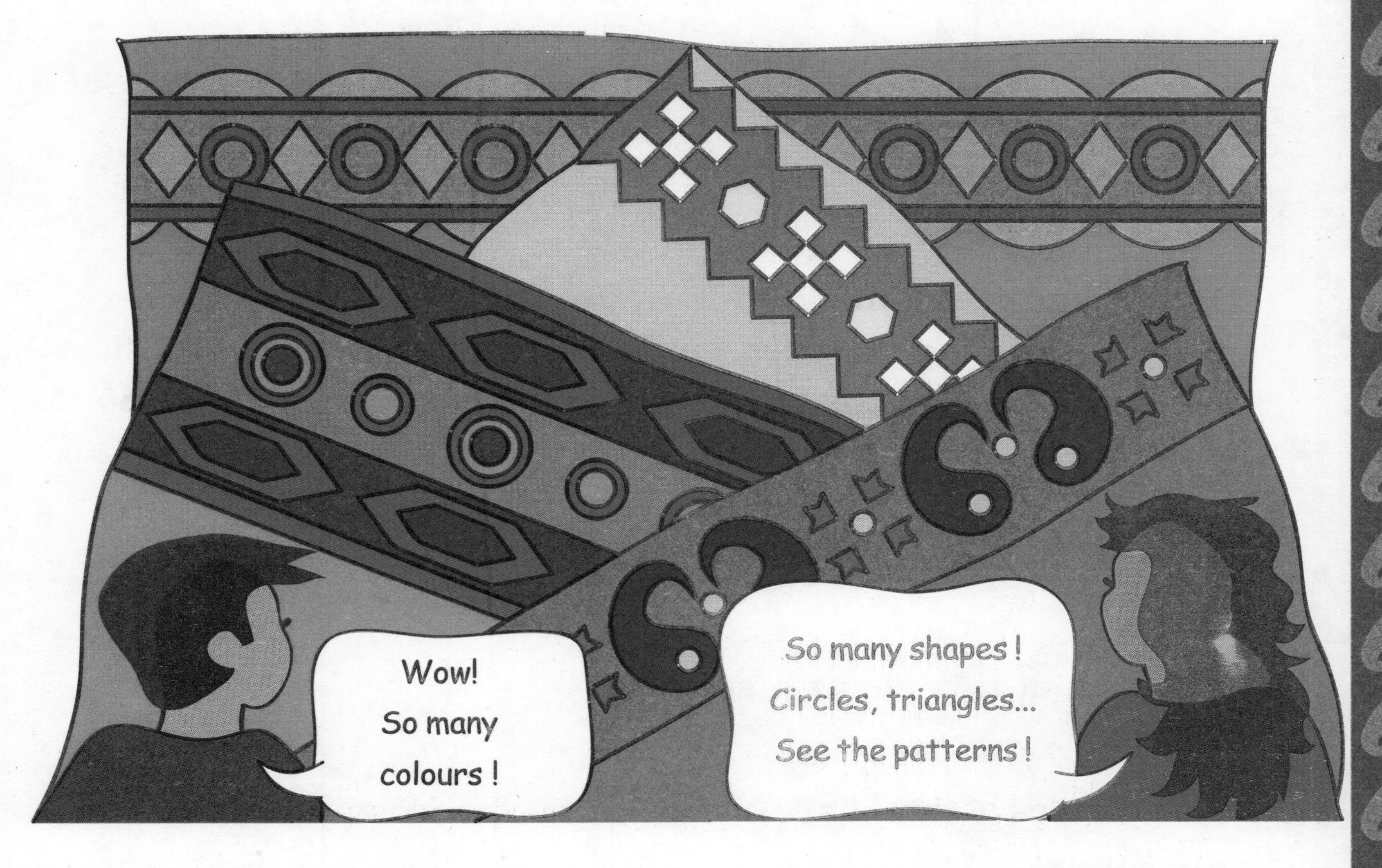

* Which geometrical shapes can you identify in these borders? Draw them in your notebook.
* Is any shape repeating in a particular pattern? Which ones?
* Are the shapes made of (i) Curved lines
  (ii) Straight lines
  (iii) Both curved and straight lines.
* Look at your clothes, your mother's saris/shawls, rugs and mats. Can you identify some patterns? Draw them in your notebook.

Floor Patterns

Have you ever seen a floor which has designs?

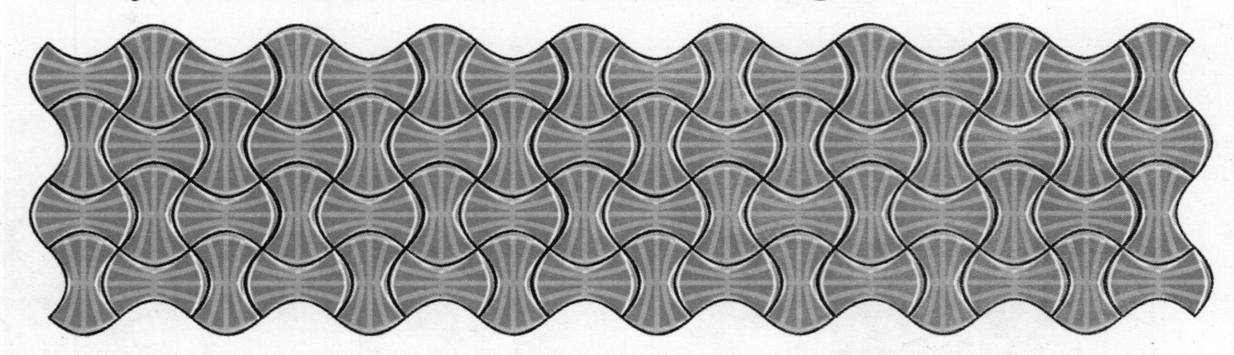

Do you know how these designs are made? These designs are made by covering the floor completely with small tiles that fit into each other without any gaps.. For example look at the shape of this tile and see how it fits.

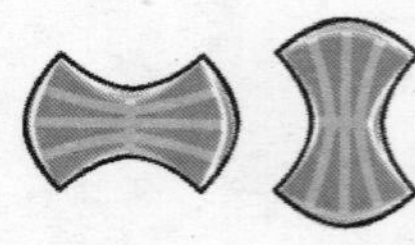

Now look at this tile with six sides.

See how tiles of this shape can cover the floor completely without any gaps.

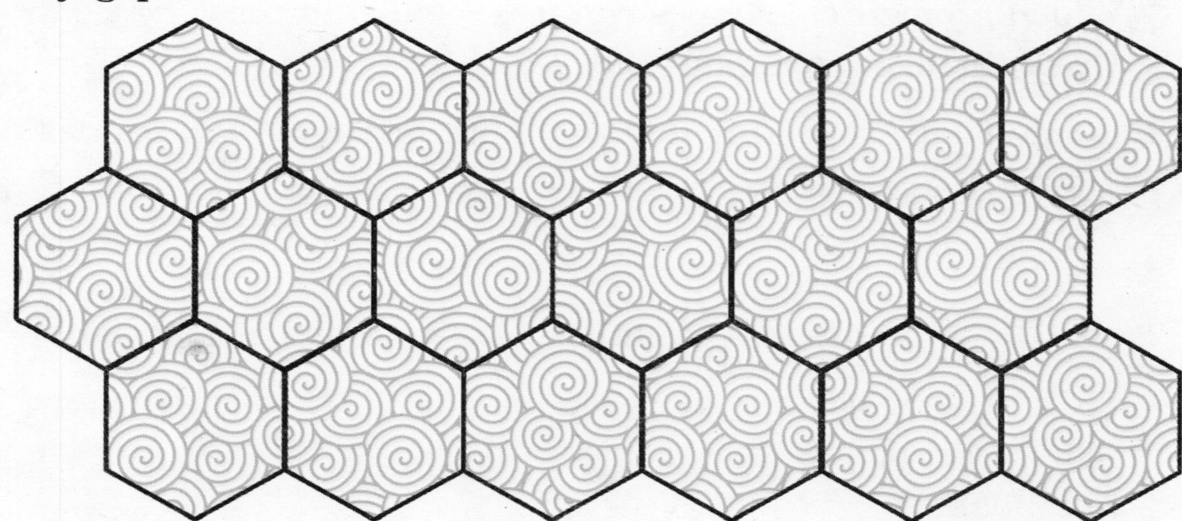

1. Among the following, can you match the tiles with the designs that they will make on the floor? Draw lines to match.

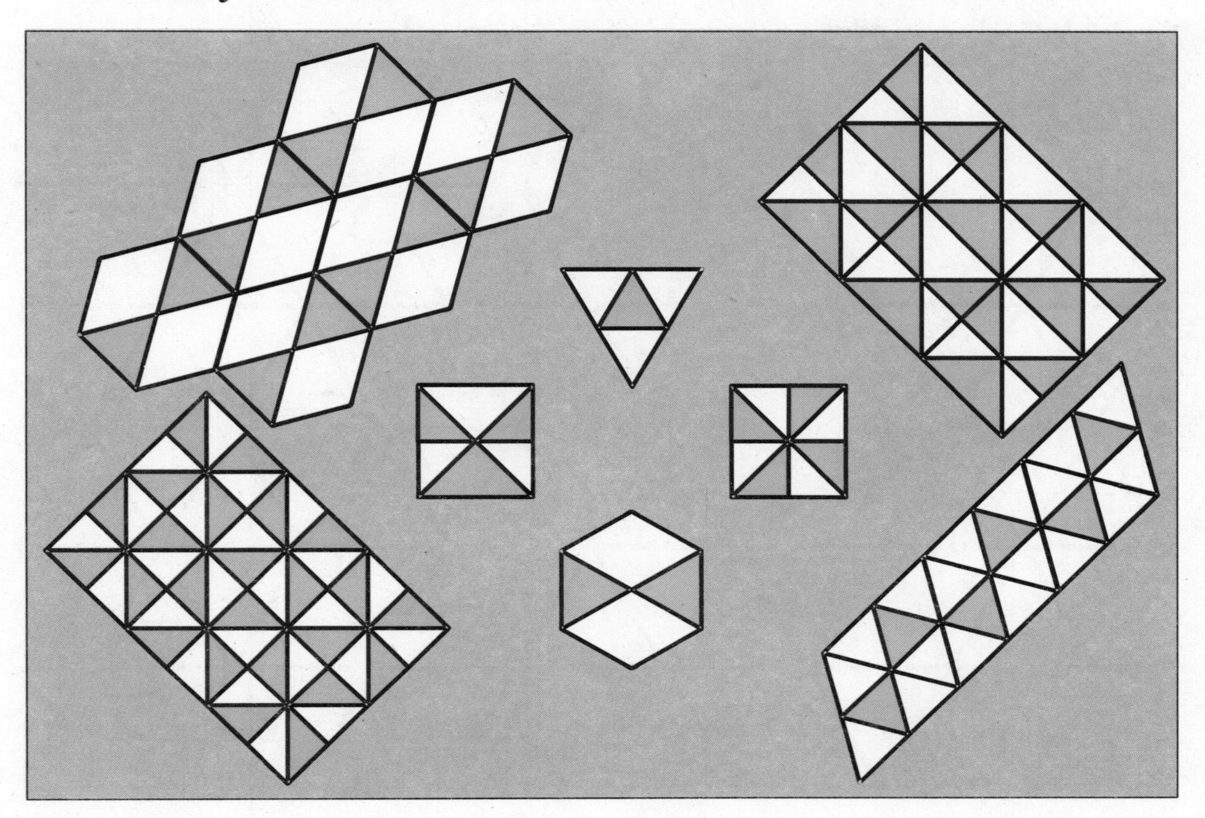

You can also make your own tiles and use them to make your own tiling patterns. You will find some such tiles at the end of the book that you can cut out, trace and colour.

2. Complete the following tiling pattern.

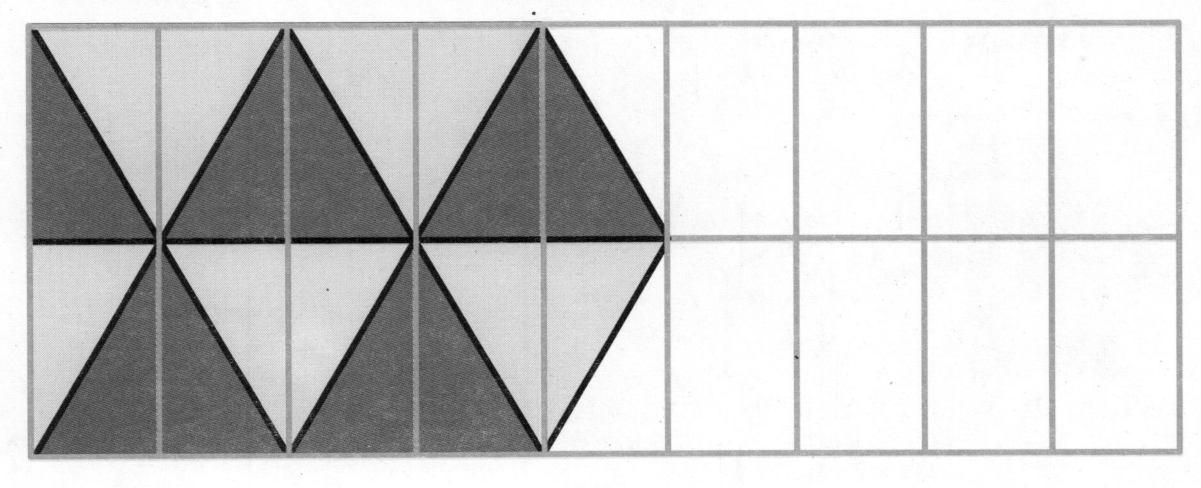

3. Complete this pattern. Compare it with the pattern on page 70 which also uses six sided shapes. What is the difference between the two?

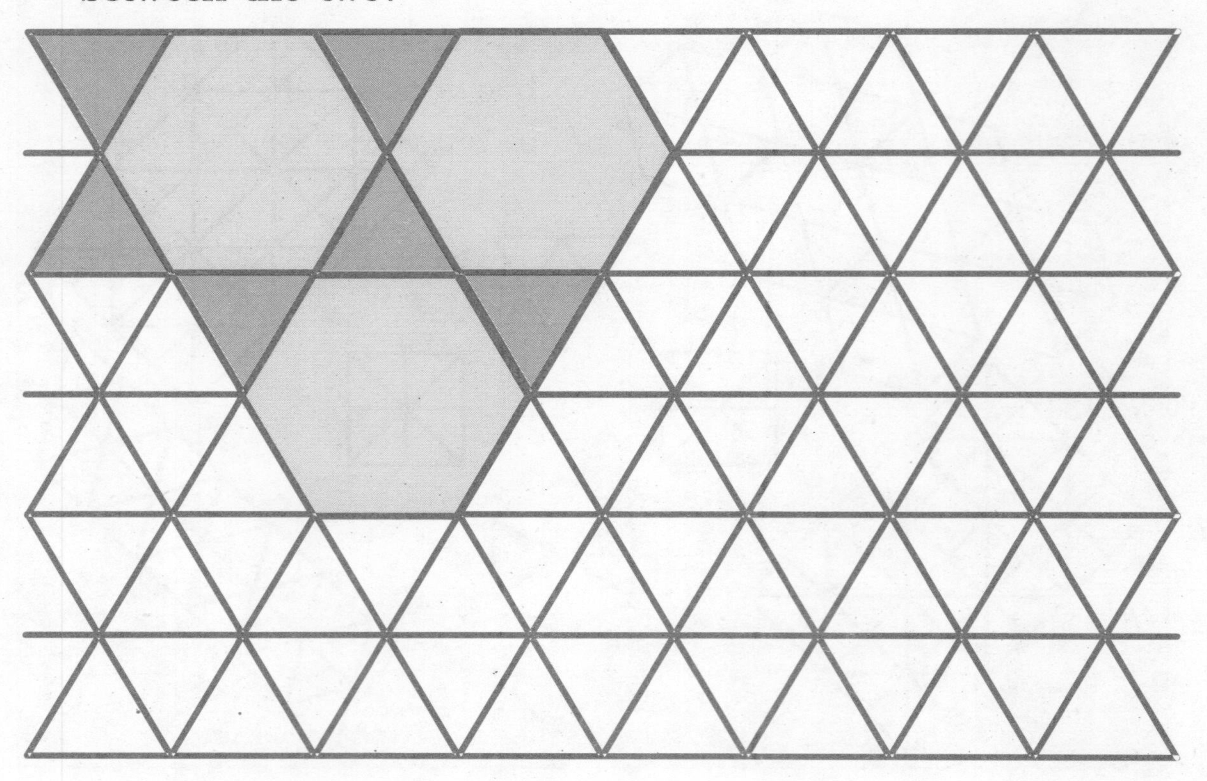

4. Khushboo and Hariz live in Agra. One day they went to see the Taj Mahal. The floor had the pattern shown below:

What do you think? Discuss with your friends.

Tiling Time

The patterns below are made from this tile. 

In this pattern three colours have been used to make it look like steps.

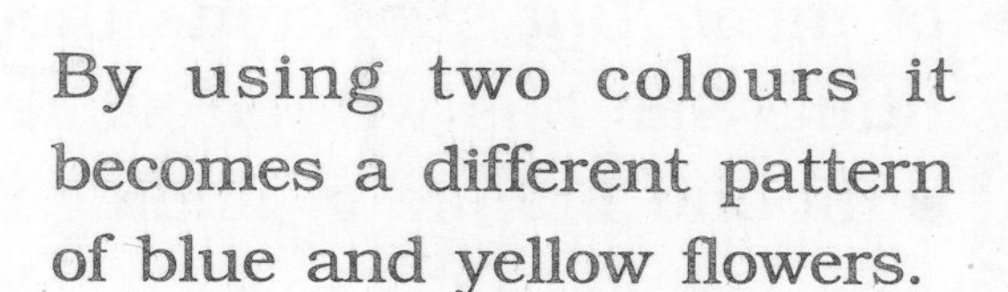

By using two colours it becomes a different pattern of blue and yellow flowers.

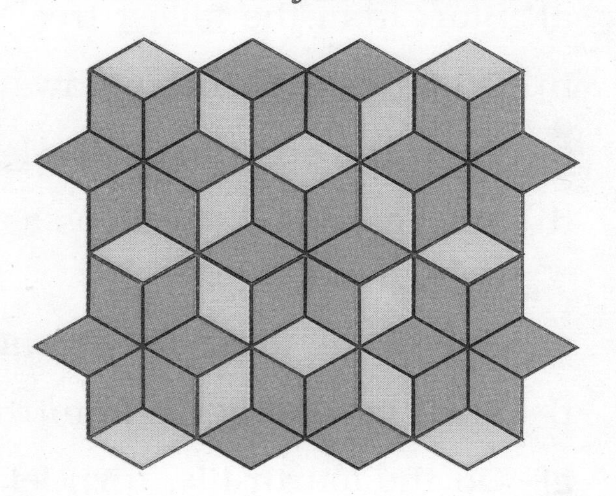

Use different colour combinations to make your own patterns.

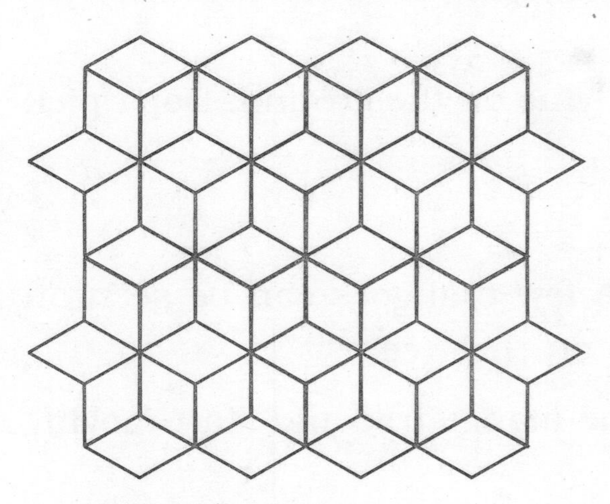

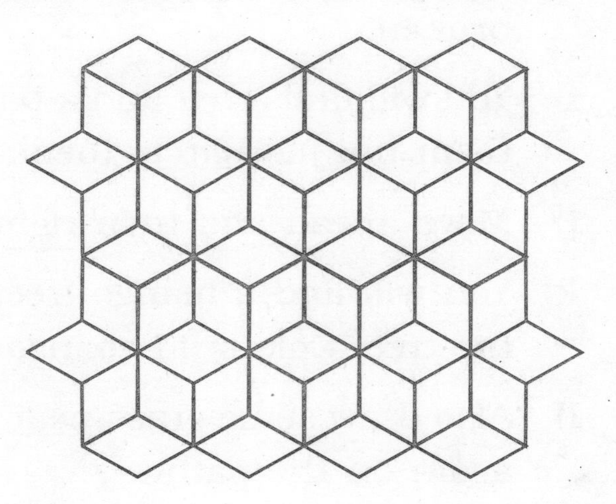

Have you seen this shape in any other design — on a wall, a dress, on a basket, a mat etc.?

Treasure Hunt

Franke and Juhi's mummy has hidden a surprise gift for both of them. But she wants them to find out through a treasure hunt. She has written some instructions here. Can you help Juhi and Franke in finding their gift?

a) Start from the tallest tree.

b) Go forward on the pathway.

c) From the sixth tile, turn left.

d) After moving a few steps again you will find a plant on your right hand side.

e) Colour the dress of the child playing closest to this plant.

f) Start moving again from the plant.

g) On the fourth tile, turn left again.

h) On the way, you will find the corner of the fourth tile is broken.

i) You will find a bat and a ball lying on the ground. Don't pick them up, just circle them.

j) Move ahead and turn right.

k) You will find a mango tree. A few mangoes can be seen on the tree. Colour 11 mangoes on the tree.

l) Also draw some grass near the mango tree and start moving again on the pathway.

m) When you go straight, you will find a house.

n) Behind that house there is a bag. Open it and you will find something sweet in it! Can you tell what their mother has kept in the bag?

Understanding of space will be facilitated if the treasure hunt worksheet is done in the class. This task will enhance skills of children in identifying positions (up, down, front, behind), distance (near, far), size (tall, small), corners and shapes. It will help if more such treasure hunts are given to children as an activity.

Fun with Give and Take

Cricket Match

In a cricket match, Sri Lanka made 235 runs.

India has made 123 runs. How many more runs does India need to win?

To win India must make 236 runs.

Runs India needs to win:

236 – 123 = ?

Guess...
To win India needs
(a) more than 100 runs
(b) less than 100 runs

Let's subtract by first taking away 1s from 1s

	100	10	1
Runs to win	2	3	6
Runs by India –	1	2	3
Runs needed	1	1	3

100 100 10 10 10 1 1 1 1 1 1

So we are left with 100 10 1 1 1

To win India must make 113 runs

Try it Yourself

Geeta had Rs 368 in her purse.

She bought a book for Rs 123.

How much money is left in her purse?

Money left in her purse is Rs 368 – Rs 123 = ?

	100	10	1	
Money in Geeta's purse	3	6	8	100 100 100 / 10 10 10 10 10 10 / 1 1 1 1 1 1 1 1
Cost of book –	1	2	3	

The teacher should discuss with students which number is to be placed above and why.

Can You Help Nabeela?

Nabeela's mother sent her to the market to buy some things. She gave her Rs 245. Nabeela bought 1 kg ghee for Rs 127. The shopkeeper gave her back Rs 98.

(Kilogram is written as kg.)

Did the shopkeeper give her the right amount?

Let's find out.

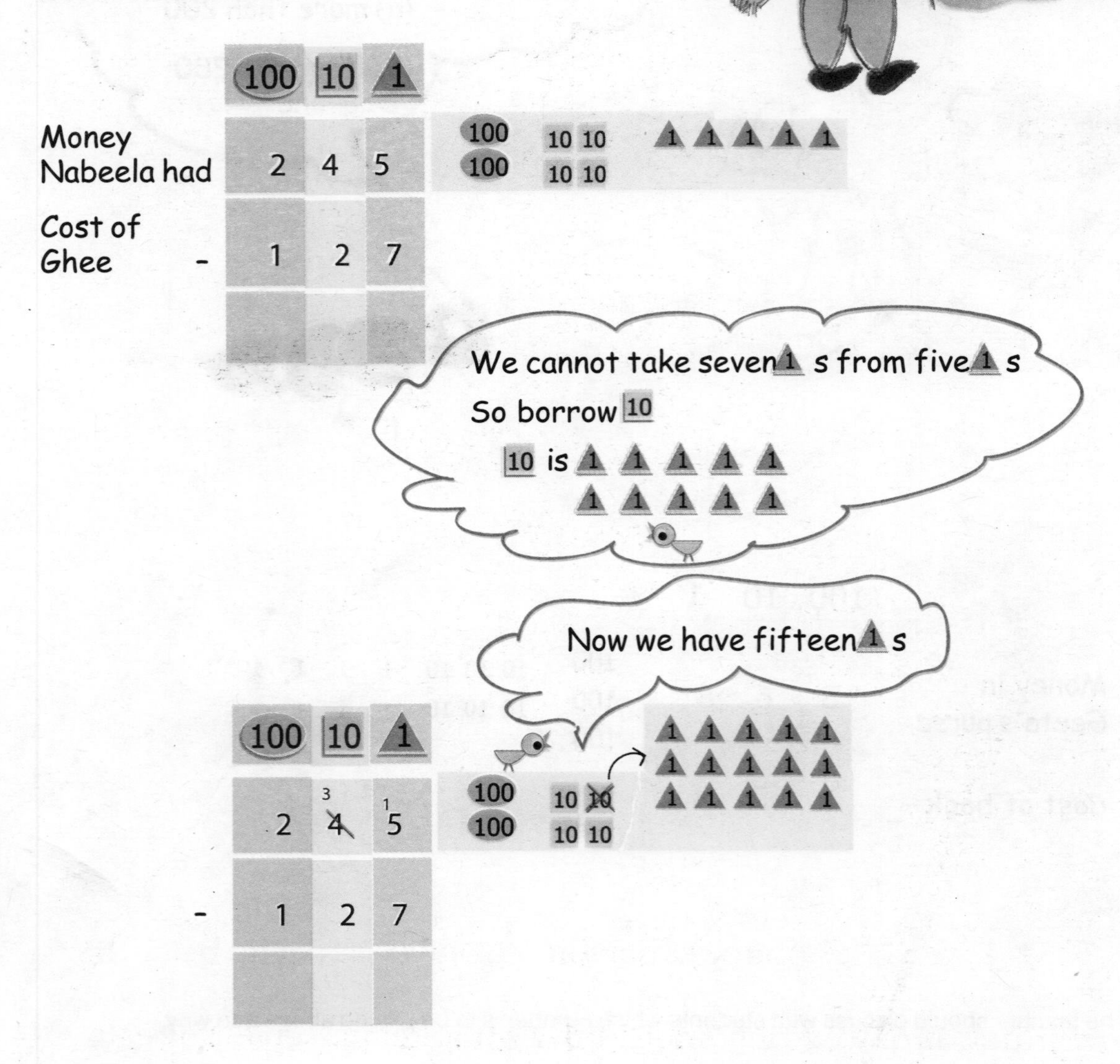

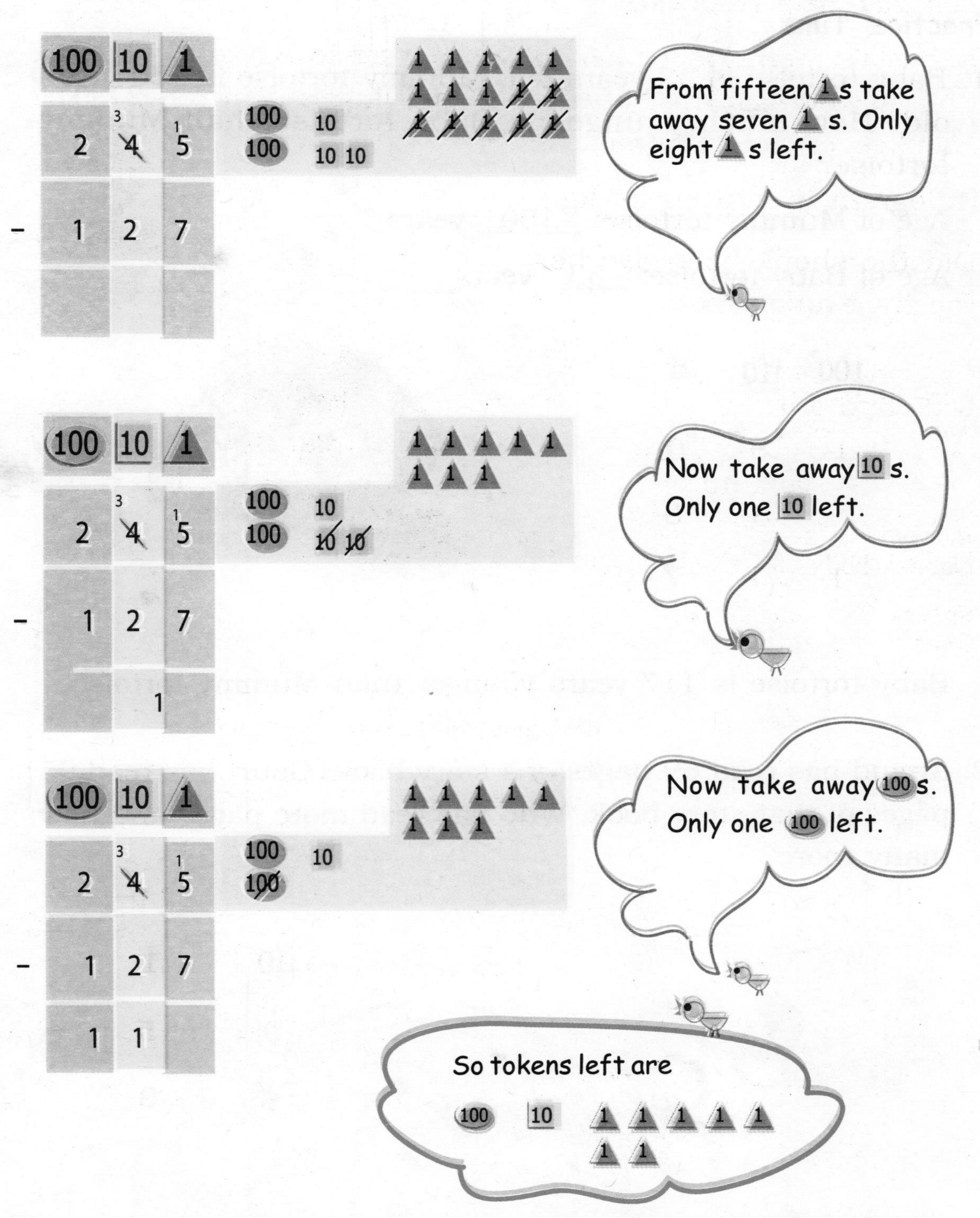

The shopkeeper had to give Nabeela Rs 118.

How much more money should the shopkeeper give Nabeela?

Practice Time

1. Baby tortoise is 33 years old. Mummy tortoise is 150 years old. How much younger is Baby tortoise than Mummy tortoise?

   Age of Mummy tortoise: 150 years

   Age of Baby tortoise: 33 years

	100	10	1
	1	[4] ~~5~~	[1] 0
–		3	3
	1	1	7

Baby tortoise is 117 years younger than Mummy tortoise.

2. Arvind has read 69 pages of a story book. Gouri has read 95 pages of that story book. Who has read more pages and how many more?

	10	1
	9	5
–	6	9

Teachers should motivate students to decide which operation they have to use to solve a problem. More such exercises can be given where students decide the appropriate operation.

3. Reena noted the electricity meter readings of her house. Last month's reading was 118 units. This month's reading is 193 units. How much electricity did she use in one month?

This month's reading ___________

Last month's reading ___________

100	10	1
1	9	3
1	1	8

She used ___________ units of electricity.

4. Khushboo bought a shirt for Rs 125 and trousers for Rs 165. How much money did she spend altogether?

Bought a shirt for Rs ___________

Bought trousers for Rs ___________

100	10	1
1	6	5
1	2	5

She spent Rs ___________ altogether.

5. Solve the following:

17	14	39	12	86
− 3	+ 3	−10	+24	−58
☐	☐	☐	☐	☐

139	237	325	474
− 110	+ 213	− 204	− 136
☐	☐	☐	☐

642	49	135
− 413	+20	+ 146
☐	☐	☐

6. Check your answers yourself:

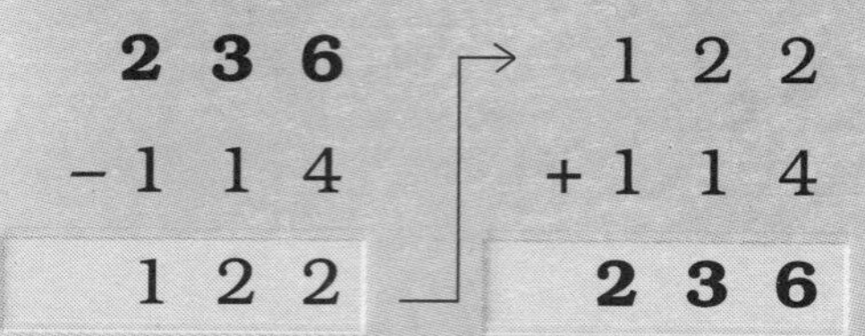

236	122	**340**	312
−114	+114	− 28	+ 28
122	**236**	312	**340**

Check Rashi's subtraction using addition. Give her a ✓ for every right answer.

	3	**8**	**4**
−	2	4	3
	1	4	1

	1	4	1
+	2	4	3
	3	**8**	**4**

✓

	4	6	8
−	1	3	9
	2	2	1

+			

	3	5	6
−	2	4	7
	1	1	9

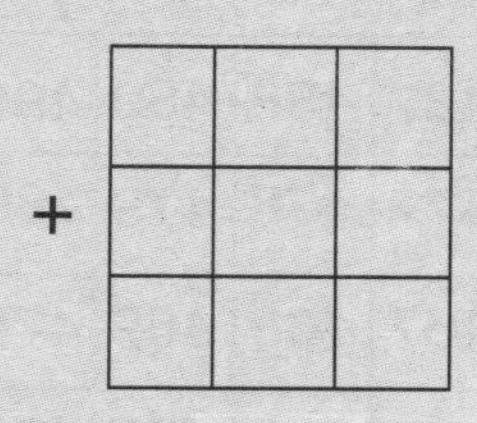

	4	6	8
−	2	2	4
	2	4	4

+			

7. Fill in the missing numbers in the coloured boxes.

	7	8
−	3	
		5

	2	1	
−	1		7
		3	2

		6
−	3	
	6	0

		4	4
−	2	3	8
	2		

The teacher should encourage students to discuss and correct the wrong answers. Children love to correct others' mistakes (for a change!) and also learn from this process.

Let's Deliver Letters

Postman Uncle is ill today. Let's deliver the letters for him.

481	482	483	484	485	486	487	488	489	490
471	472	473	474	475	476	477	478	479	480
461	462	463	464	465	466	467	468	469	470
451	452	453	454	455	456	457	458	459	460
441	442	443	444	445	446	447	448	449	450
431	432	433	434	435	436	437	438	439	440

Write the correct room numbers on the letters. Then find the rooms in the above building and circle them.

Make a circle on room 455.

The teacher should encourage students to solve the problems mentally using the above chart.

Find the Missing Numbers

Look at the number patterns. Write the missing numbers.

a) 100, 200, 300, ____, ____, 600, ____

b)

c) 50, 100, 150, 200, ____, ____, ____, ____

d)

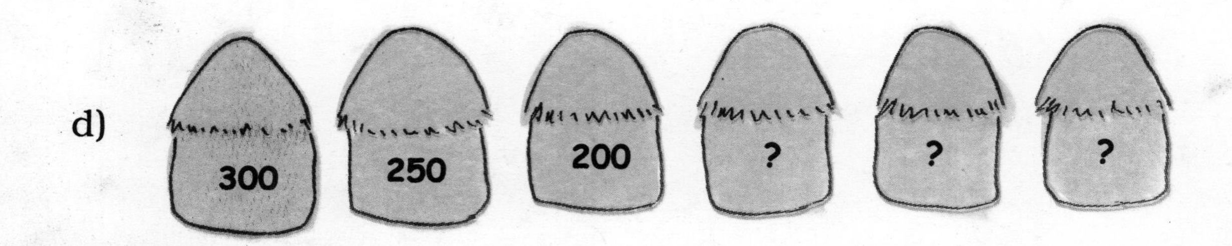

e)

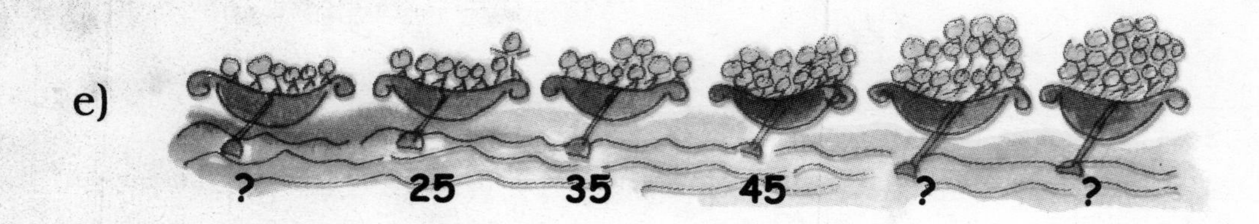

f) 280, 260, 240, ____, ____, ____, ____

g) 125, 150, 175, 200, ____, 250, ____, ____

Mental Maths

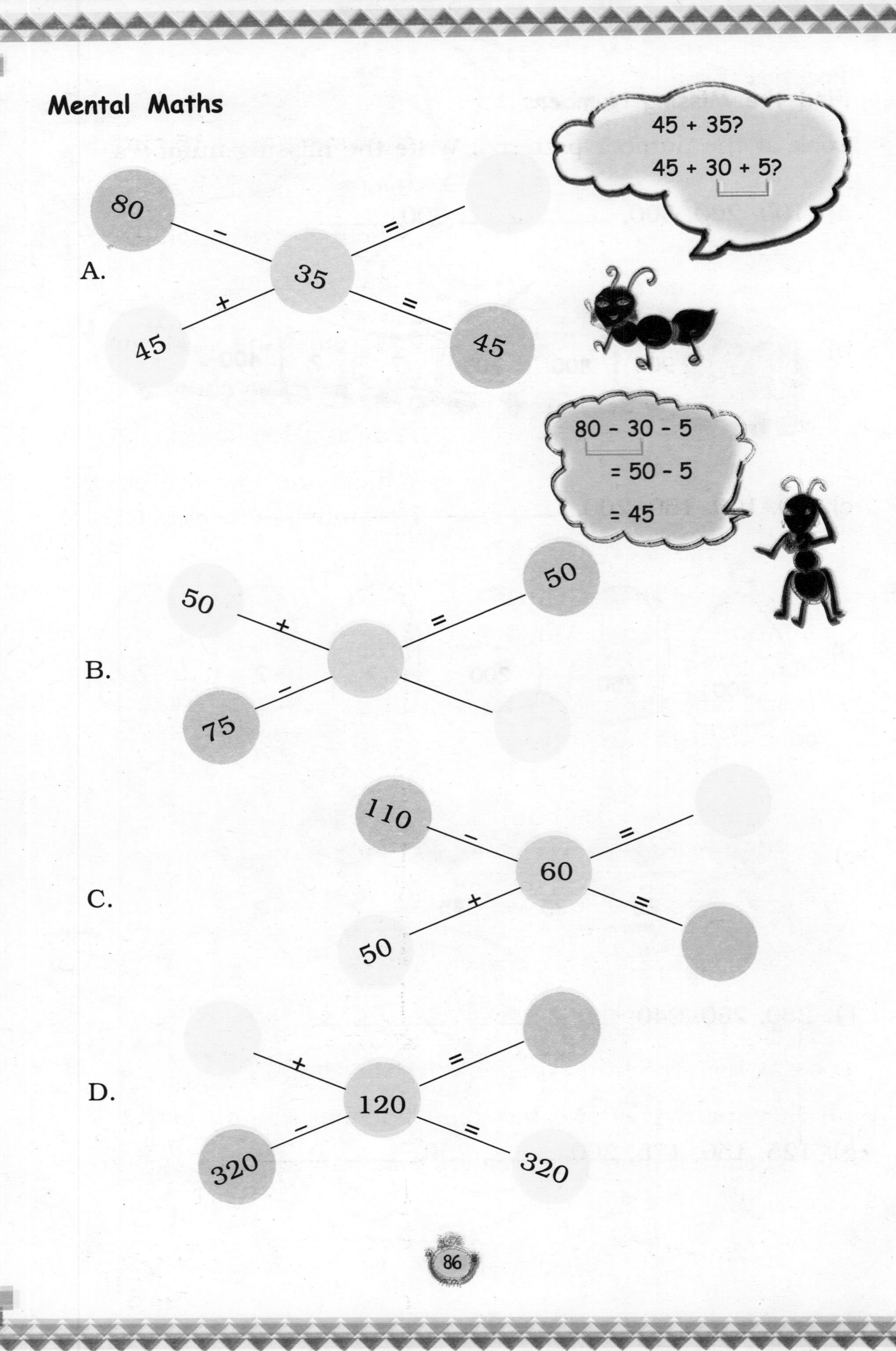

Practice Time

1. Indu's pencil is 15 cm long.

   Jyoti's pencil is 8 cm long.

   Whose pencil is longer?

   How much longer?

2. Ask your Papa or Mummy

   Price of 1 kilo salt –

   Price of 1 kilo sugar –

   Which one is more costly?

   How much more does it cost?

3. Ajay cooked *chapatis* in 25 minutes. Then he made *daal* in 15 minutes. How much time did he take to cook both things?

4. Chanchal sells school sweaters. In 2 days she sold some red, blue and grey coloured sweaters.

	Red	*Blue*	*Grey*
Sweaters sold on first day	38	66	74
Sweaters sold on second day	40	23	89

Look at the above and answer the following:

(a) How many grey sweaters did Chanchal sell in 2 days?

(b) Did she sell more red sweaters than blue sweaters in 2 days?

(c) How many red and grey sweaters did she sell on the first day — more than 120 or less than 120? Tick (✓) the right answer.

more than 120 ☐ less than 120 ☐

(d) How many sweaters in all did she sell on the second day — more than 140 or less than 140? Tick (✓) the right answer.

more than 140 ☐ less than 140 ☐

5. *Is Sangeeta right?*

Sangeeta went to the market with her grandpa.

She looked at the prices and said to her grandpa —

(a) Ghee is Rs 102 rupees costlier than biscuits. ☐

(b) Price of oil and ghee altogether is more than Rs 200. ☐

(c) Price of ghee and 10 kg rice is less than Rs 300. ☐

(d) Oil costs Rs 40 more than a pack of biscuits. ☐

Is Sangeeta right? Mark (✓) or (×) in the box.

Can you find this without using paper and pencil?

Story Problems

Nisha and Sonu were making story problems. Nisha said — 13 boys and 14 girls in a class. Sonu, can you make a problem on it?

Sonu wrote

There are 13 boys and 14 girls in a class.
How many students are there altogether?

You can also make story problems with your friends. Look at each picture and the words next to it. Write your problem below it.

A. 36 men and 52 women waiting for their turn

B. We have our mid-day meal in 20 minutes and play for 15 minutes.

C. The post office is 1 kilometre from Shahid's home and 2 kilometres from his school.

D. Bunty has read 27 books and Babli has read 34 books.

Count to Subtract!

Dolma bought 4 dozen (48) bananas and gave one to each of her friends. 13 bananas were left. How many friends got a banana?

As you know, this can be found by counting forward from 13. It is easier to count in jumps of 10. You can also use Kittu's home shown on page 29 to solve these problems.

48 – 13

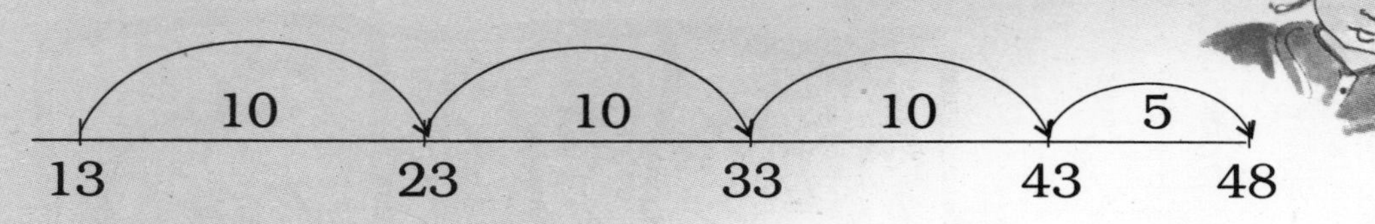

10 + 10 + 10 + 5 = <u>35</u>

So 48 – 13 = [35]

A. 56 – 37 = [ ]

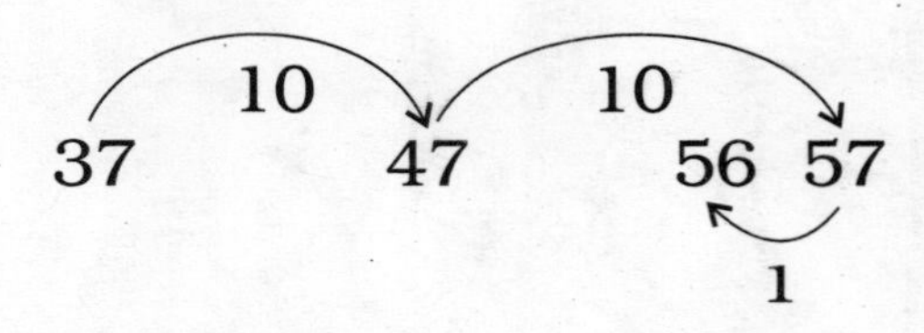

10 + 10 – 1 = ______

So 56 – 37 = [ ]

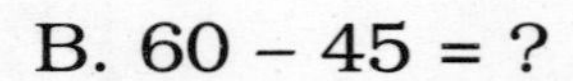

B. 60 – 45 = ?

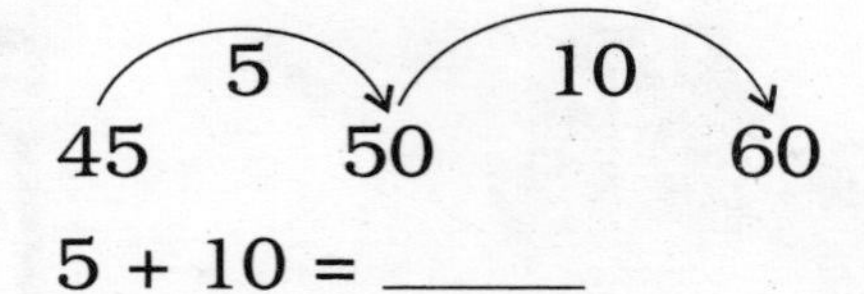

5 + 10 = ______

So 60 – 45 = [ ]

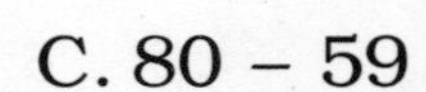

C. 80 – 59

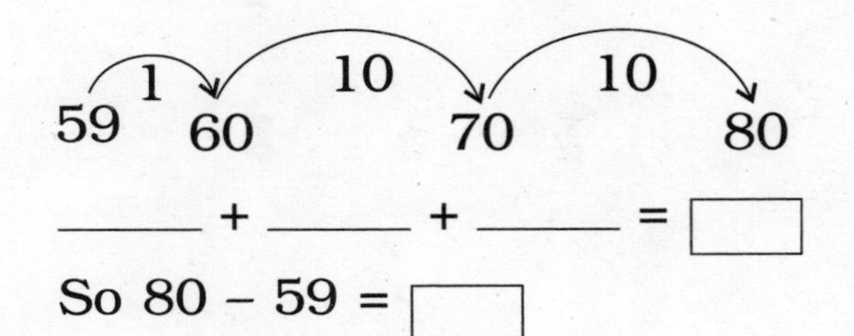

______ + ______ + ______ = [ ]

So 80 – 59 = [ ]

D. 85 – 63 = [ ]

E. 84 – 69 = [ ]

F. 60 – 20 = [ ]

G. 90 – 50 = [ ]

All the King's Horses....

Once there was a king who could count only up to 9. Up to what number can you count?

The king loved horses. But he could never count all of them. He kept them in such a way that he needed to count only up to 9 from each side.

How many horses in all did the king have? _______

One day a visitor with 4 horses came there. It was getting dark so he wanted to stay there at night. But the horse-keeper was scared. If the king saw these extra horses he would be very angry! The visitor said — do not worry. The king will never know. So he arranged the horses like this:

How many horses are there now? _______

At night the king came to count the horses. Along each side he counted 9 horses. Ah! That's fine – he said. Then he happily went to sleep.

In the morning the clever visitor tried another trick. He took out his own 4 horses. But he also ran away with some of the king's horses. He left the king's horses standing in this way.

The silly king did not find any horse missing. Can you help him?

How many horses are now left? ________

How many of the king's horses were taken away?

(Based on a Tamil folk story from the book "Numeracy Counts!")

Pu^{ZZ}le

What numbers are we?

If you add us both you get 100.

The difference between us is also 100.

7 Time Goes On.......

Ulta Pulta Time — This is a story with topsy turvy time.

As the sun sets ______________ Sumana wakes up. What a lovely evening! ______________ She washes her face fast in 2 hours ______________ and runs out. She goes straight to the bird's nest. She has been watching the eggs for the last few months ______________. She was waiting for the baby birds to come out. But before she can blink her eyes, in a week ______________ a cat jumps on to the tree. The mother bird cries loudly and Sumana rushes to shoo away the cat. As the cat jumps, it hits the big green mango. **Dhum!** ...

Dhum!

... In two days ______________ it is on the ground ! Oh, how sad! The mango is still not fully ripe. It needed one more year ______________ to become sweet. Suddenly Sumana's sister calls out — Are you still not hungry? Has your stomach clock gone to sleep? Come and eat hot upma for dinner ______________.

Wasn't that funny? You must have guessed that the coloured words are wrong. Choose the correct word from the box given below and write it next to the wrong word.

days	rises	seconds	morning
breakfast	moment	minutes	week

How Long does it Take?

Have you seen someone knitting a sweater? Or someone weaving a cloth? Do try to find out from a potter how long it takes to make a pot. Also tell us if you take hours or minutes to have your bath! (Is it years since you last had a bath? Ha, ha!)

Think of many different things that can take different times. Make your table as long as you can.

Takes minutes	*Takes hours*	*Takes days*
a bath	to stitch a shirt	to knit a sweater
to boil milk	to set curd	to weave a sari
	a school day	for a banana to become ripe

Think of some other things, some faster and some slower. Make a long list.

Takes seconds

to blink my eyes   to snap my fingers   to gulp my medicine

for fruit to fall from a tree

Takes months
to grow wheat (from seed to big plant)
to change from summer to winter
for a baby to come out of its mother's stomach

Clap! Clap! — Before you Catch

Play this game

Throw a stone into the air. Clap once before you catch it.

Now try to clap 2 times before the catch.

Try more claps. How many times can you clap before you catch the stone?

Ta Thai — Different Claps

Clap 2 times and say 1 2

Keep clapping 1 2, 1 2, 1 2, ...

or say *Ta Thai, Ta Thai, Ta Thai,* ....

Also stamp your feet Left Right, Left Right, Left Right,.....

Now clap with three beats 1 2 3, 1 2 3, 1 2 3, ...

Say: *Ta Thai Tut, Ta Thai Tut, Ta Thai Tut,* ....

Can you stamp your feet Left Right Left, Left Right Left, ...

How many of you can speak and stamp at the same time?

Find Out

Have you heard people playing a *tabla* or the drums? Find out a few different beats they play. Also ask what 'bols' they say for the beats they play.

How Old are We?

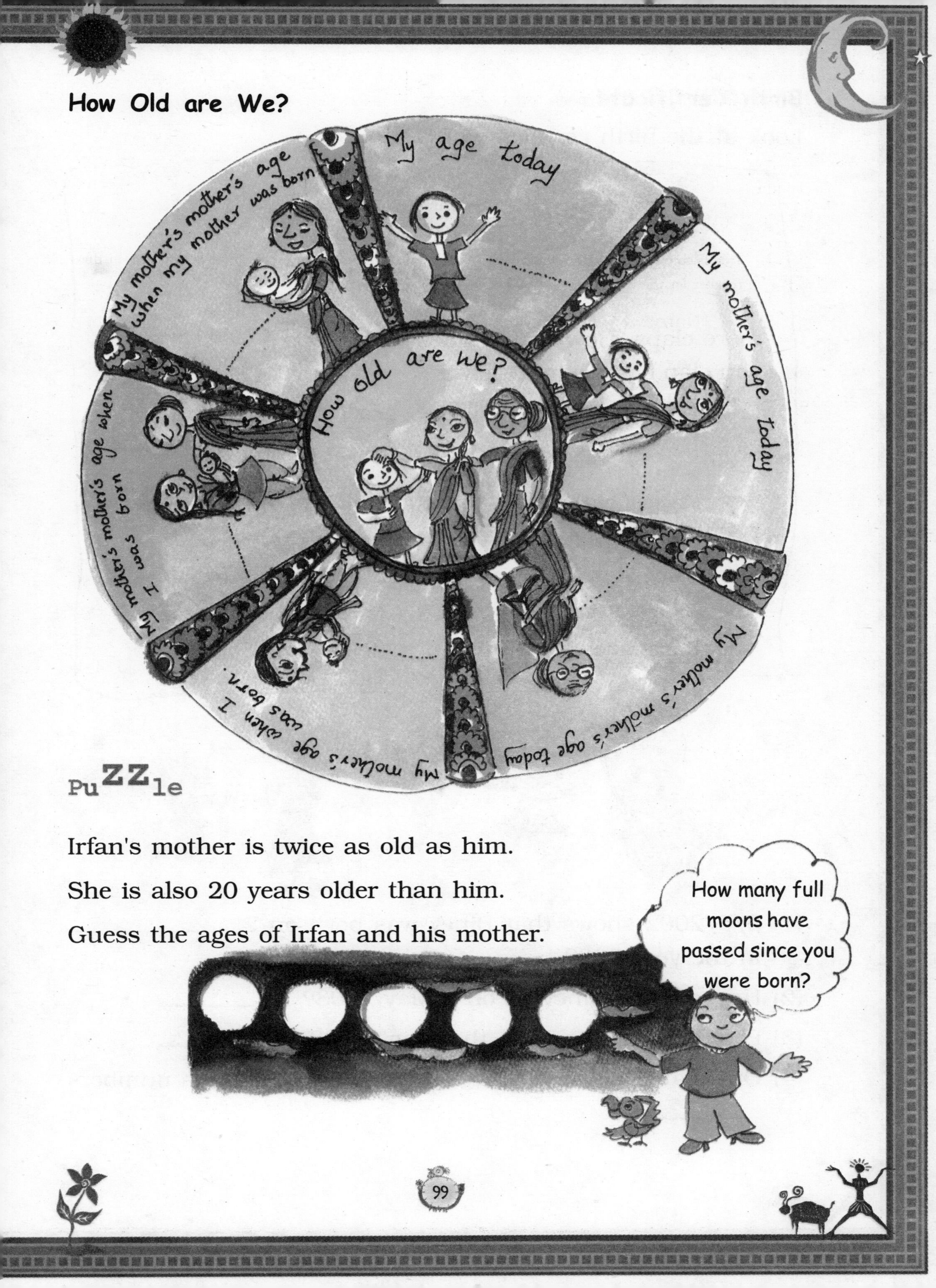

PuZZle

Irfan's mother is twice as old as him.

She is also 20 years older than him.

Guess the ages of Irfan and his mother.

Birth Certificate

Look at the birth certificate of Bincy.

Form Number 5

Government of Kerala

Birth Certificate

This is to certify that this information is taken from the original record of birth which is in the register for the year 2002 of Kottayam Panchayat.

Name	Bincy Thomas Jacob
Sex	Female
Date of birth:	02/05/2002 (Second May, Two Thousand Two)
Place of birth:	Kadampuzha Hospital
Name of Father:	Jacob Tharakan
Name of Mother:	Lara Thomas
Date of Registration:	02/05/2002
Registration Number	815/02

Date 05.08.2002 Signature of issuing authority

(1) 2/5/2002 shows that Bincy was born on 2 ____________, in the year 2002.

(2) How old will Bincy be on 2 May 2008? __________

(3) How old will she be in the year 2052? __________

(4) On what date will she be eight years old? Write in numbers.

____

(5) How many months old was Bincy on 2 August 2002? ____________

(6) How many years old is Bincy now? ____________

(7) After how many months of her birth was the certificate issued? ____________

(8) What is the registration number of her certificate? ________

Find Out

When were you born? ____________

Write your date of birth in numbers. ____________

Do you have a birth certificate? Ask your parents and make one for yourself.

Form Number ____

Government of ______

Birth Certificate

This is to certifiy that this information is taken from the original record of birth which is in the register for the year ____________ of ____________

Name

Sex

Date of birth:

Place of birth:

Name of Father:

Name of Mother:

Date of Registration:

Registration Number

Date

Signature of issuing authority

Calendar 2006

January

S	M	T	W	T	F	S
1	2	3	4	5	6	7
8	9	10	11	12	13	14
15	16	17	18	19	20	21
22	23	24	25	26	27	28
29	30	31				

February

S	M	T	W	T	F	S
			1	2	3	4
5	6	7	8	9	10	11
12	13	14	15	16	17	18
19	20	21	22	23	24	25
26	27	28				

March

S	M	T	W	T	F	S
			1	2	3	4
5	6	7	8	9	10	11
12	13	14	15	16	17	18
19	20	21	22	23	24	25
26	27	28	29	30	31	

April

S	M	T	W	T	F	S
						1
2	3	4	5	6	7	8
9	10	11	12	13	14	15
16	17	18	19	20	21	22
23	24	25	26	27	28	29
30						

May

S	M	T	W	T	F	S
	1	2	3	4	5	6
7	8	9	10	11	12	13
14	15	16	17	18	19	20
21	22	23	24	25	26	27
28	29	30	31			

June

S	M	T	W	T	F	S
				1	2	3
4	5	6	7	8	9	10
11	12	13	14	15	16	17
18	19	20	21	22	23	24
25	26	27	28	29	30	

July

S	M	T	W	T	F	S
						1
2	3	4	5	6	7	8
9	10	11	12	13	14	15
16	17	18	19	20	21	22
23	24	25	26	27	28	29
30	31					

August

S	M	T	W	T	F	S
		1	2	3	4	5
6	7	8	9	10	11	12
13	14	15	16	17	18	19
20	21	22	23	24	25	26
27	28	29	30	31		

September

S	M	T	W	T	F	S
					1	2
3	4	5	6	7	8	9
10	11	12	13	14	15	16
17	18	19	20	21	22	23
24	25	26	27	28	29	30

October

S	M	T	W	T	F	S
1	2	3	4	5	6	7
8	9	10	11	12	13	14
15	16	17	18	19	20	21
22	23	24	25	26	27	28
29	30	31				

November

S	M	T	W	T	F	S
			1	2	3	4
5	6	7	8	9	10	11
12	13	14	15	16	17	18
19	20	21	22	23	24	25
26	27	28	29	30		

December

S	M	T	W	T	F	S
					1	2
3	4	5	6	7	8	9
10	11	12	13	14	15	16
17	18	19	20	21	22	23
24	25	26	27	28	29	30
31						

Calendar

Let us look at the calendar for the year 2006.

- How many months does a year have? ____________
- List the months which have 30 days. ____________
  ____
- List the months which have 31 days. ____________
  ____
- How many days does the month of February have?
  ____
- How many days makes a week? ____________
- How many weeks are there in July? ____________ Is it true for all the months? ____________
- In which month did you come to Class III?
- Make a circle on these dates in the calendar:

  26th January

  14th November

  31st December.

Is there something special about these dates?

Fill in the blanks with the correct year:

2005 2008 2007 2004 2009 2010

1. Which year was it two years back? ____________
2. In which year were you in Class II? ____________
3. Which year will be the next year? ____________
4. Which year will come after 3 years? ____________

This chapter encourages children to look at different cultural contexts in which the idea of elapsed time occurs in their lives. It is more important for them to be able to develop an intuitive estimate of seconds, minutes, months etc. than to actually measure. The chapter also helps them to understand the use of a clock and calendar through interesting exercises. Teachers could create more such exercises related to number patterns and symmetries.

Which Festival comes First?

Given below are some festivals we celebrate during the year. Look at the calendar (2006) to find the days on which these fall.

Name of the festival	*Date*	*Day*
Diwali	October 21	
Pongal	January 14	
Raksha Bandhan	August 9	
Gandhi Jayanti	October 2	
Milad-Ul-Nabi	April 11	
Onam	September 5	
Guru Nanak's Birthday	November 5	
Guru Ravidas's Birthday	February 13	
Christmas Day	December 25	
Bihu	April 14	

- Arrange the festivals in the order in which they come in the year.

1. ____________ 6. ____________

2. ____________ 7. ____________

3. ____________ 8. ____________

4. ____________ 9. ____________

5. ____________ 10. ____________

- Which festival comes in the beginning of the year?

____

- Which festival comes at the end of the year?

____

Calendar Magic

Here is the calendar for the month of February 2007.

Let us mark a square on the calendar and see some magic.

February 2007

S	M	T	W	T	F	S
				1	2	3
4	5	6	7	8	9	10
11	12	13	14	15	16	17
18	19	20	21	22	23	24
25	26	27	28			

Which is the number in the centre of the square? __________

Join three numbers by drawing a line. The line must pass through the number at the centre.

5	6	7
12	13	14
19	20	21

How many such lines can you draw?

Add the three numbers on each of these lines.

What do you notice?

5 + 13 + 21 =

6 + 13 + 20 =

19 + 13 + 7 =

12 + 13 + 14 =

- Now look at the calendar of 2006. Also look for the present month and draw any similar square in your notebook. Does the magic work for these?
- Is this magic possible on a 10 × 10 number chart? Go to the chapter 'Fun with Numbers' and check.

More Magic!

March 2007

S	M	T	W	T	F	S
				1	2	3
4	5	6	7	8	9	10
11	12	13	14	15	16	17
18	19	20	21	22	23	24
25	26	27	28	29	30	31

See if this magic works for other lines which have five numbers. What about five numbers on a slanting line? Try this trick with your family and friends.

Can you find other magic patterns in the calendar?

Complete the Calendar for August 2006

Sunday	Monday	Tuesday	Wednesday	Thursday	Friday	Saturday
		1		3		
	7					
					18	
				24		

Colour all the Sundays in red.

On which day does this month end? ____________

Write the number of days in this month. ____________

What day is it on 13th August? ____________

What is the date on the second Saturday? ____________

Is the 21st a Sunday? ____________

What is the day on the 29th? What will be the date on the same day next week? ____________

How many Thursdays are there in this month? ____________

Find Out!

Which months in the calendar (2006) have 5 Sundays?

Is there any other day in any month which comes 5 times?

Can there be 6 Sundays in a month? Why?

Ask such questions for the current month and also other months. Encourage students to discover more patterns through a calendar.

The True Story of Pedki Devi

My Time Line

My name is Pedki Devi. I live in a village in Dhanbad district (Jharkhand). I never got a chance to go to school. I remember that when I was 5 years old I broke my foot. I had climbed a tree to eat the jamun fruit. But the branch broke and I fell down. My foot still hurts in winter.

While grazing our goats we often got busy in playing. Once at the age of 10 years I got a big scolding — I had lost one goat! At the age of 15 years I was married. My husband was much older than me. My first daughter was born three years after my marriage. Later I had three more children when I was 20, 22 and 24 years old.

Time passed very fast then. I was busy with my farm, housework and looking after my animals. But at the age of 35 years my world came to a stop. My husband fell ill and died. His brothers tried to take away our farm. They beat me badly and said I was a witch! Some good people saved me. We fought a case against those who beat me up. At the age of 40 years I saw a police station for the first time. When I was 45 I learnt to read and write. 2 years later I got my eldest daughter married. Now I am 50 years old. I enjoy playing with my grandchild. Two of my children are studying in school.

Some things that happened in her life are given below. Mark these on her time line. For example, when she was 5 years old Pedki broke her foot. A is marked at 5 on the time line.

A. Broke her foot

B. Lost one goat

C. Got married

D. Had her fourth child

E. First saw a police station

F. Learnt to read and write

G. Eldest daughter got married

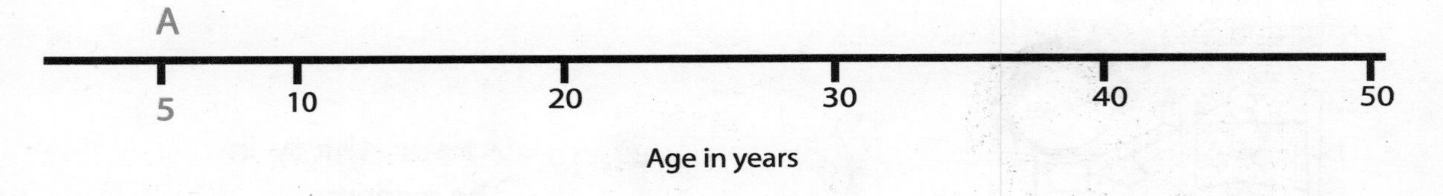

* Mark on the time line when she was born.
* In the blank box draw a picture of Pedki as a new born baby.
* Make your own time line. Ask people around you and mark at least one thing that happened in each year of your life.

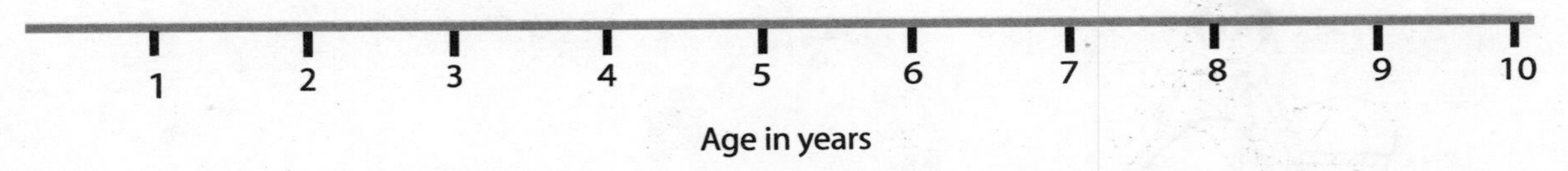

* Make time lines of people you admire. These can be from among your family, friends, teachers, etc.

One Day in the Life of Kusum

Let's see what Kusum does every day.

Write down the time for each picture.

For some pictures the time is already written and you must draw the hands on the clock. In others you have to write the time shown by the clock.

Kusum gets up early in the morning.

She brings water from the well.

At six -thirty in the morning

She cleans her house.

She goes to school.

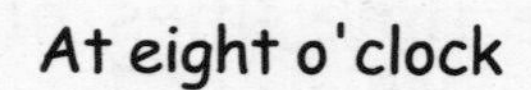

At eight o'clock

She is studying in school.

1 o'clock in the afternoon

She comes back from school.

She takes lunch with her brother and grandmother.

Five-thirty in the evening

She plays with her friends.

9 o'clock at night

She listens to a story from her grandmother before she sleeps.

Now prepare a chart showing your own daily routine.

Time of the day		
In words	*On the clock*	*What do you do at this time?*

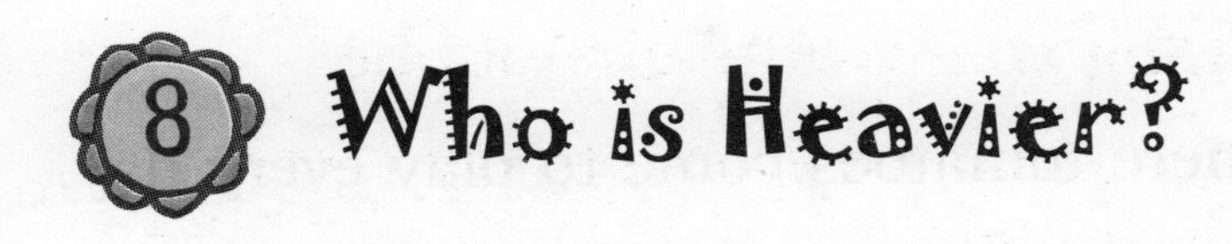

8 Who is Heavier?

Gur (jaggery) and Groundnuts

Shabnam loved to eat jaggery (gur) and groundnuts.

One day she bought 1 kg of jaggery and 1 kg of groundnuts.

(You know that kilogram is also written as kg.)

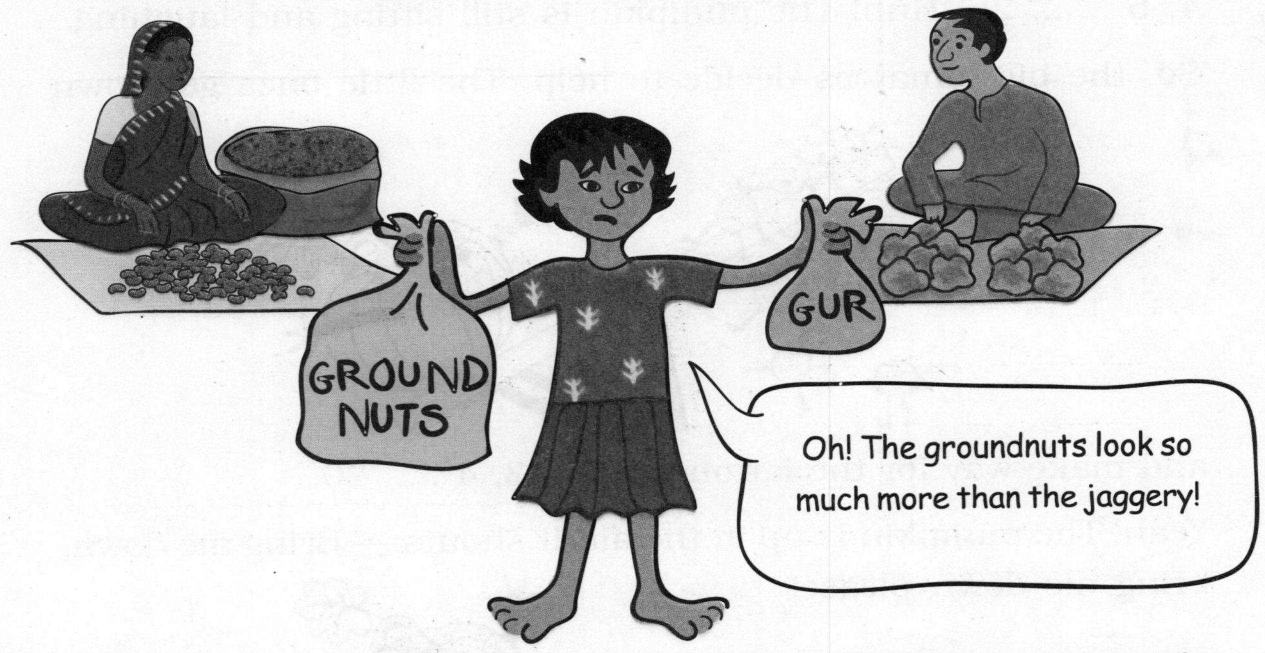

* Are the groundnuts really more than the jaggery (gur) in weight or do they just look more?

Now guess, for which of these you need a bigger bag:

(1) 1 kg popcorn or 1 kg sugar?

(2) 1 kg peas or 1 kg potatoes?

Go to the market and check if your guess is right.

Pumpkin Tomato '*Panga*'

This is the playground where tomatoes come to play every day.

They love playing on the see-saw. One day a big pumpkin comes and sits on one side of the see-saw. When he does not get up for a long time, the tomatoes decide to sit on the other side and lift the pumpkin up so that he falls off.

The little tomatoes start climbing on to the other side...1, 2, 3, 4, 5 .... 25. Huh! The pumpkin is still sitting and laughing.

So, the big tomatoes decide to help. The little ones get down

and make way for the fat ones. 1, 2, 3, 4 ..... 20.

Yeah! The pumpkin is up in the air. It shouts — Bring me down, bring me down please!

'*Panga*' is a colloquial word which gives the sense of a problem or a quarrel. It has been used deliberately because children can find it amusing.

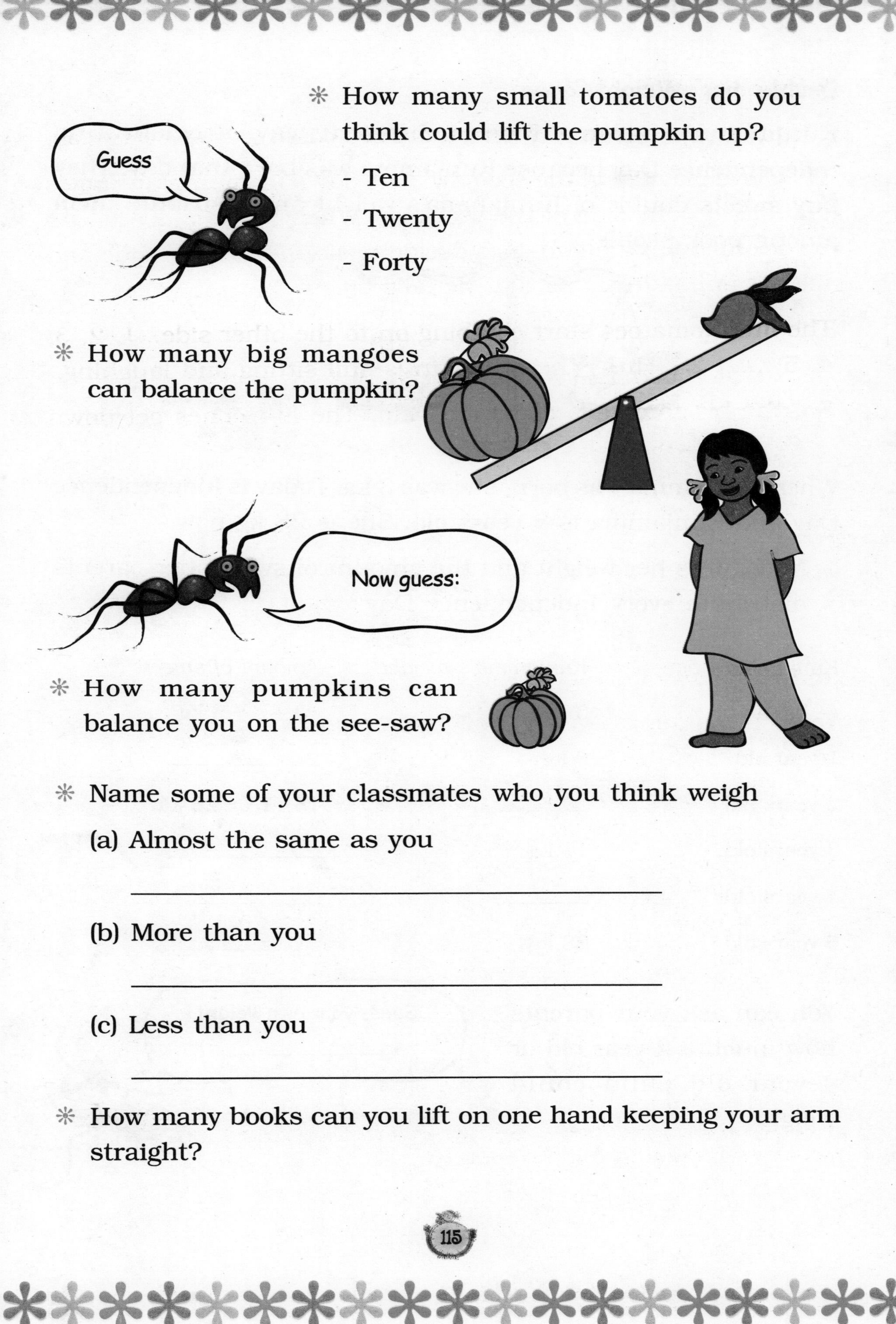

* How many small tomatoes do you think could lift the pumpkin up?
  - Ten
  - Twenty
  - Forty

* How many big mangoes can balance the pumpkin?

* How many pumpkins can balance you on the see-saw?

* Name some of your classmates who you think weigh

  (a) Almost the same as you

  ____

  (b) More than you

  ____

  (c) Less than you

  ____

* How many books can you lift on one hand keeping your arm straight?

Double her Weight

Kunjamma's parents have a different way of celebrating Independence Day because Kunjamma was born that day. They buy sweets double of Kunjamma's weight and distribute them among poor people.

When Kunjamma was born, she was 3 kg. Today is Independence Day and Kunjamma is 5 years old. She is 28 kg now.

- Now guess her weight and the amount of sweets her parents distribute every Independence Day.

Kunjamma's age	*Kunjamma's weight*	*Amount of sweets*
At birth	3 kg	3 + 3 = 6 kg
1 year old	9 kg	________
2 years old	________	13 +13 = 26 kg
3 years old	17 kg	________
4 years old	________	________
5 years old	28 kg	________

You can ask your parents how much a 2-year old or 4-year old child could weigh.

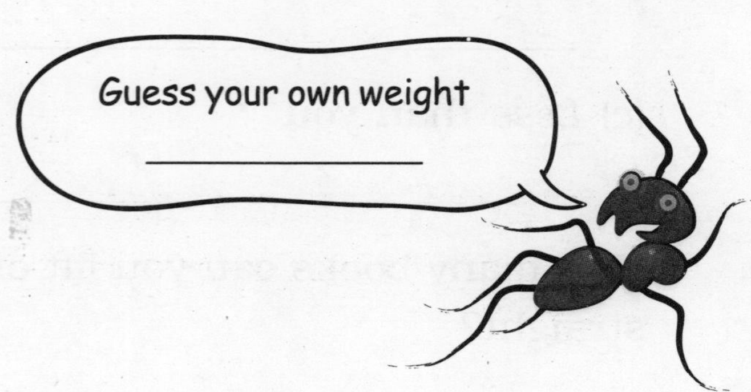

Yum-yum Rice

Shugoto heard about a new dish on the radio. He wants to try making it. When he notes down how to make it, he gets confused.

This is what he notes down —

(1) Pour **2 spoons** of water in the pot

(2) Boil the water and add

- **1 pinch** of *daal*
- **half kg** red chilli powder
- **1 bowl** salt

(3) Now put **a spoon** of rice

(4) Add **2** peas and **8 glasses** of mustard seeds

(5) Finally add **1 kg** of onions

Mix everything and boil for 15 minutes.

But Shugoto feels there is something VERY wrong in the amounts of everything!!!

✻ Help him match the things with their right amounts.

1 kg	rice
half kg	*daal*
________	peas
________	water
________	onions
________	salt
________	mustard seeds
________	red chilli powder

Activity Time

A. Make a list of things bought at your home. Find out how much of each thing is bought at one time. These things can be rice, oil, chilli powder, sugar, milk, onions, ginger, etc.

Name of thing	*How much bought*

B. Guess their weights and match.

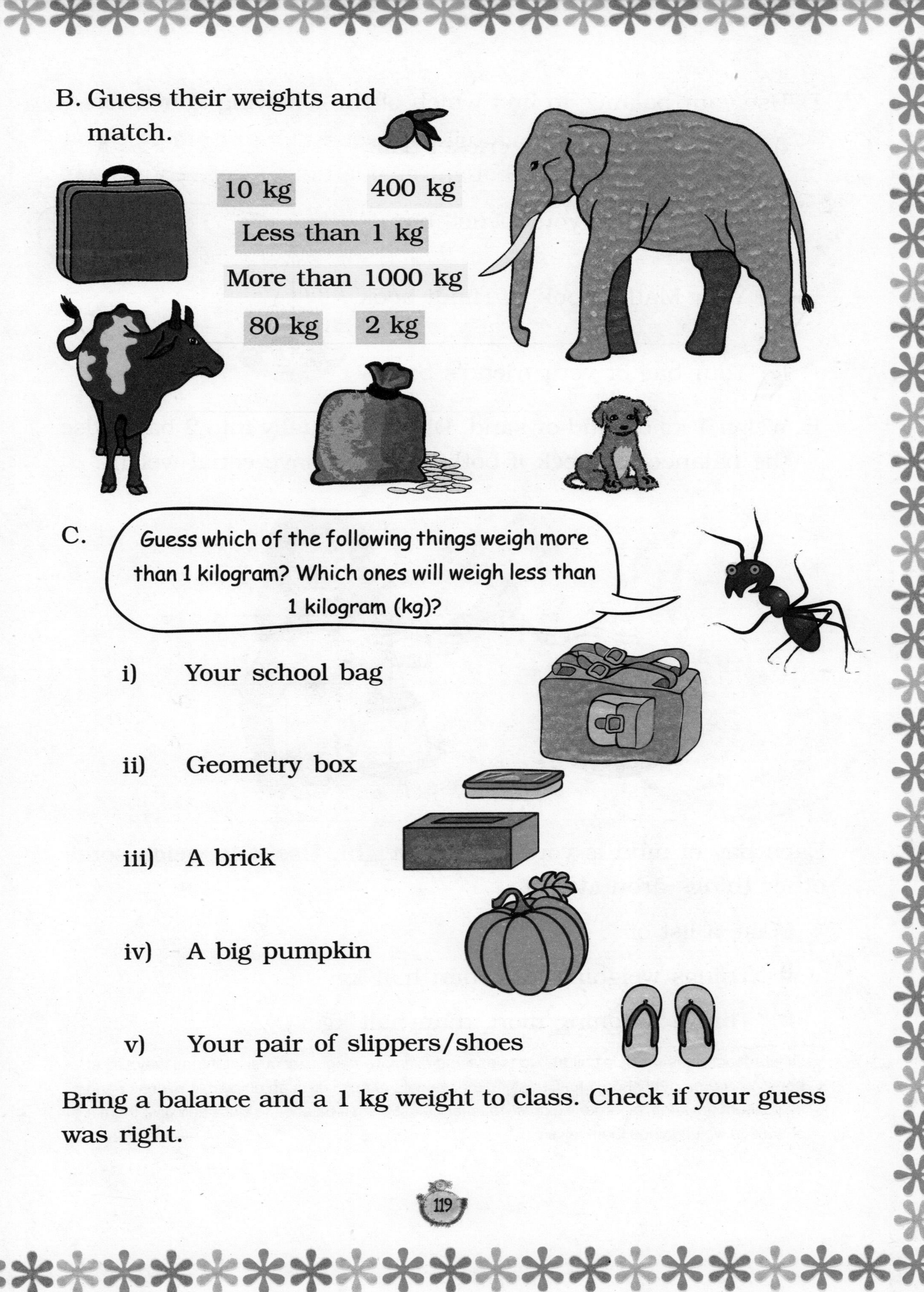

C.

i) Your school bag

ii) Geometry box

iii) A brick

iv) A big pumpkin

v) Your pair of slippers/shoes

Bring a balance and a 1 kg weight to class. Check if your guess was right.

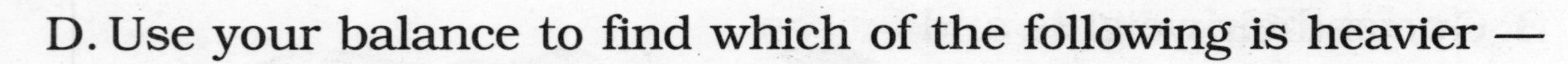

D. Use your balance to find which of the following is heavier —

i) A water bottle or a cricket ball

ii) Your shoe or your pencil box

iii) Your Maths book or Hindi book

iv) Your bag or your friend's bag

E. Weigh 1 kg of mud or sand. Divide it equally into 2 bags. Use the balance to check if both the bags have equal weight.

Each bag of mud is your half-kg weight. Use it to weigh some other things around you.

* Make a list of

  i) Things weighing less than half kg.

  ii) Things weighing more than half kg.

Different activities will help children to guess and estimate weights of familiar things they see at home, at the grocery shop, etc. Guessing the weights of animals is an enjoyable exercise and helps them get a feel of larger weights. Teachers must bring a balance to class and give them a chance to weigh things themselves.

Look for Weights and Balances

Make a trip to your nearest junk dealer, vegetable shop and grocery shop. Have a look at the weights they use. Find out:

i) Who uses the biggest weight?

ii) Who uses the smallest weight?

Have you seen any of these balances?

In which shop would you find the following types of weights? Discuss with your friends.

9 How Many Times?

Leggy Animals

There are 5 goats.

How many legs altogether?

$4 + 4 + 4 + 4 + 4 = 20$

or 5 times 4 is 20

or $5 \times 4 = 20$

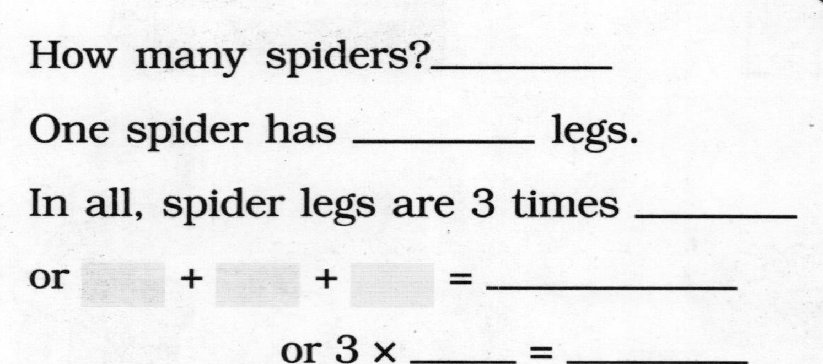

How many spiders?________

One spider has ________ legs.

In all, spider legs are 3 times ________

or ☐ + ☐ + ☐ = ____________

or 3 × _____ = _________

Do you know this leggy fellow?

This is an octopus.

It lives in the sea.

It also has 8 legs.

So how many legs altogether do 5 octopuses have?

☐ + ☐ + ☐ + ☐ + ☐ = _________

or 5 times ________ = _________

or 5 × _________ = _________

Give me your hand, hand, hand, ...!

Find the Number without Counting

How many flowers in a flower bed?

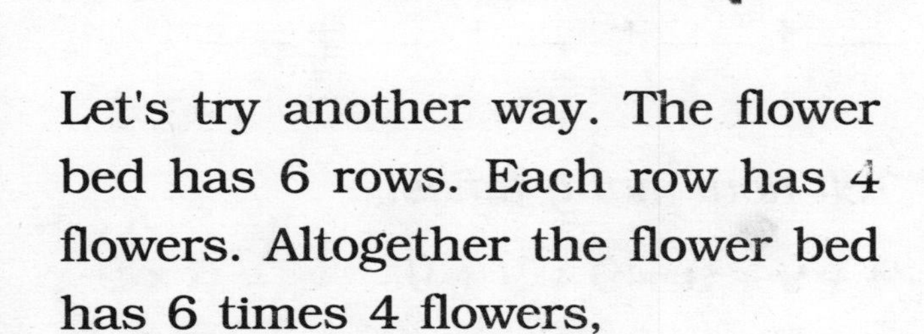

It has 4 columns. Each column has 6 flowers. So altogether the flower bed has 4 times 6 flowers,

$6 + 6 + 6 + 6 = 24$ or

$4 \times 6 = 24$

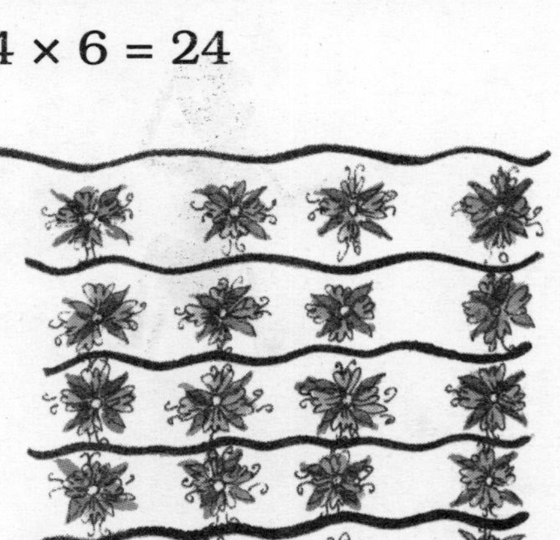

Let's try another way. The flower bed has 6 rows. Each row has 4 flowers. Altogether the flower bed has 6 times 4 flowers,

$4 + 4 + 4 + 4 + 4 + 4 = 24$

or $6 \times 4 = 24$

In the same way, how many bottles are these?

_____ times _____ = _____ bottles

How many eggs?

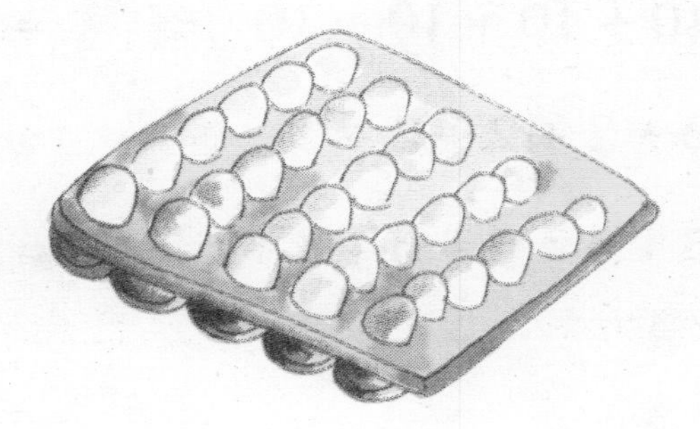

_____ times _____ = _____ eggs

Practice Time

A. *Rewrite using the + sign.*

2 × 5 is 2 times 5 or 5 + 5

4 × 18 is 4 times ____ or ____ + ____ + ____ + ____

3 × 20 is ____ times ____ or ____ + ____ + ____

8 × 9 is ____ times ____ or ____ + ____ + ____ +

____ + ____ + ____ + ____ + ____

B. *Tell how many times!*

9 + 9 + 9 + 9 + 9 + 9 = 6 × 9 = 54

4 + 4 + 4 + 4 + 4 = 5 × 4 = 20

8 + 8 + 8 = ____ × 8 = ______

3 + 3 + 3 + 3 + 3 = 5 × ____ = ______

30 + 30 + 30 = ____ × ____ = ______

7 + 7 + 7 + 7 + 7 + 7 = ____ × ____ = ______

12 + 12 + 12 + 12 = ____ × 12 = ______

6 + 6 + 6 = ____ × ____ = ______

10 + 10 + 10 + 10 = ____ × ____ = ______

2 + 2 + 2 + 2 + 2 = ____ × ____ = ______

6 + 6 + 6 + 6 + 6 + 6 + 6 = ____ × ____ = ______

C. Ramu bought 4 packets of biscuits. Each packet has 4 biscuits. How many biscuits did Ramu buy?

D. There are 12 desks in a classroom. Each desk has 4 legs. What is the total number of legs of the desks?

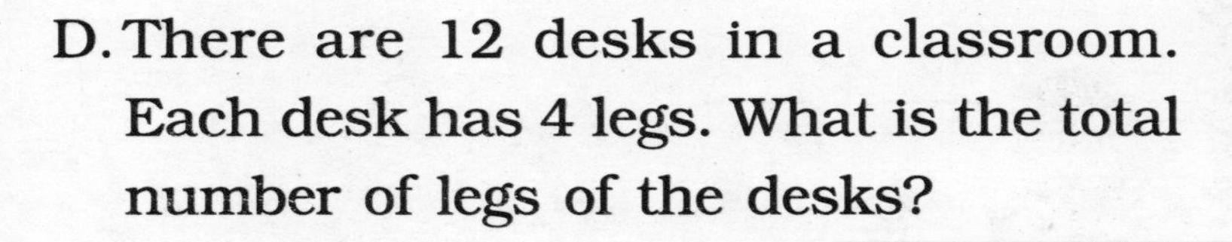

E. Sabiha brought home 3 bunches of flowers. Each bunch has 4 flowers. How many flowers were there?

F. One rail coach has 8 wheels. How many wheels in all in 6 coaches?

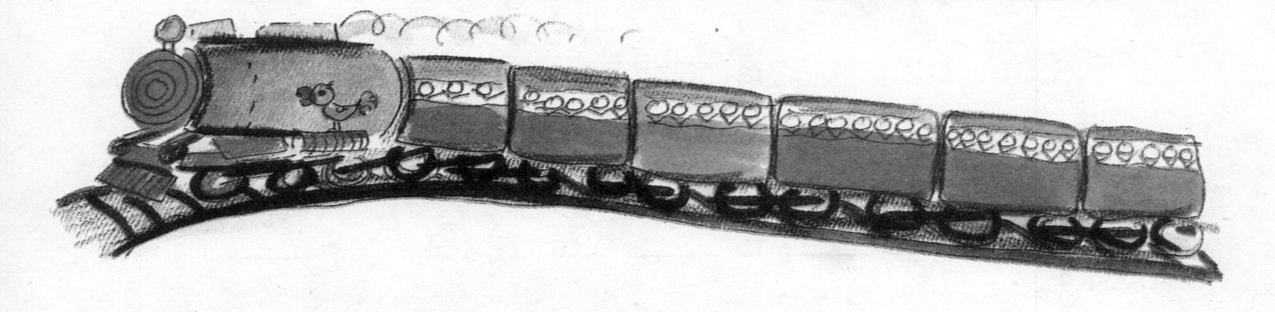

After children attempt word problems, there should be a discussion on how they arrived at their answers. This will help children develop a conceptual understanding of multiplication.

How Many Times 2?

1 time 2	is 2	or	1 × 2	= 2
2 times 2	is 4	or	2 × 2	= 4
3 times 2	is 6	or	3 × 2	= 6
4 times 2	is ____	or	4 × 2	= ____
5 times 2	is ____	or	5 × 2	= ____
6 times 2	is ____	or	6 × 2	= ____
___ times 2	is ____	or	___ × 2	= ____
____ times ____	is ____	or	8 × 2	= ____
____ times ____	is ____	or	9 × 2	= ____
____ times ____	is ____	or	10 × 2	= ____

Jump with Me

Tarru Frog jumps
3 steps each time.
Which numbers will
Tarru touch?

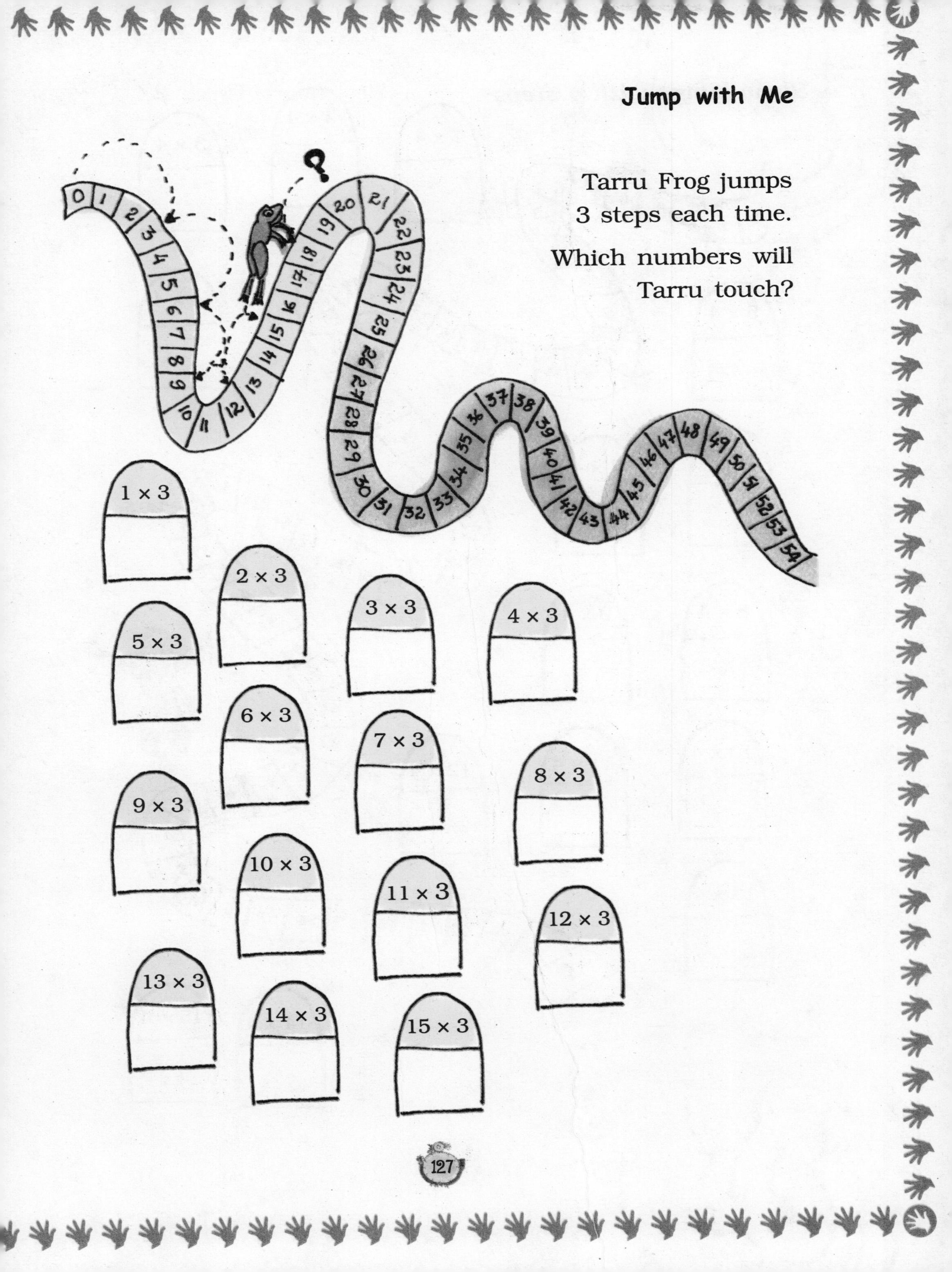

Show jumps with 4 steps

Try jumps with seven steps

1×7

2×7

3×7

4×7

5×7

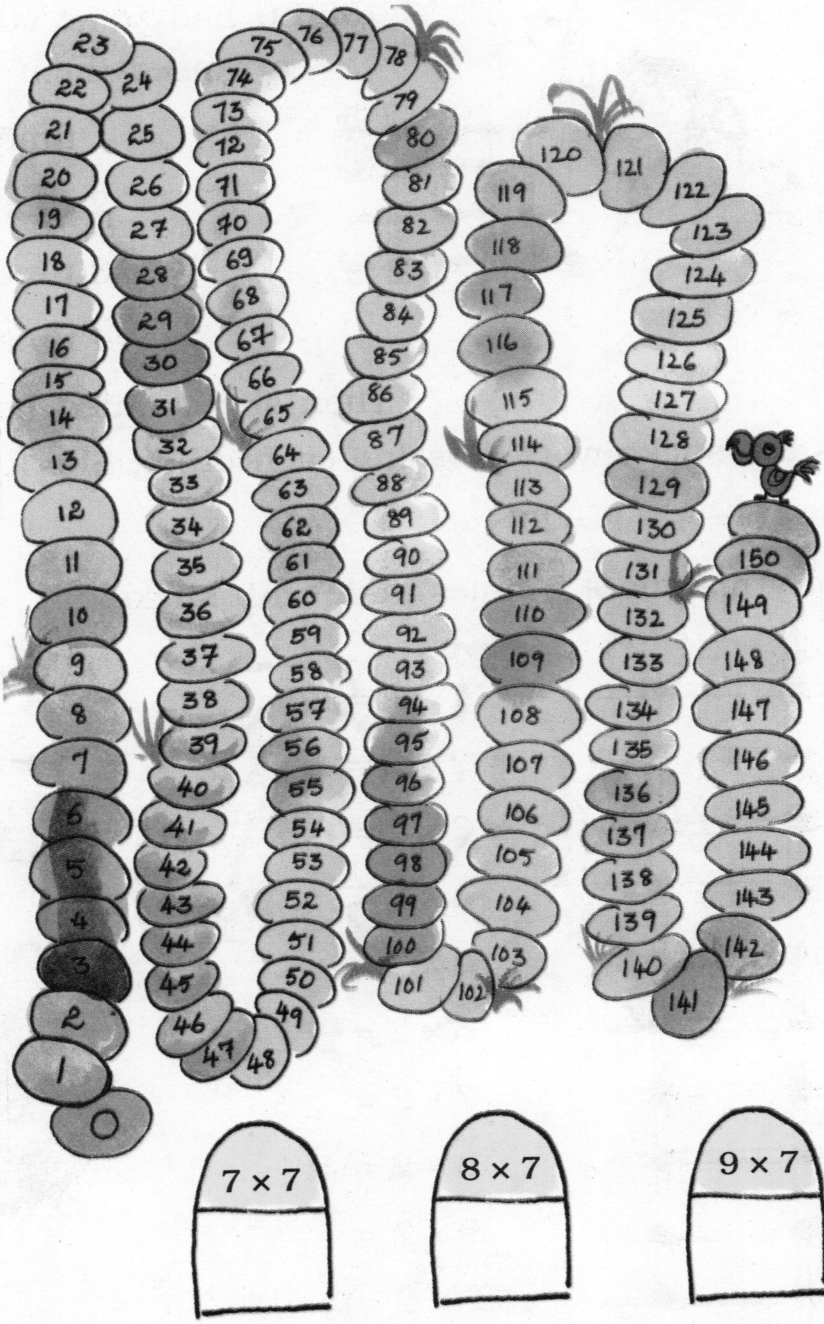

6×7

7×7

8×7

9×7

10×7

11×7

12×7

13×7

14×7

15×7

Stick Play

Mithu had some sticks. She arranged them like this:

1 time 5 = 5

2 times 5 = 10

3 times 5 = 15

4 times 5 = 20

Then she counted how many times the sticks were crossing each other. She found that

4 times 5 = 4 × 5 = 20

Let's try making a 2 times table with sticks:

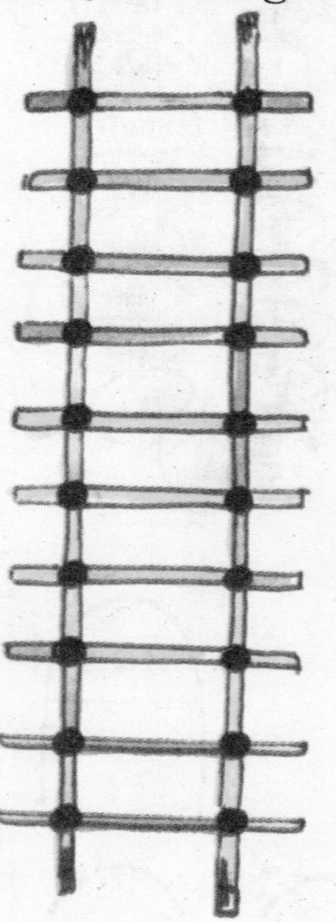

1 × 2 = 2

2 × 2 = 4

3 × 2 = 6

4 × 2 =

5 × 2 =

6 × 2 =

7 × 2 =

8 × 2 =

9 × 2 =

10 × 2 =

Children can be given 16 and 24 sticks to arrange and encouraged to try different arrangements like 4 × 4, 2 × 8, 8 × 2 for 16 sticks and 12 × 2, 8 × 3, 4 × 6, 6 × 4, 3 × 8, 2 × 12 for 24 sticks.

Now draw sticks to make the multiplication table of 6:

Shopping with Tables

How much do these things cost?

4 toffees cost __________ rupees.

[Hint: 4 × 2]

3 pencil boxes cost ________ rupees.

10 pencil boxes cost ________ rupees.

9 balloons cost ________ rupees.

5 toys cost ________ rupees.

7 face masks cost ________ rupees.

Practice Time

A. Complete the following:

2×7 = ________ 3×9 = ________

4×9 = ________ 5×2 = ________

5×8 = ________ 3×10 = ________

10×6 = ________ 2×8 = ________

5×9 = ________ 10×8 = ________

B. Look at the patterns and complete them.

3, 6, 9, ________, ________, ________.

2, 4, 6, ________, ________, ________.

10, 20, 30, ________, ________, ________.

4, 8, 12, ________, ________, ________.

5, 10, 15, ________, ________, ________.

30, 60, 90, ________, ________, ________.

C. Complete the multiplication tree

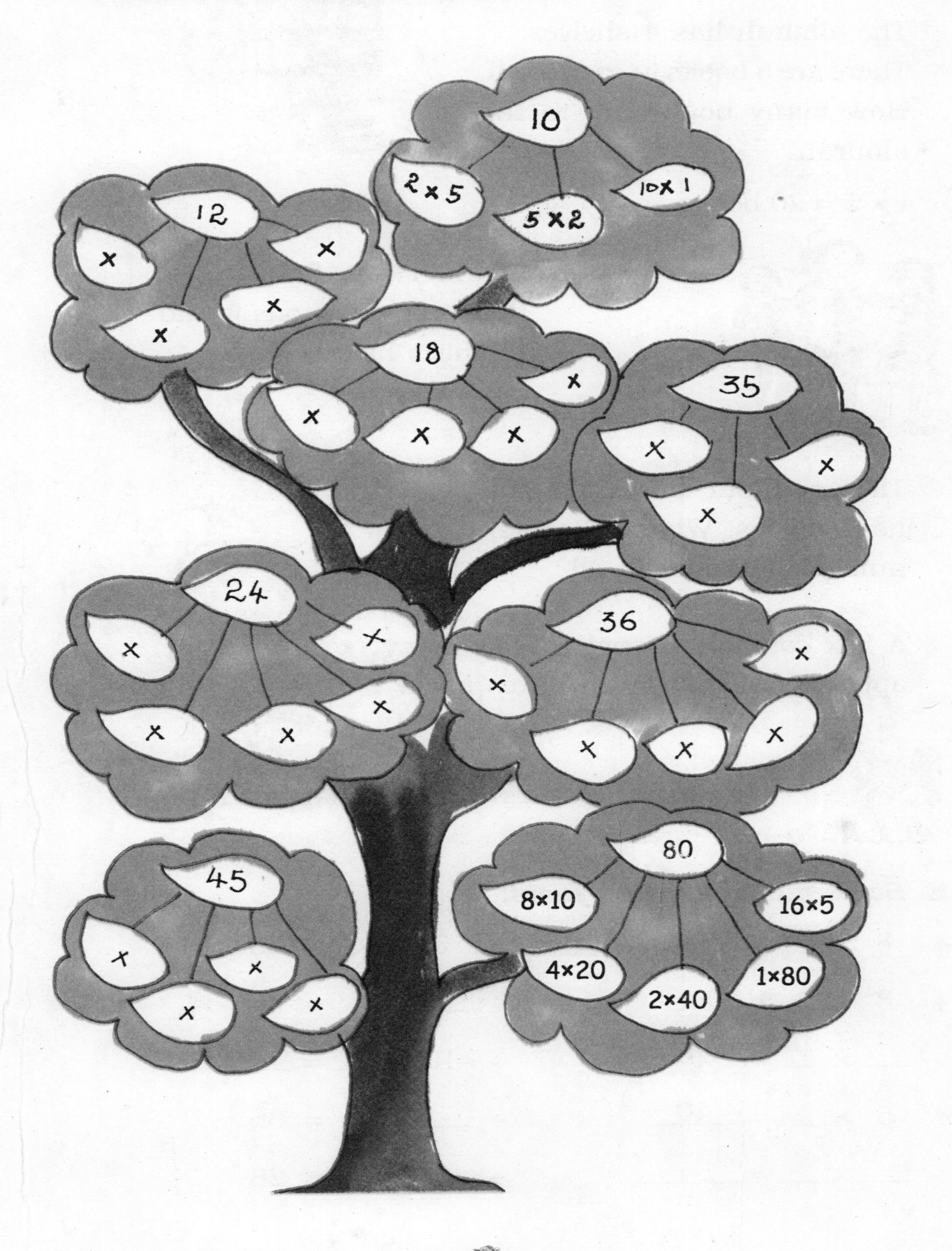

D. How many in all?

- The almirah has 4 shelves. There are 5 books in each shelf. How many books are in the almirah?

$4 \times 5 = 20$ books

- A shirt has 5 buttons. How many buttons would 3 shirts have?

- There are four fans. Each fan has 3 blades. What is the total number of blades in all?

- A box contains 6 apples. How many apples in all will seven boxes have?

- How many corners would 4 triangles have?

E. Some multiplication facts:

8 × 3 = ______	5 × ____ = 35
3 × ____ = ______	____ × 6 = 36
____ × ____ = 42	10 × ____ = ______
5 × ____ = 40	____ × 9 = 36
____ × ____ = 54	____ × 7 = 28

Multiplication Table of 1

one time one is	1 × 1 =	1
two times one is	2 × 1 =	2
three times one is	3 × ____	= ____
four times one is	____ × ____	= ____
_____ times one is	____ × ____	= ____
_____ times one is	____ × ____	= ____
_____ times one is	____ × ____	= ____
_____ times one is	____ × ____	= ____

Multiplying Big Numbers

A. Two toffees were given to each student in the class. If there were 34 students, how many toffees were given in all?

Total students present = 34

Each student gets 2 toffees.

So total number of toffees given is 34 × 2.

34x2 is 34 times 2

30 times 2 is 60.

So the answer is more than 60.

40 times 2 is 80.

So the answer is less than 80.

What is the answer?

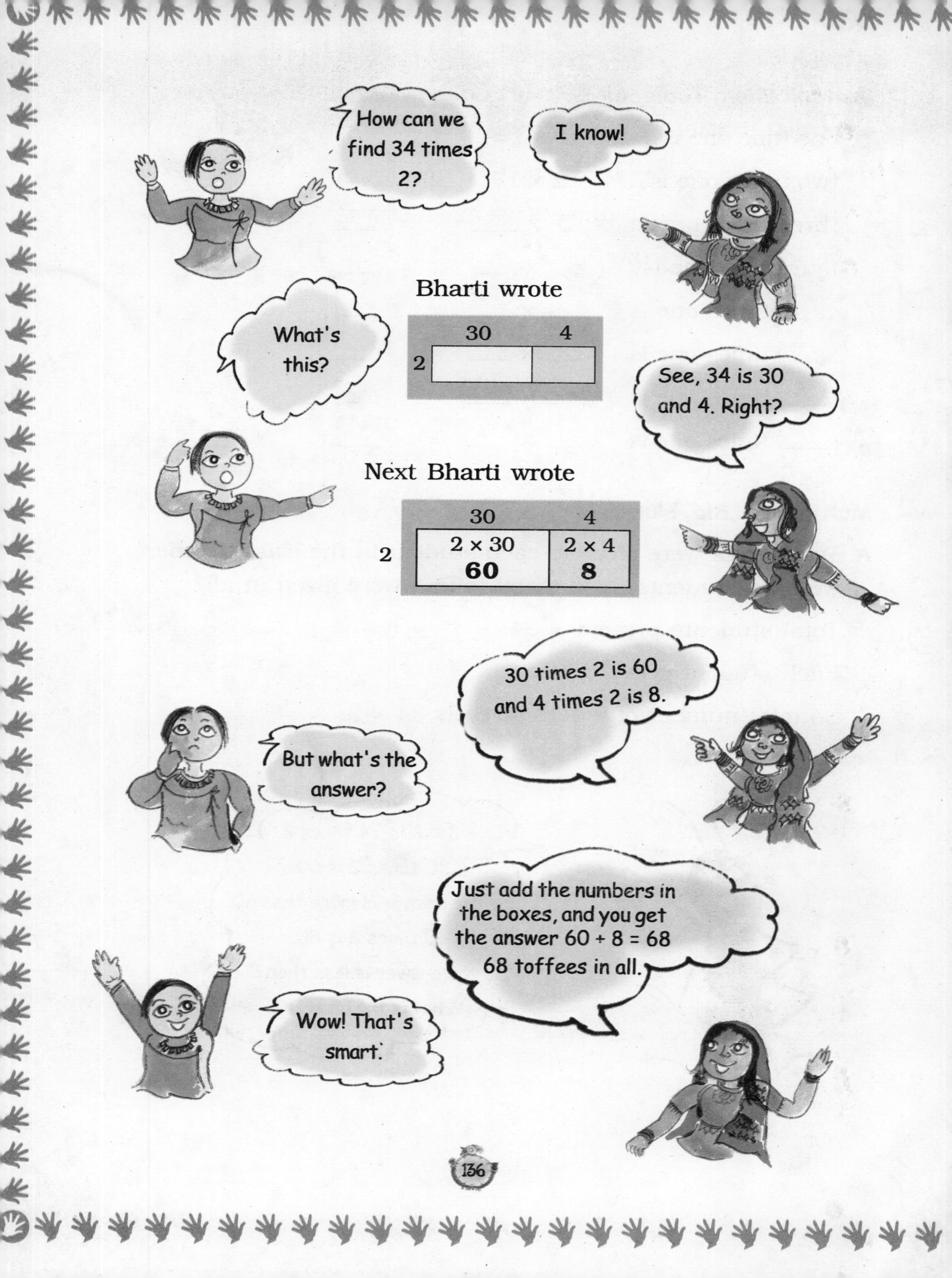
How can we find 34 times 2?
I know!
Bharti wrote
What's this?
30 4
2
See, 34 is 30 and 4. Right?
Next Bharti wrote
30 4
2 2 × 30 2 × 4
60 8
30 times 2 is 60 and 4 times 2 is 8.
But what's the answer?
Just add the numbers in the boxes, and you get the answer 60 + 8 = 68
68 toffees in all.
Wow! That's smart.

B. In a picnic 4 fruits were given to every student. The number of students was 23. Find out the total number of fruits given.

Number of students in the picnic = 23

Fruits given to each student = 4

Total number of fruits = 23 × 4

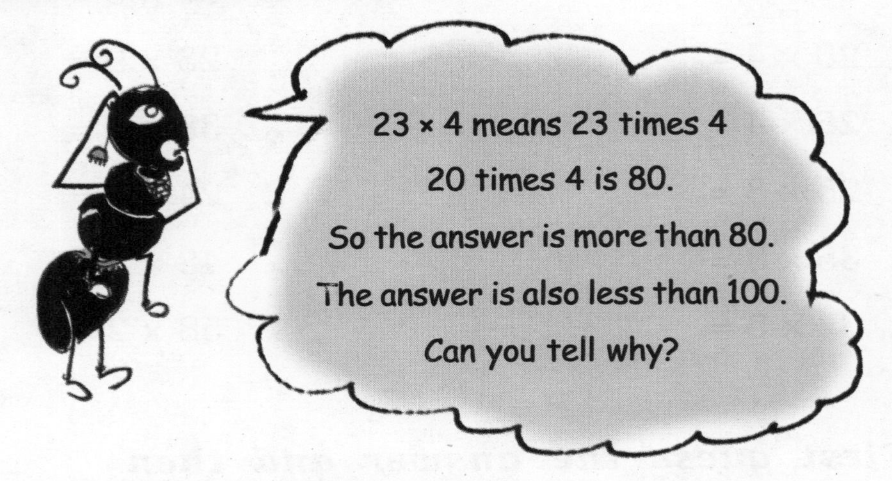

Let us try if we can do this by Bharti's method.

	20	3
4	20 × 4 **80**	3 × 4 **12**

Adding 80 and 12 gives

$$\begin{array}{r} 80 \\ +\ 12 \\ \hline 92 \\ \hline \end{array}$$

So 23 times 4 is 92.

The activities given in this chapter are designed to develop children's conceptual understanding of multiplication. The standard method for multiplying larger numbers may be efficient, but teaching it too early may actually hinder learning. The method given here builds on children's growing sense of two-digit and three-digit numbers. Children should also be encouraged to estimate the result of the operation.

Practice Time

A. *Multiply:*

- $22 \times 3 =$
- $21 \times 4 =$
- $11 \times 5 =$
- $20 \times 4 =$
- $26 \times 4 =$
- $25 \times 3 =$
- $35 \times 3 =$
- $32 \times 5 =$
- $43 \times 2 =$
- $24 \times 2 =$
- $30 \times 5 =$
- $23 \times 9 =$
- $38 \times 2 =$
- $24 \times 5 =$
- $48 \times 4 =$
- $58 \times 2 =$

B. *First guess the answer and then calculate:*

- A flower has five petals. A bunch of flowers has 13 flowers. How many petals are there in the bunch?

- A book has 64 pages. What will be the total number of pages in 8 such books?

- Students stand in rows in the assembly. There are six rows of students. Each row has 17 students. How many students are there?

✳ A design has 3 flowers in it. A piece of cloth has 17 such designs. How many flowers will be on the cloth?

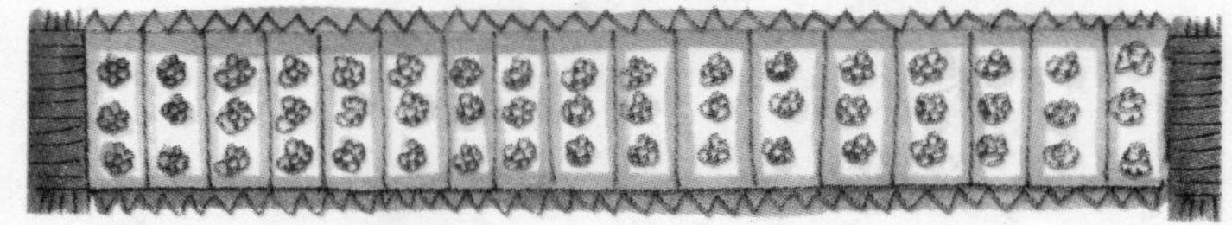

How many in 23 dozen?

Many things are sold by the dozen. For example, bangles and bananas are often sold by the dozen.

1 dozen bananas means 12 bananas.

So 23 dozen bananas is

23×12 bananas.

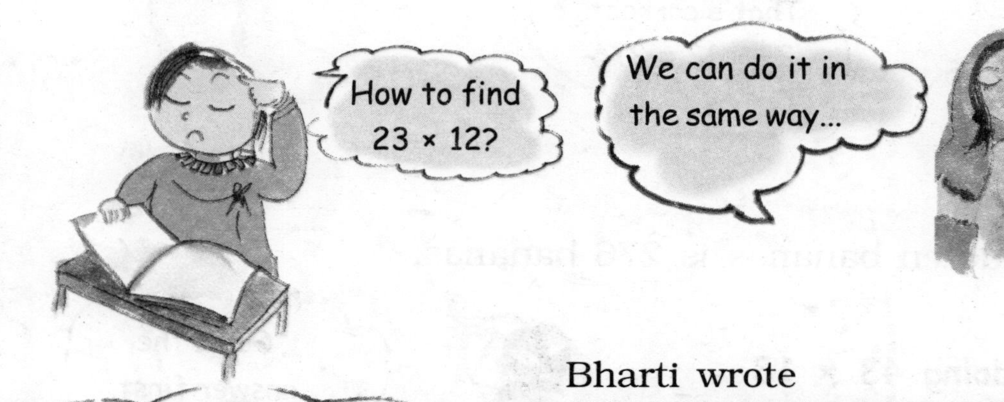

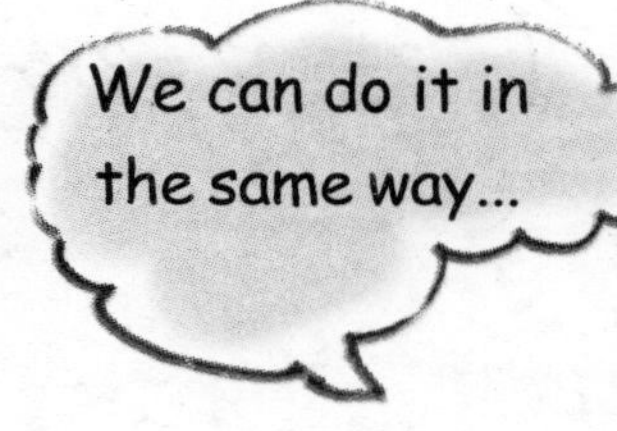

Bharti wrote

	20	3
10		
2		

Next Bharti wrote

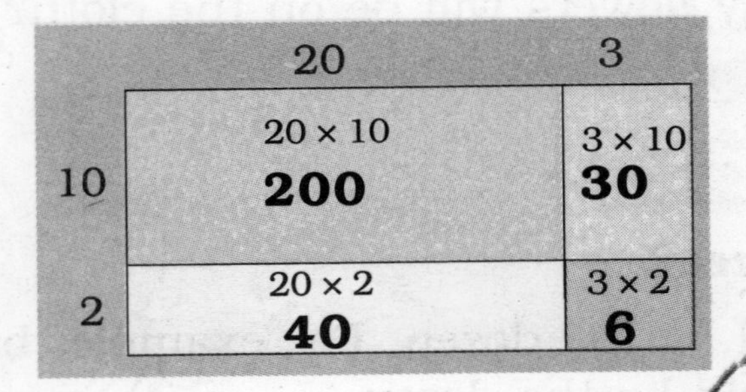

	20	3
10	20 × 10 **200**	3 × 10 **30**
2	20 × 2 **40**	3 × 2 **6**

And Bharti wrote

$$\begin{array}{r} 200 \\ 40 \\ 30 \\ +\ 6 \\ \hline 276 \end{array}$$

We will add the numbers in the boxes to get the answer.

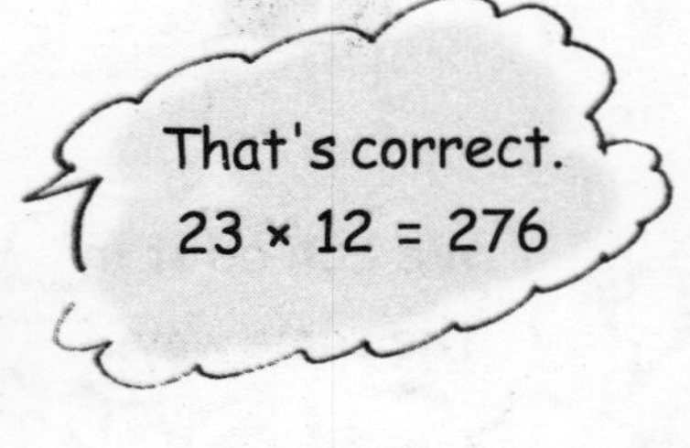

So 23 dozen bananas is 276 bananas.

Now try doing 43 × 13

43 is 40 and 3

13 is 10 and 3

We write the numbers in the boxes as shown.

	40	3
10	40 × 10 **400**	3 × 10 **30**
3	40 × 3 **120**	3 × 3 **9**

Add the numbers in the boxes:

$$\begin{array}{r} 400 \\ 120 \\ 30 \\ +\ 9 \\ \hline 559 \end{array}$$

So 43 × 13 = 559

Practice Time

First guess the answer and then check it by calculating :

42 × 23 = ______ 73 × 11 = ______

51 × 13 = ______ 54 × 12 = ______

25 × 36 = ______ 12 × 14 = ______

Multiplication Patterns

A. 9 × 1 = 9

9 × 2 = 18 1 + 8 = 9

9 × 3 = 27 2 + 7 = 9

9 × 4 = 36 3 + 6 = 9

9 × 5 = 45 4 + 5 = 9

9 × __ = ___ __ + __ = ___

9 × __ = ___ __ + __ = ___

9 × 8 = ___ __ + __ = ___

Did you see the pattern in the 9 times table? What numbers are adding up to 9?

Observing patterns in multiplication tables deepens the understanding of the number system.

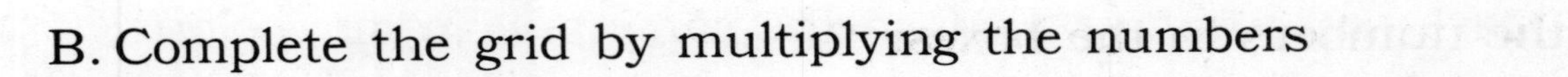

B. Complete the grid by multiplying the numbers

×	1	2	3	4	5	6	7	8	9	10
1	1	2	3	4	5	6	7	8	9	10
2	2	4	6	8	10	12	14	16	18	20
3	3	6	9	12	15	18	21	24	27	30
4										
5										
6										
7										
8										
9										
10										

Look at the cross in your grid.

	3	
4	6	8
	9	

Add the numbers together from top to bottom.

3 + 6 + 9 = 18

Add the numbers together from left to right.

4 + 6 + 8 = 18

The total is the same.

Look for other such crosses and copy them in your notebook.

C. * Mark the numbers 1–10 in the same grid in one colour.

* Mark the numbers 12–20 in another colour.
* Similarly mark 21–30 in a third colour.

Do you see any colour pattern?

Patterns Around Us

In everyday life, we see many patterns.

For example, we see:

Barbed wire

Grills of a window

A snake

Look around you and list three things in which you find some pattern. ___________ ___________ ___________

Draw some patterns which you have found around yourself.

Hello! I am Pallavi. I live in Jaipur. My city is known for clothes with block prints. Have a look at some of the block print designs made by my mother.

She makes these designs by using blocks again and again. One day I got hold of the blocks and made a beautiful design.

You will see that these designs have been made by using the same block in different ways.

Can you see a pattern in the way each block is repeated?

Pictures in a Pattern

I have made some patterns of pictures. I have used a rule for each pattern.

The rule for this pattern is — There is one girl after every 2 boys. Then this is repeated.

In this pattern there is one arrow up and one down. Then this is repeated.

Practice Time

◆ Given below are some patterns.

Figure out the rule for each and continue the pattern.

a) 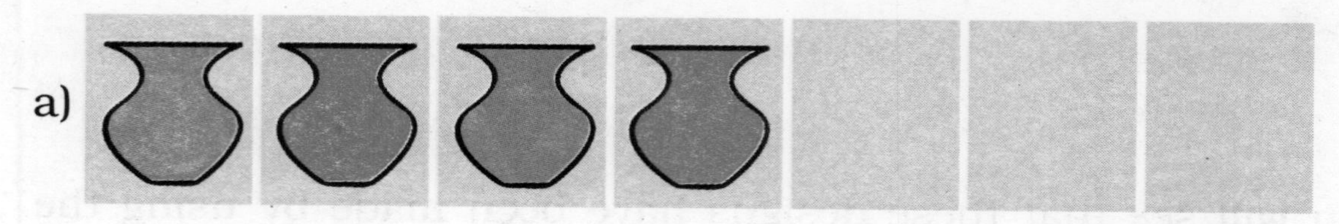

b) A A B A A B

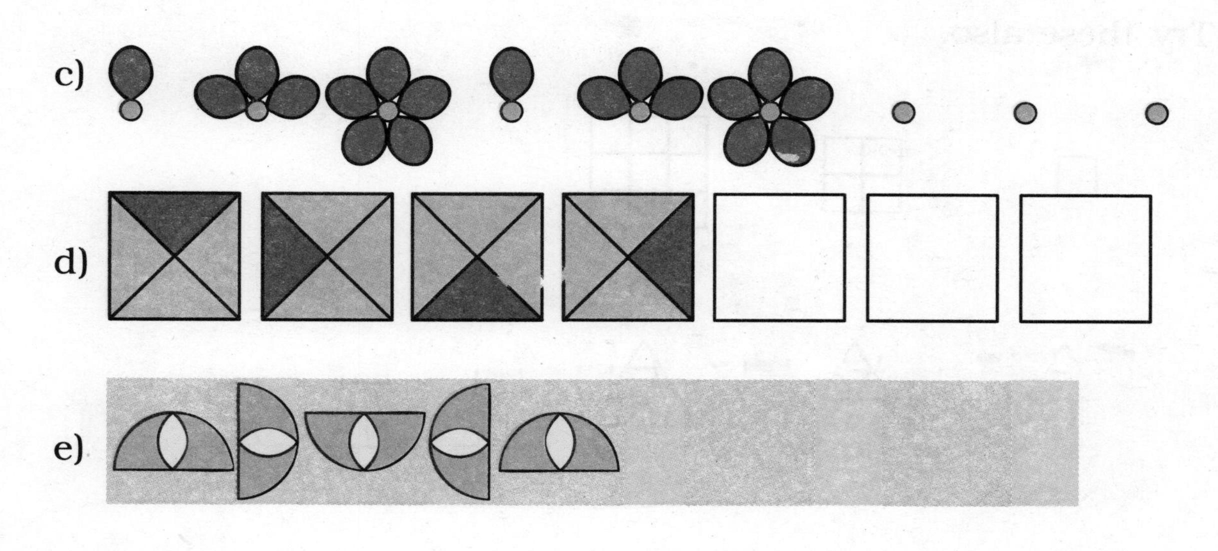

f) Morning, afternoon, evening, night, morning, ________........

Growing Patterns

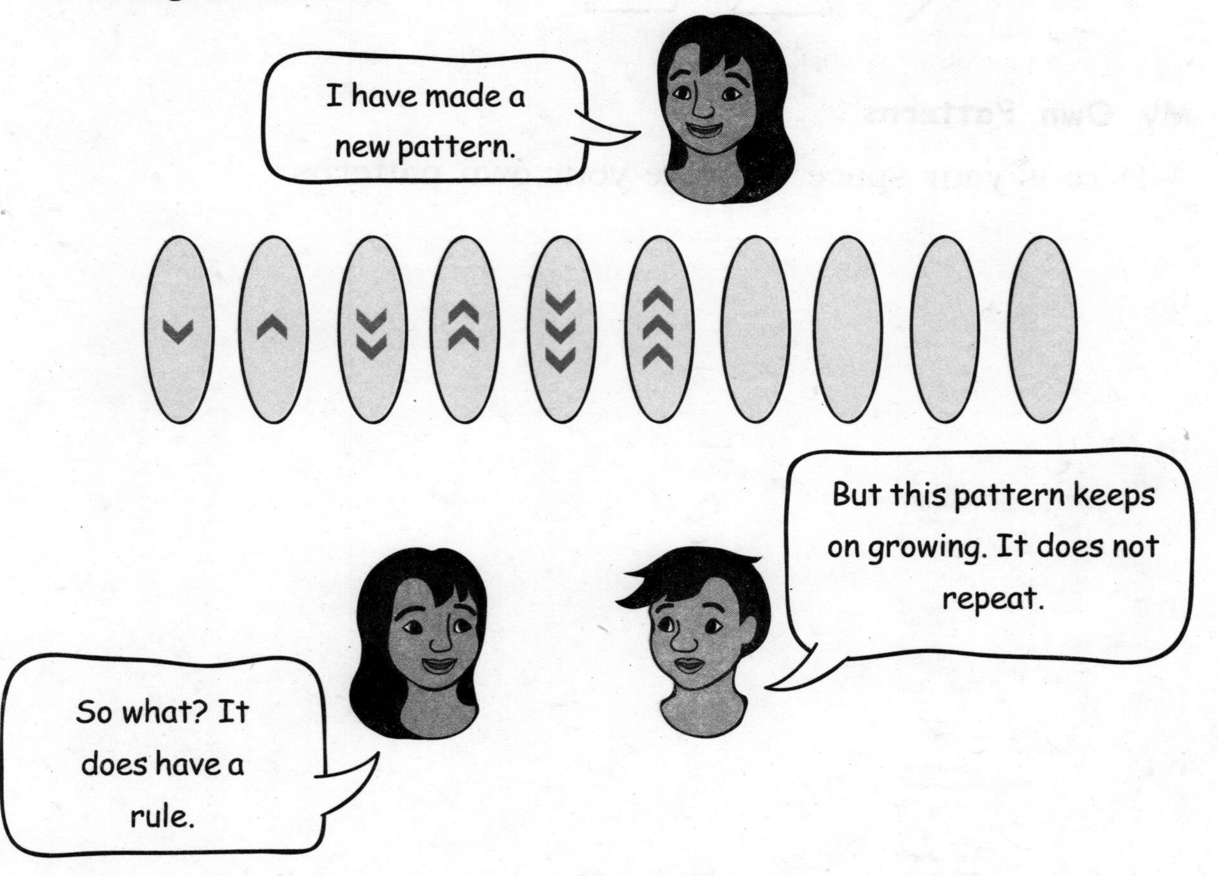

Can you see the rule and continue the pattern?

Try these also.

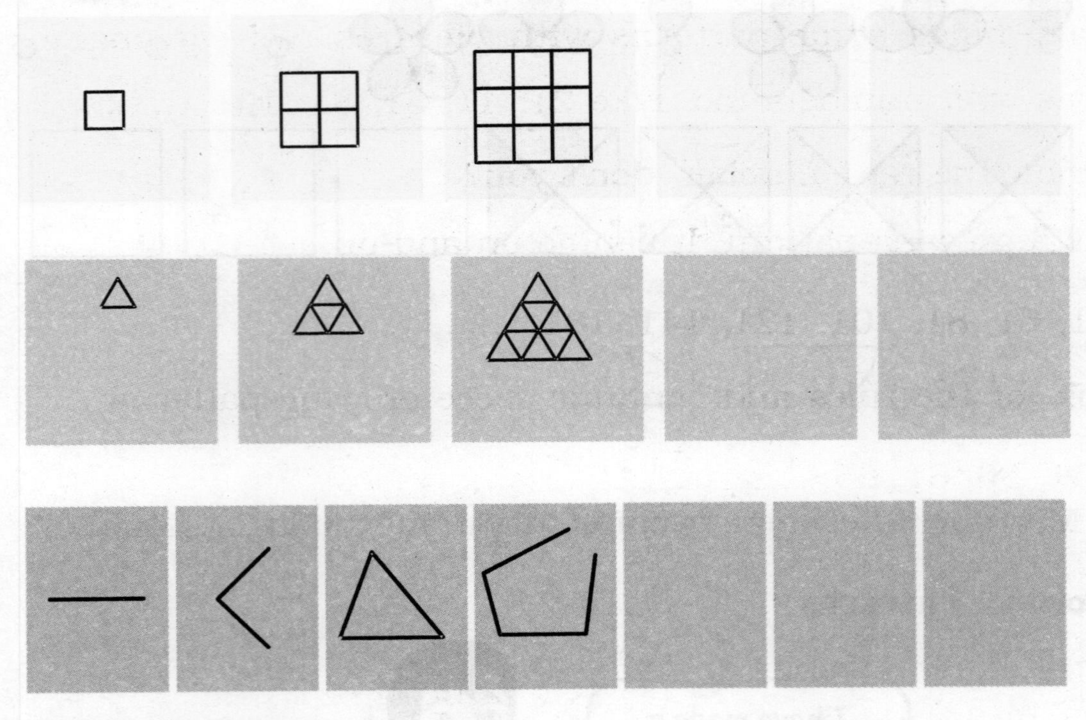

My Own Patterns

◆ Here is your space to make your own patterns:

i)

ii)

iii)

iv)

◆ Ask your friends to continue the patterns made by you.

Number Patterns

We have made some patterns with pictures. We can make patterns with numbers too. Like 21, 41, 61, 81, 101, ...

You know the next number don't you?

This is a growing pattern. It can go on and on.

21, 41, 61, 81, 101, 121, 141, 161, ...

A. Look for the rules and continue these growing patterns:

a) 51, 56, 61, 66, _____, _____ ....

b) 7, _____, 21, 28, 35, _____, _____ ....

c) 2, 4, 8, 16, 32, _____, _____, _____

d) 12A, 13B, 14C, _____, _____.

B. Look at these growing patterns. Find out what to add to each number to get the next one:

a) 1, 3, 6, 10, _____, _____, _____, _____, _____

b) 0, 2, 6, 12, _____, _____, _____, _____, _____

c) 1, 3, 7, 13, _____, _____, _____, _____, _____

d) 2, 3, 6, 11, 18, _____, _____, _____, _____, _____

This chapter helps children observe and understand patterns around them. They can be given more examples of repeating or growing patterns to recognise the motif or basic unit which generates the patterns. Making secret messages or codes also helps pattern recognition. As their algebraic thinking develops, they will realise that the pattern created by the rule **boy boy girl** is the same as **A A B** or ↑↑↓. Some interesting and important number patterns that relate to mathematical operations are given.

Secret Messages

Amrita and Paritosh are writing secret messages.

3W3H3E3R3E
3A3R3E 3Y3O3U

3I3N 3T3H3E
3C3A3N3T3E3E3N

Can you tell what they are trying to say?

These are two secret messages. Look for the patterns and find the hidden sentences.

1 I 2 L 3 O 4 V 5 E 6 Y 7 O 8 U

ATBHCIDS EBFOGOHK IIJS KFLUMN

Now you also make your own secret messages.

____

____

____

Even and Odd Number Patterns

91	92	93	94	95	96	97	98	99	100
81	82	83	84	85	86	87	88	89	90
71	72	73	74	75	76	77	78	79	80
61	62	63	64	65	66	67	68	69	70
51	52	53	54	55	56	57	58	59	60
41	42	43	44	45	46	47	48	49	50
31	32	33	34	35	36	37	38	39	40
21	22	23	24	25	26	27	28	29	30
11	12	13	14	15	16	17	18	19	20
1	2	3	4	5	6	7	8	9	10

Half these numbers are in yellow. What patterns do you see in these numbers? Continue the same pattern and fill in the blanks:

96, 98, ____, 102, ____, ____, ____, ____, ____

How far can you continue this pattern?

These numbers have a special name. They are called **even** numbers.

Do any of these even numbers end with 3 or 5?
What do even numbers end with?

Look at the pattern of numbers in blue. Continue the pattern and fill in the blanks:

99, 101, ____, 105, 107, ____, ____, ____

What do the numbers in blue end with?

All numbers that end with 1, 3, 5, 7 or 9 are called **odd** numbers.

Write all odd numbers between 400 and 410.

____

Write all even numbers between 155 and 165.

____

If we add 1 to any odd number we get an ________ (even/odd) number.

If we add 1 to any even number we get an ________ (even/odd) number.

What do you get if you add an even number to an odd number?

Names in an Order

Adil has to arrange this list so that the names starting with A come first and then come those with B, C, D and so on. Number these names in the order in which they will come.

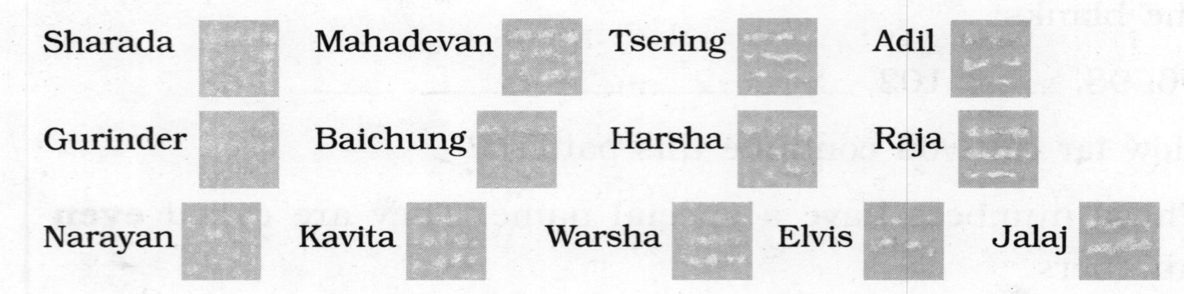

Jalaj is proud to have a special name. He says if you read it backwards it is still the same.

Which of the following names have the same pattern? Mark ✓.

Harsh, Anna, Kanak, Munna, Ongbi

11 Jugs and Mugs

Wedding in Bunny's Family

There is a wedding in Bunny's family, a family of rabbits. Many guests are invited — deer, monkeys, elephants, cats, dogs, mice, foxes, camels, mongoose etc. A special drink is served to all the guests — one glass each. Everyone finds the drink very tasty but some small guests like _____, _____ cannot finish a full glass. But ______________ is able to finish his glass.

Some others like __________ , __________, _ ________ ask for more than one glass.

Now the trouble begins !!!

There are some big guests who go on gulping down glass after glass...!

Bunny wants to guess who drank how much.

Help him fill the table. Have fun! 

Drank how much	*Name of guest*
Less than 1 glass	__________, __________
Between 1-5 glasses	__________, __________
Between 5-10 glasses	__________, __________
More than 10 glasses	__________, __________

Water In, Water Out?

Have you ever thought like Laddu?

About how many glasses of water do you drink in a day?

Summer day : _____ glasses

Winter day : _____ glasses

Can you guess how much water goes out of you?

Bottles and Buckets

Get a 1 litre bottle (can be an empty bottle of water, oil etc.). Now collect some bottles and a mug, jug, glass, bowl, etc. at your house. Use the 1 litre bottle to check which of these holds more than 1 litre and which one holds less than 1 litre. Make a small drawing if you like.

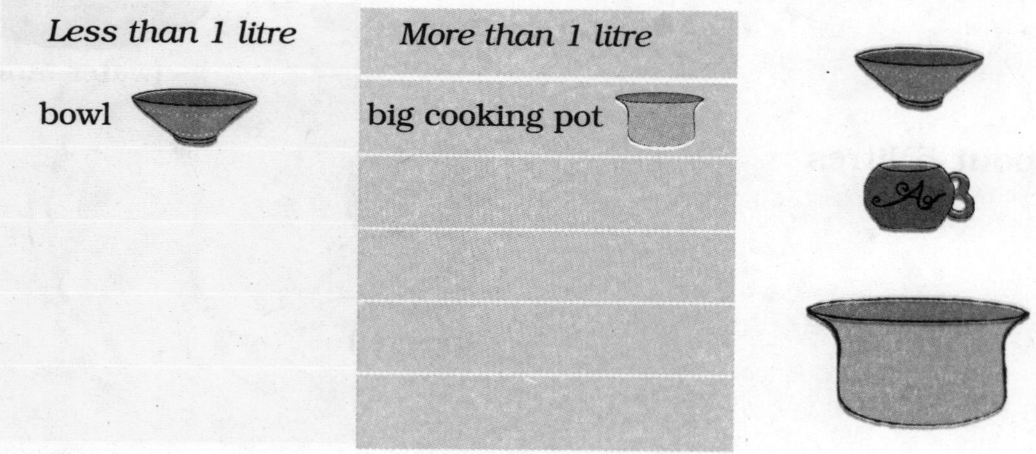

Less than 1 litre	*More than 1 litre*
bowl	big cooking pot

- Now look at the buckets in your house.
- Guess how many litres of water they can hold.
- Use a 1 litre bottle and check if your guess is right for all the buckets.

Bucket	My guess	My measure
Bucket 1		
Bucket 2		
Bucket 3		

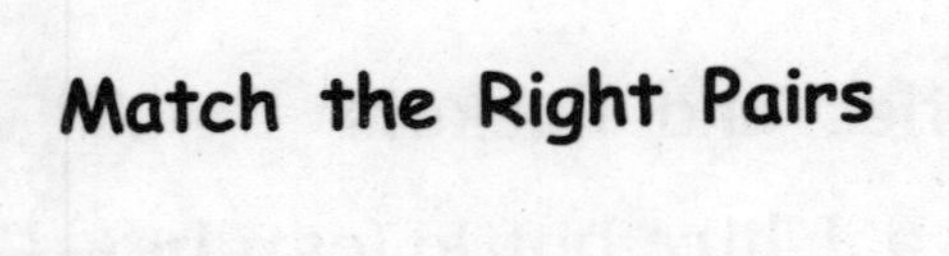

Match the Right Pairs

About 12 litres

(to measure milk)

Less than ½ litre

(water tank)

About 5 litres

(bucket)

1000 litres

(eye drops bottle)

½ litre

(water *suraahi*)

Whose Jug Holds More?

What are Naima and Jeetu doing?

If Naima pours one glass of water in her jug, it looks like this:

Naima thinks she will have to pour around 3 glasses of water to fill the jug. What do you think? ______________

If Jeetu pours one glass of water in his jug, it looks like this:

- Whose jug holds more water? ______________
- How many glasses of water do you think Jeetu should pour to fill his jug? ______________
- If Jeetu pours one more glass of water his jug will be around ______________ full.

Filling Pots

Naseem and Abdul had to fill their pots each with water. Both pots were equally big and heavy. So they went to the tap again and again, filled their own bottles and poured water into the pots.

Naseem had to fill her bottle 16 times from the tap. But Abdul had to fill his bottle only 8 times.

* Why did Naseem go more times than Abdul?
* Naseem's bottle can hold ______________ (twice/half/three times) as much water as Abdul's bottle.

How Many Glasses?

Pot B holds 11 glassfuls of water. Pot A holds twice as much water as pot B. How many glasses of water are needed to fill pot A? ________

In class, children need to speak about their own daily experiences of measuring liquids and comparing the sizes of different containers. They must get many opportunities to use words like 'glassful', 'bucketful' etc. They will also get familiar with ideas such as 'half', 'twice', 'four times' the amount of water, and a sense of roughly how much one litre is.

Filling Potholes

This is a small town near Kohima. There are some potholes in the road. Before the rains come, children want to fill the holes with pebbles. They bring pebbles in mugs of the same size.

Hole A gets filled with 9 mugs of pebbles.

Hole B gets filled with 18 mugs of pebbles.

Hole C gets filled with 12 mugs of pebbles.

- Mark A, B, C on the right hole in the picture.
- Which is the biggest pothole? ________
- If jugs are used, hole A gets filled with 5 jugs. How many jugs of pebbles are needed to fill hole B? ________

12 Can We Share?

How Many in Each Group?

- There are 10 butterflies.

  They are in 2 groups.

  There are 5 butterflies in each group.

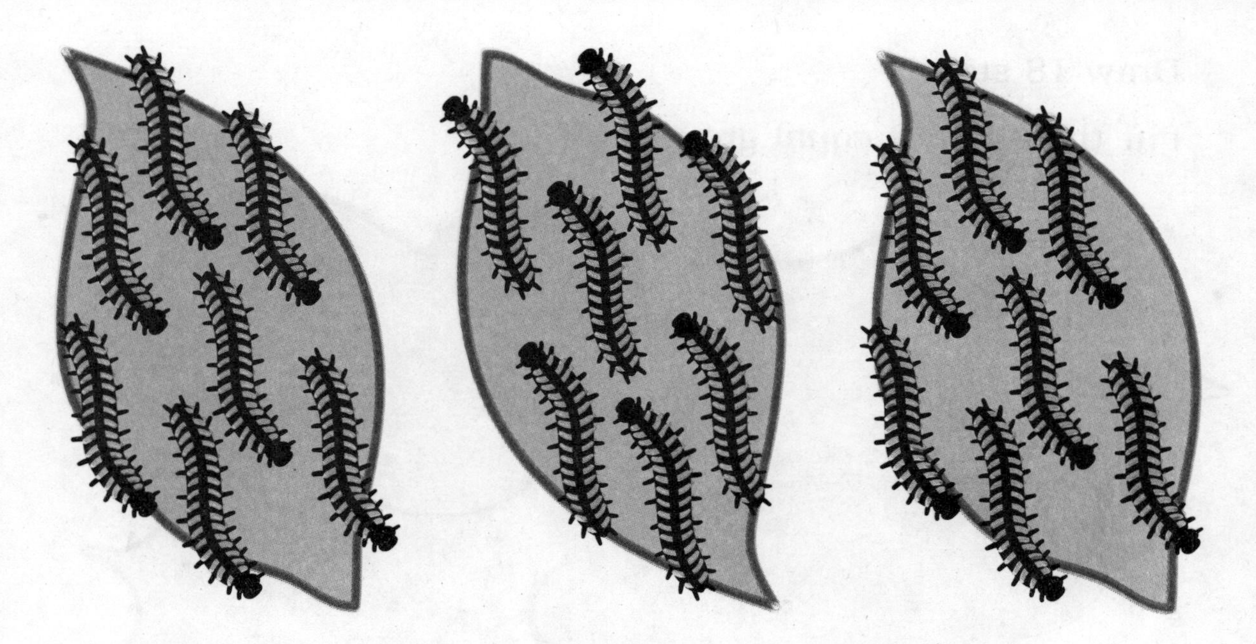

◆ There are __________ caterpillars.

They are in __________ groups.

There are __________ caterpillars in each group.

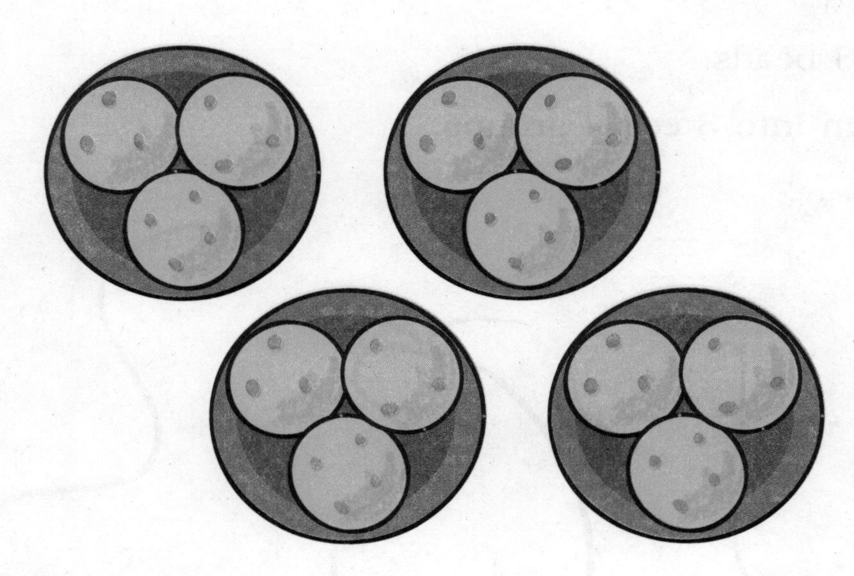

◆ There are __________ laddoos.

They are in __________ groups.

There are __________ laddoos in each group.

◆ Draw 18 stars.

Put them into 2 equal groups.

There are __________ stars in each group.

◆ Draw 18 beads.

Put them into 3 equal groups.

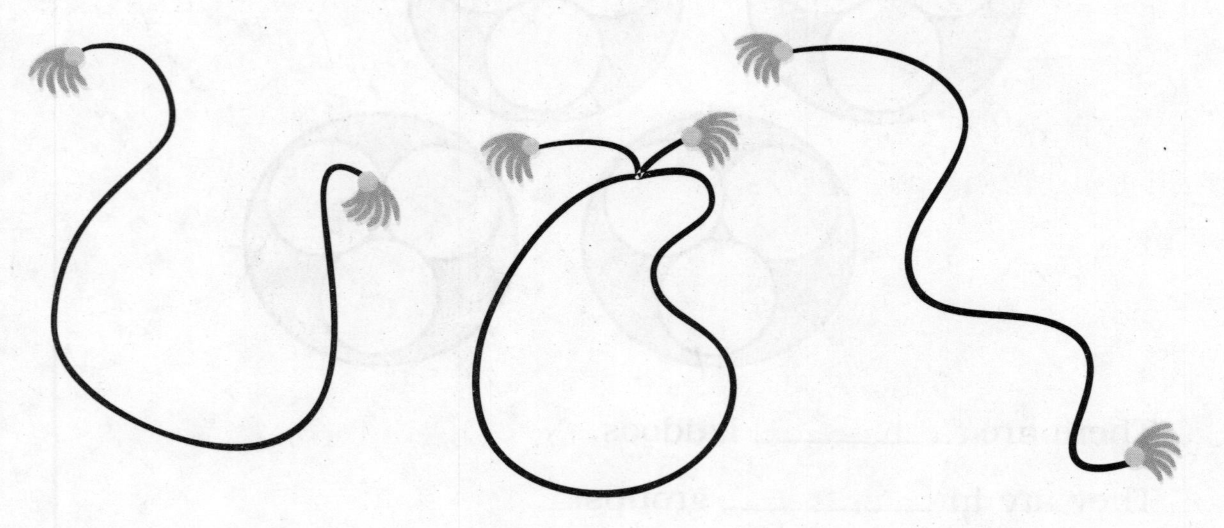

There are __________ beads in each group.

Share the Grains

Mummy bird brings 12 grains.

How to distribute equally?

Mummy bird starts by giving 1 grain to each baby.

Then Mummy bird gives one more grain to each baby.

Each baby has got 2 grains now. How many grains are left?_______

She puts one more grain in each baby's mouth.

All the grains are finished.

12 grains have been **divided** among 4 baby birds.

Each baby has got 3 grains.

$12 \div 4 = 3$

Try These Now.......

- Gopu has 3 plates of *jalebis*.

Each plate has a different number of *jalebis*.

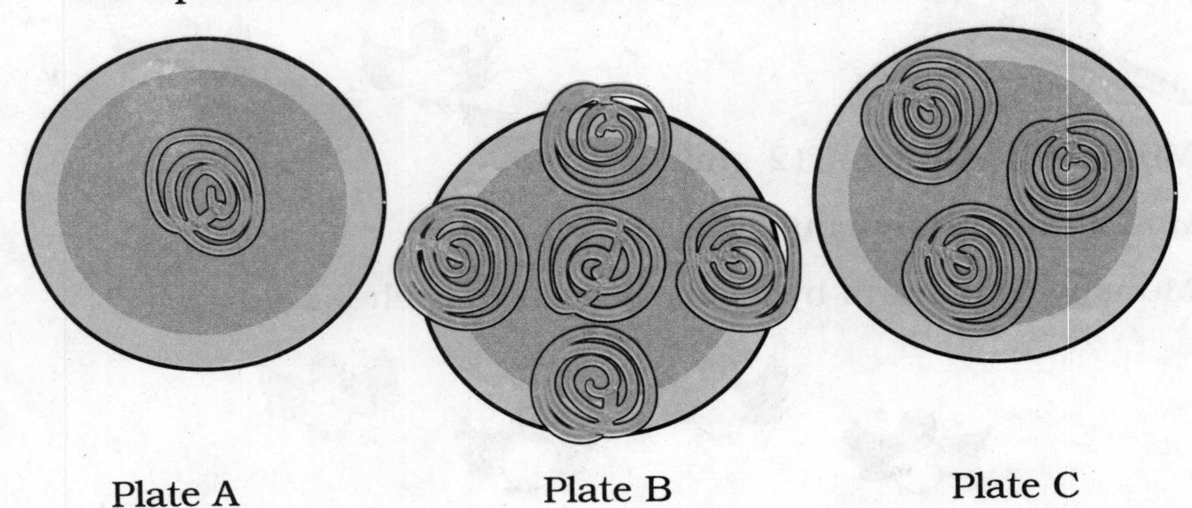

Now draw the *jalebis* on the plates below, so that each plate has the same number of *jalebis*.

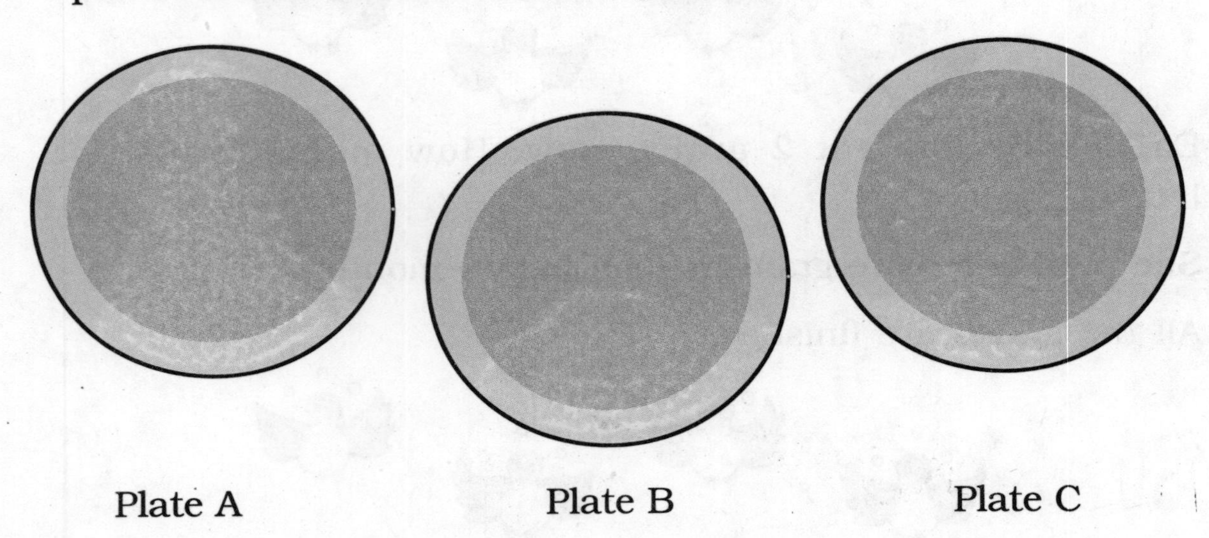

How many *jalebis* are there altogether? ________

How many *jalebis* are there in each plate? ________

Discuss in the class how you found the answer.

Sharing them Equally

◆ Here are six bananas.

Here are three monkeys.

If they share the bananas equally, each monkey will get two bananas.

6 bananas divided into 3 equal parts = 2 bananas each

$6 \div 3 = 2$

If there are six bananas

and two monkeys,

each monkey will get three bananas.

Six bananas $\div$ 2 = 3 bananas each

$6 \div 2 = 3$

Give children the experience of sharing things equally and writing corresponding division statements.

If there are 60 bananas and two monkeys, how many will each monkey get?

________ bananas.

What if there are 600 bananas and two monkeys?

- Five friends found 10 five-rupee coins on the ground.

They shared them equally.

Each friend got ten rupees.

$50 \div 5 = 10$

If there are 16 ten-rupee notes and four friends to share, then

$16 \div 4 =$ ________ and $4 \times 10 = 40$

so each friend gets __________ rupees.

Five friends found Rs 100. If they share it equally, how much will each get? __________

- Hari Prashad has 30 metres of rope.

He distributes it equally among his three children.

Each child gets __________ metres of rope.

If there is 36 metres of rope, how much of rope will each child get? __________

And if there is 60 metres of rope,

how much will each child get? __________

How Many Shelves?

I have 20 books. I can keep 5 books in one shelf, so how many shelves do I need in my almirah?

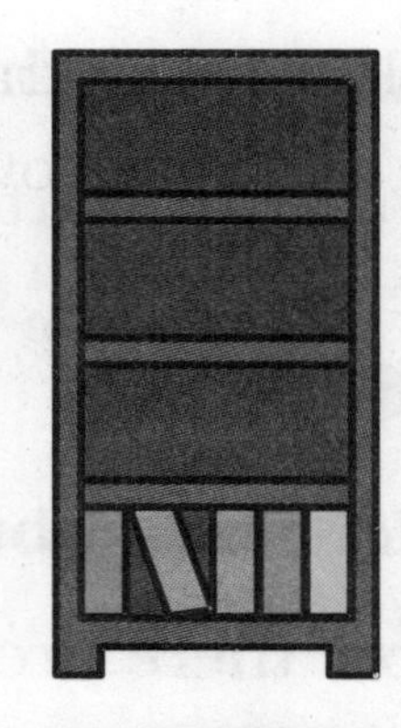

Five books in the first shelf.

15 books are left.

5 more books in the second shelf.

10 books are left.

5 more books in the third shelf.

5 books are left.

5 more books in the fourth shelf.

20 books have filled up 4 shelves of the almirah.

20 books put into equal groups of 5 each take 4 shelves.

On this and the following page, division is done by making equal groups. For instance, here equal groups of 5 books each have been made. This process is different from sharing them equally (by distributing them into 4 shelves).

◆ Now let us try this.

Here are 28 buttons.

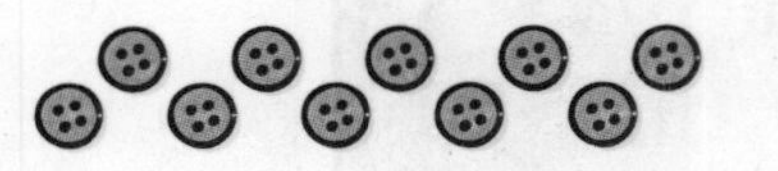 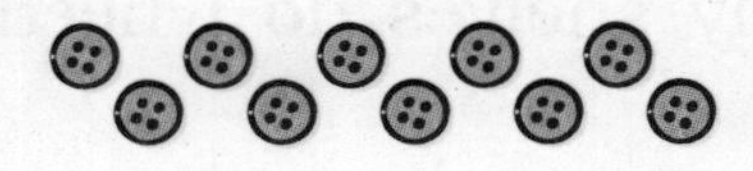 

A tailor puts 4 buttons on one shirt.

So now there are 7 shirts with buttons.

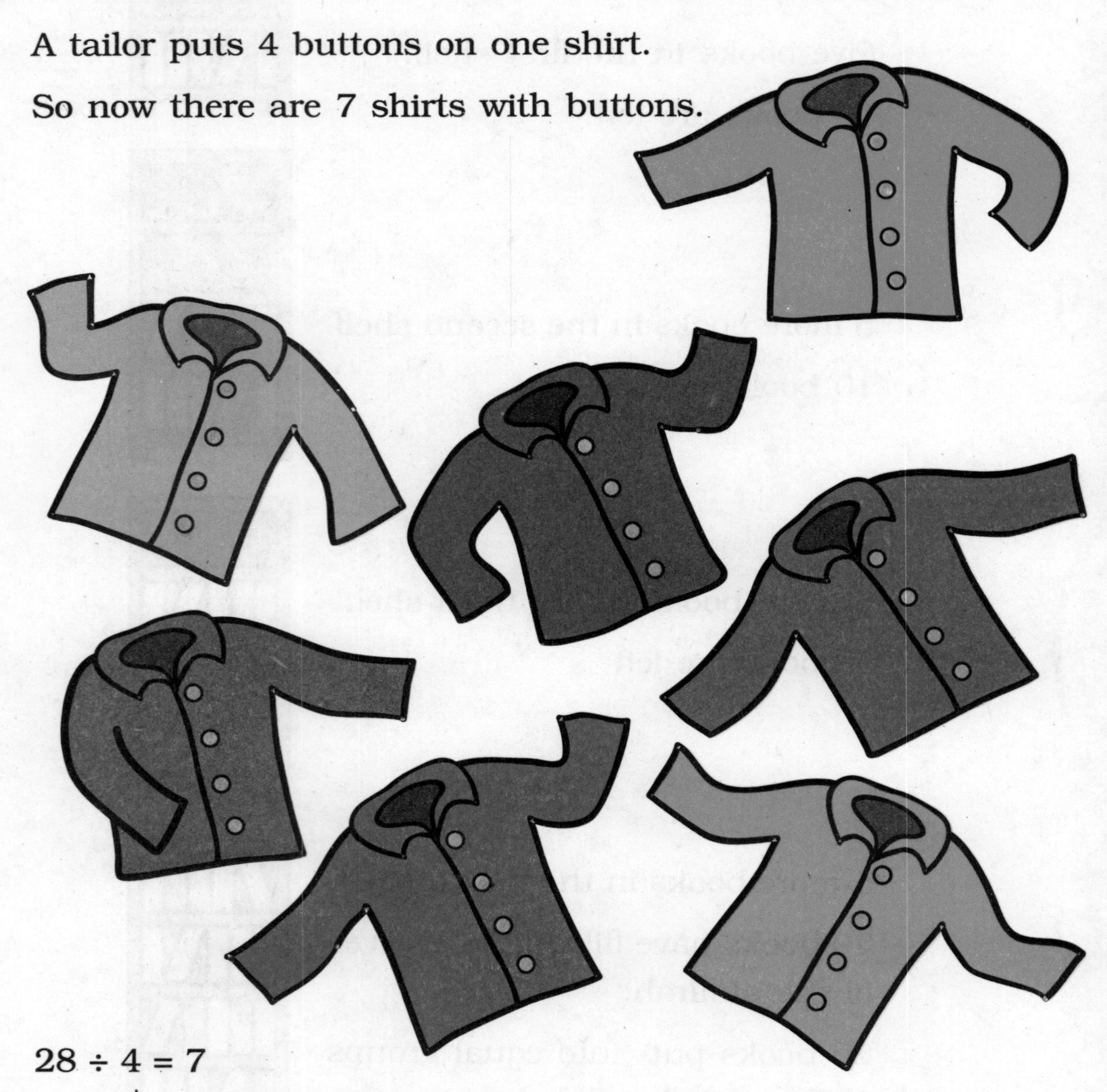

28 ÷ 4 = 7

If there are 28 buttons, and the tailor puts 7 buttons on each shirt, there will be __________ shirts with buttons.

28 ÷ 7 = __________

Practice Time

1. Minku puts her 15 laddoos equally into 5 boxes.

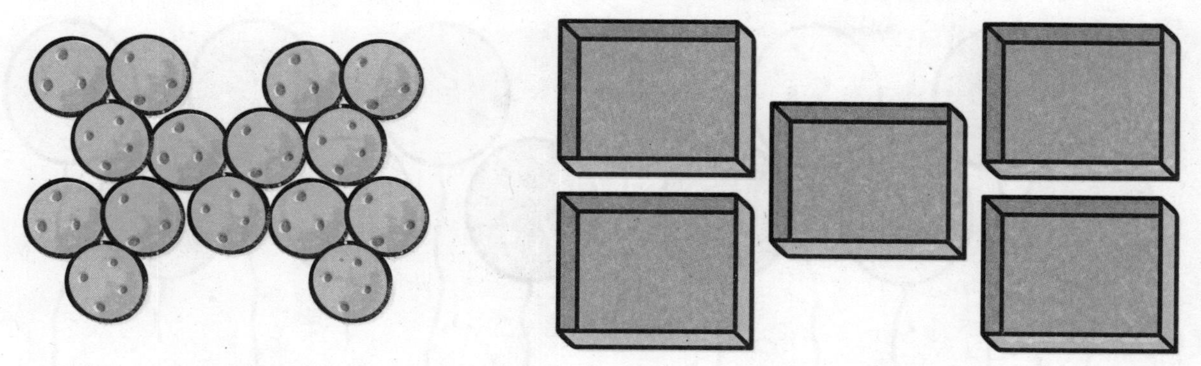

(i) How many laddoos will there be in each box?

There will be __________ laddoos in each box.

$15 \div 5 =$ _____

(ii) If she uses only 3 boxes, how many laddoos will there be in each box?

There will be __________ laddoos in each box.

_____ $\div 3 =$ _____

2. Share 25 bananas among 5 monkeys. How many bananas for each monkey?

_____ $\div 5 =$ _____

Each monkey has __________ bananas.

3. Share 12 balloons among 3 boys. How many balloons for each boy?

_____ ÷ _____ = _____

Each boy has __________ balloons.

4. There are 21 candles. Put them equally in 3 boxes. How many candles are there in each box?

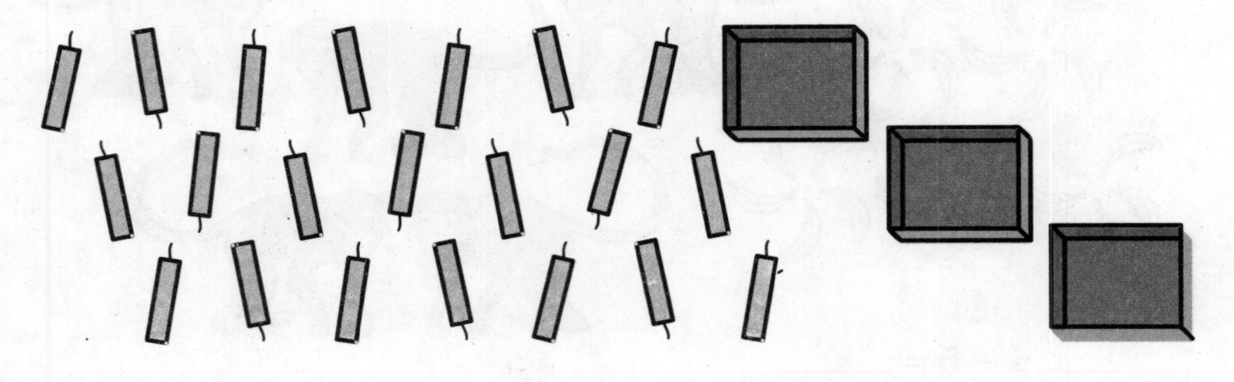

_____ ÷ _____ = _____

5. There are 18 socks.

How many girls can wear these socks?

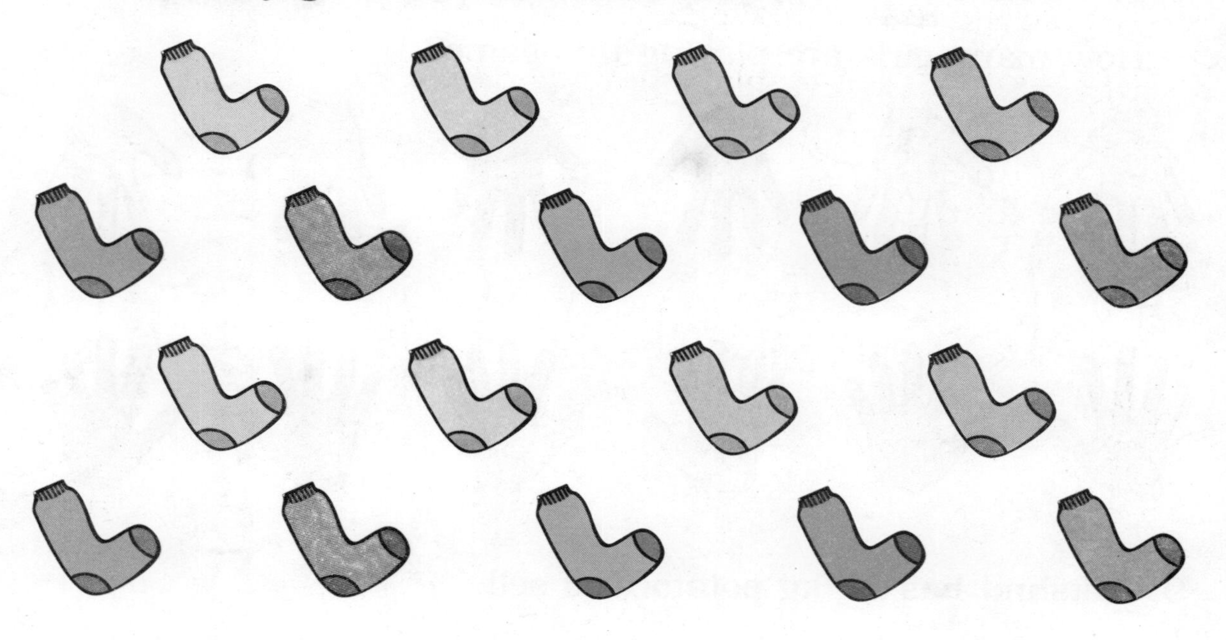

6. Raj has 36 minutes to make rotis. One roti takes 3 minutes. How many rotis can he make in this time?

He can make __________ rotis.

7. These are 24 footmarks of goats.

So how many goats were there?

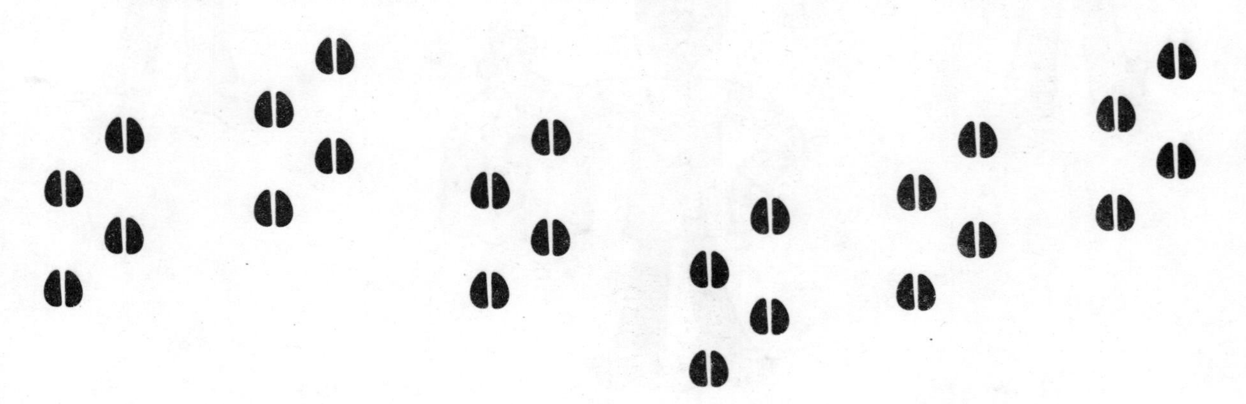

8. Some girls are playing a game with both their hands.

The girls who are playing have 60 fingers altogether.

How many girls are playing this game?

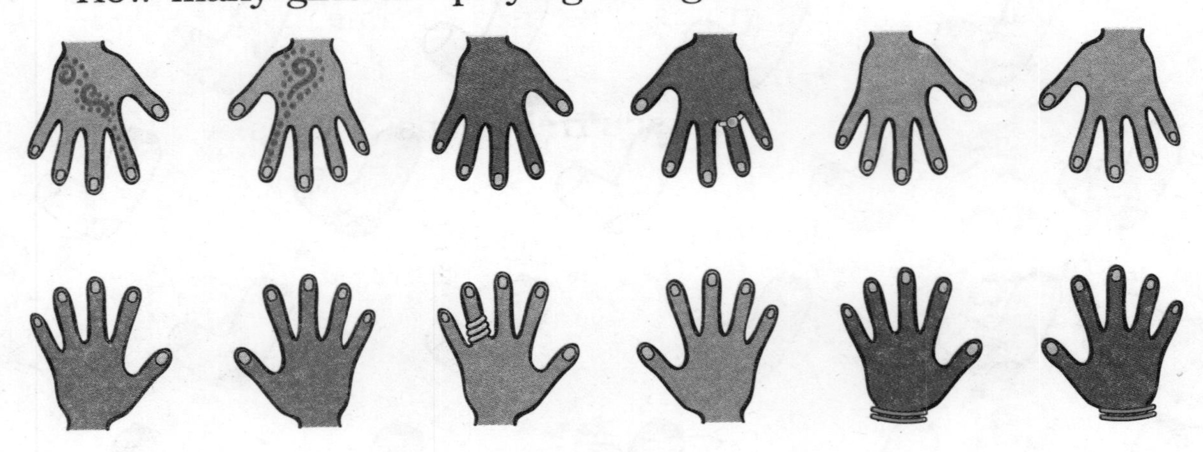

9. Lakshmi has 27 kg potatoes to sell.

Three men came and bought equal amounts of potatoes.

Each man bought _______ kg of potatoes.

Jumpy Animals

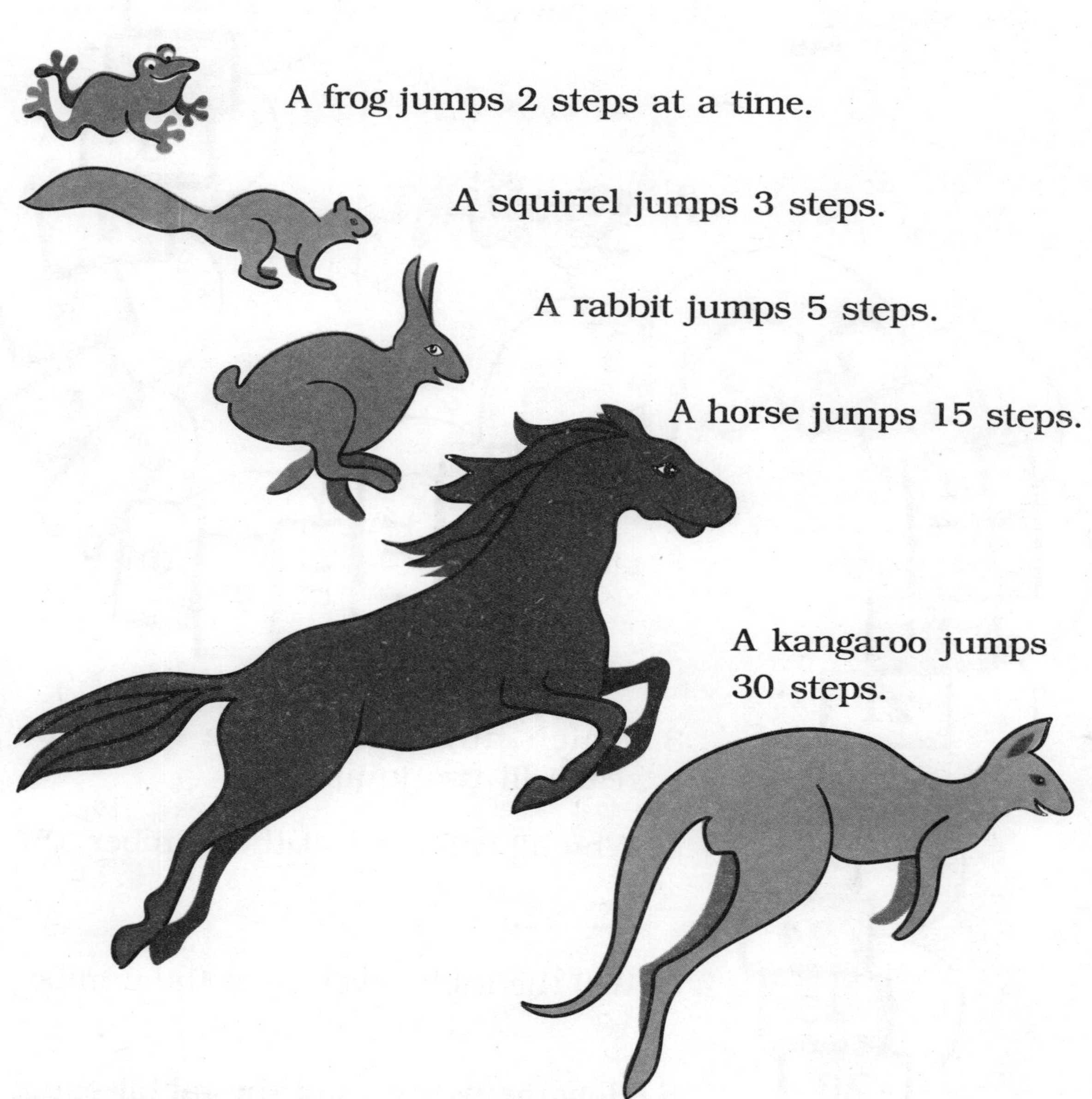

A frog jumps 2 steps at a time.

A squirrel jumps 3 steps.

A rabbit jumps 5 steps.

A horse jumps 15 steps.

A kangaroo jumps 30 steps.

Use the path on the next page to find out:

1. In how many jumps will the frog reach 30?

   $30 \div 2 =$ ______

2. In how many jumps will the squirrel reach 27?

   $27 \div 3 =$ ______

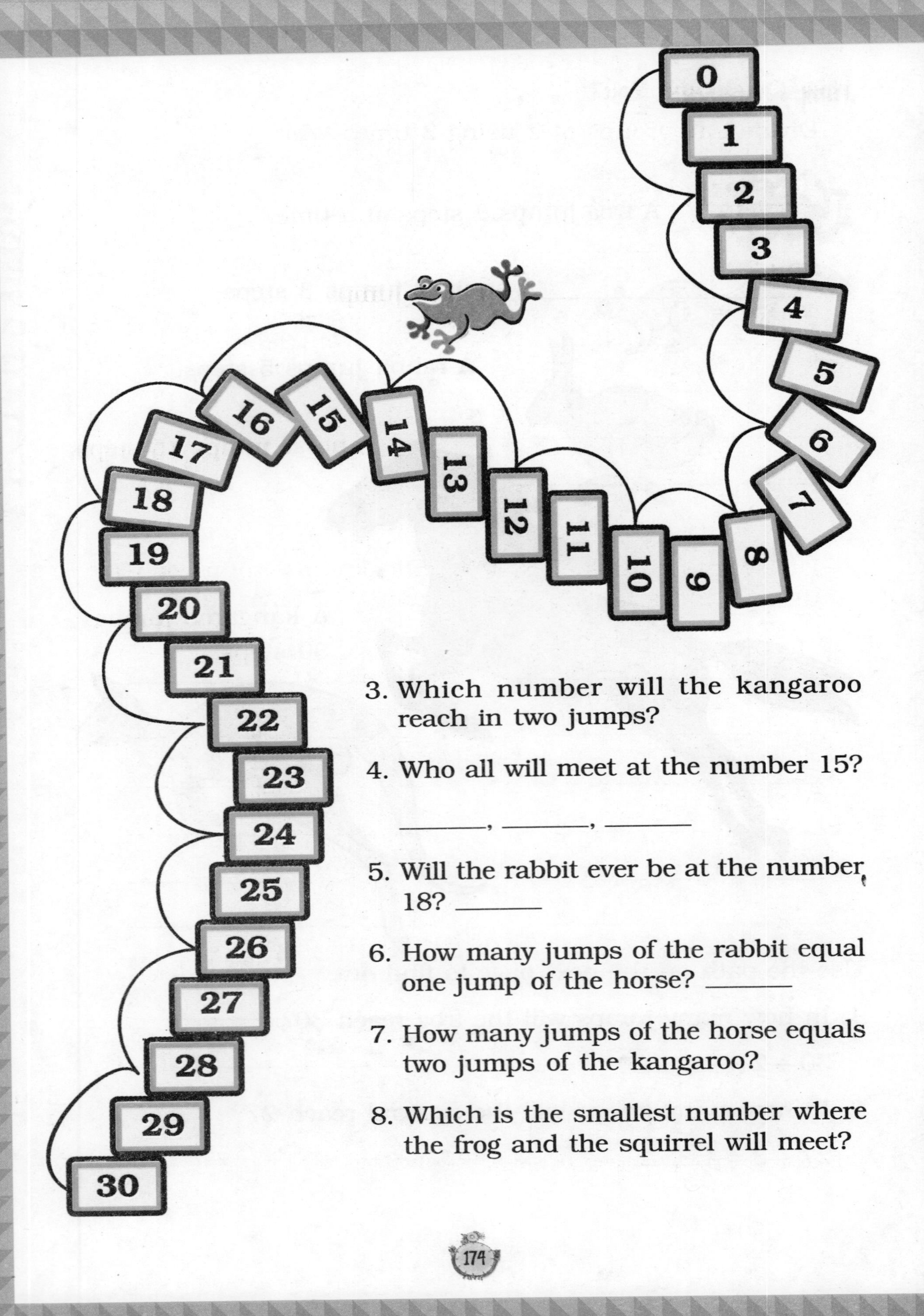

3. Which number will the kangaroo reach in two jumps?

4. Who all will meet at the number 15?

   _______, _______, _______

5. Will the rabbit ever be at the number 18? ______

6. How many jumps of the rabbit equal one jump of the horse? ______

7. How many jumps of the horse equals two jumps of the kangaroo?

8. Which is the smallest number where the frog and the squirrel will meet?

How Quick Are You?

◆ Divide into groups of 2 using 2 times table.

18 ÷ 2 =	9	Hint: 2 × 9 = 18
18 ÷ 9 =	2	
16 ÷ 2 =		
20 ÷ 2 =		
÷ 2 =	7	
÷ 2 =	10	
8 ÷ =	4	
÷ 2 =	5	

◆ Divide into groups of 5 using 5 times table.

10 ÷ 5 =		Hint: 5 × 2 = ?
20 ÷ =	4	
15 ÷ 5 =		
40 ÷ =	8	
20 ÷ 5 =		
÷ 5 =	6	
25 ÷ 5 =		
÷ 5 =	3	
35 ÷ 5 =		
÷ 5 =	2	

◆ Divide into groups of 10 using 10 times table.

20 ÷ 10 =		
30 ÷ 10 =		
40 ÷ 10 =		
50 ÷ 10 =		
40 ÷ =	4	
÷ 10 =	8	
÷ 10 =	5	
÷ 10 =	3	
÷ 10 =	2	
60 ÷ =	6	

Encourage children to explore the use of multiplication facts for division through mental computation.

◆ Try these.

4 ÷ = 2	9 ÷ 3 =
14 ÷ 7 =	18 ÷ 9 =
6 ÷ 3 =	÷ 2 = 5
÷ 2 = 7	20 ÷ 5 =
÷ 2 = 3	12 ÷ 4 =
15 ÷ 3 =	20 ÷ 4 =
8 ÷ 4 =	12 ÷ = 2
15 ÷ 5 =	
8 ÷ = 4	
÷ 2 = 8	

Puzzle

Divide the clock face into three parts so that the sum of the numbers in each part is the same.

Smart Charts!

Flowers of Different Colours

Have you been to a park?

What coloured flowers did you see?

Were most of the flowers yellow in colour?

Look at the different flowers in the picture. Complete the table:

Colour of flowers	*Number of flowers*
Blue	
Red	
Orange	
Purple	

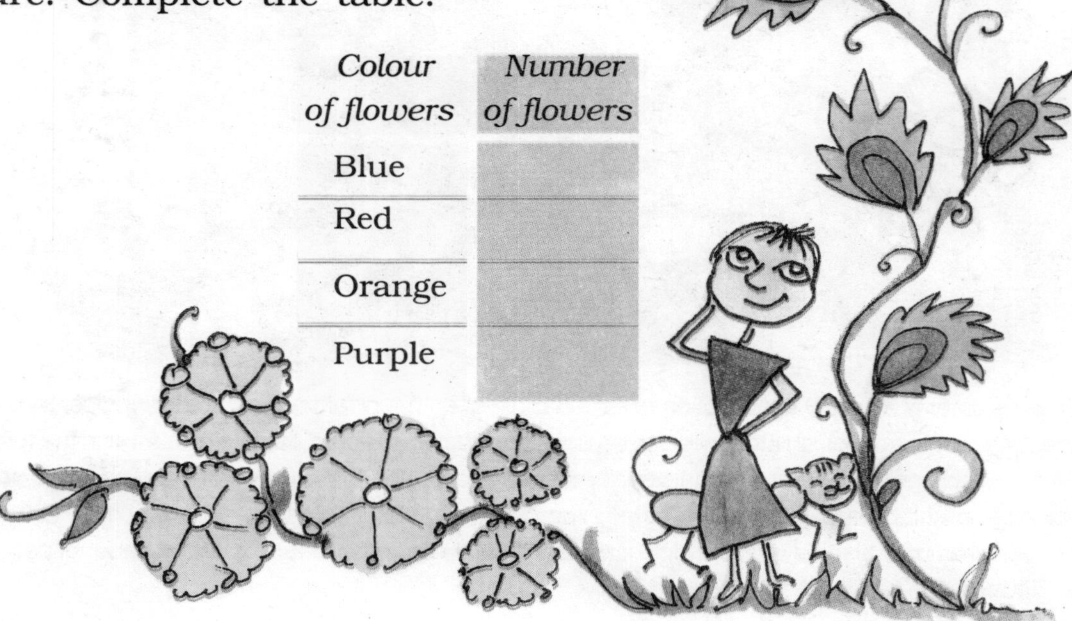

Draw the right flower. Write how many there are.

a) ________ are the most in number. How many?________.

b) ________ are the least in number. How many?________.

c) ________ are more than ________

d) ________ are more than ________

What do We See on the Road?

Look at the traffic scene in the picture and fill in the table.

This chapter is an early introduction to data handling, an important area of mathematics. By the end of primary school, children need to be able to collect and record data, to present it in the form of bar charts and tables, to recognise patterns in the data and to draw inferences. Teachers can take several interesting and even funny examples from chilldren's own experiences. Pictures given here could also be used for different classification exercises, such as the number of petals of flowers.

Way of Travel	*How many*
Walking (people)	
Bicycles	
Scooters	

Answer the following questions.

a) In the picture which way of travel do you see the most? ________

b) Which way of travel (vehicle) do you see the least? ________

c) The number of people walking is more than the number of ________

d) The number of buses is less than the number of ________

How Many Times do You Get 6?

Have you played any games with dice?

How many dots are there on the different faces of a die?

* Throw a die.
* Look at the number of dots you get on the face of your die.
* For each throw draw a mark / in front of that number in the table.
* Throw the die 30 times and mark in the table each time.

For example, Rabia threw her die 30 times. She got [3] five times. In her table she marked:

[3]	/////

Now fill in the table:

Face of the die	*Number of times (/ for each throw)*
[1]	
[2]	
[3]	
[4]	
[5]	
[6]	

a) Which face of the die did you get the most number of times?

______

b) How many times did [6] come up? ______ times

c) [4] came up more number of times than [ ]

d) Compare your table with that of the student sitting next to you. Do you find any difference in the two tables?

Find out from People Around You

1. Talk to people around you about their favourite sweets.

   Fill in the table:

Favourite sweet	*Number of people*
Jalebi	

From the above table answer the following:

a) Most favourite sweet ________________

b) Least favourite sweet ________________

c) ______________ is liked more than ______________

(Name of the sweet) (Name of the sweet)

d) ______________ is liked more than ______________

e) ______________ is liked more than ______________

f) ______________ is liked more than ______________

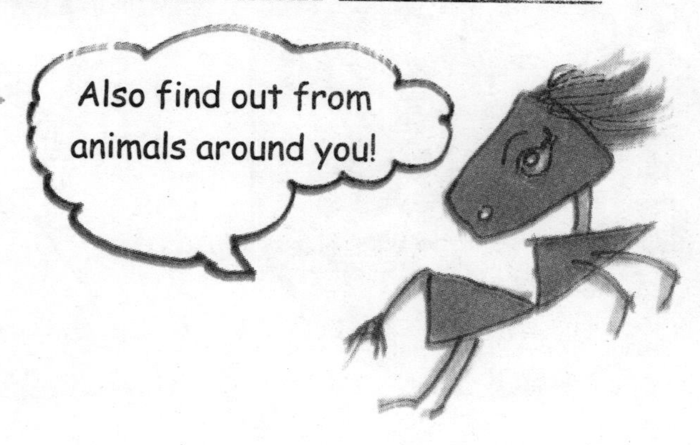

2. Ask your friends about the number of people living in their homes. Fill in the table.

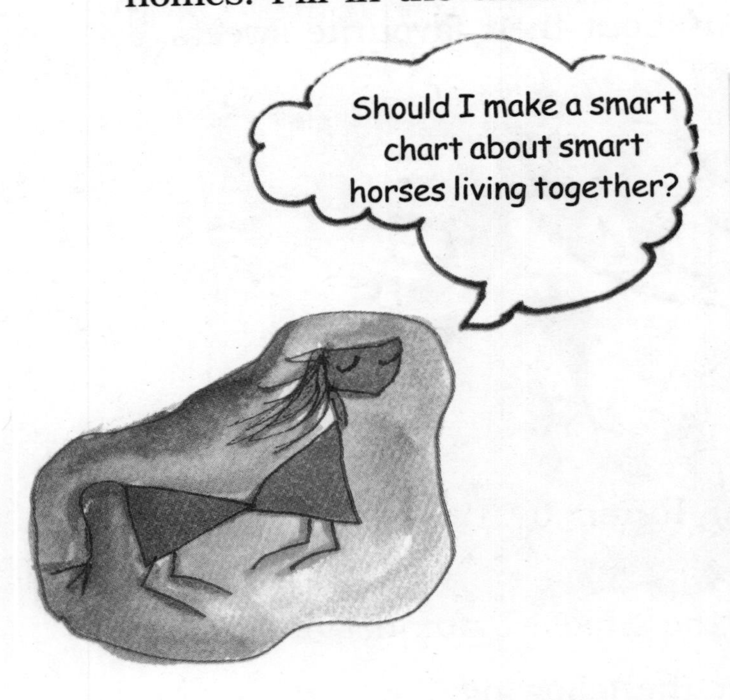

Number of people living together	*How many families*
1 alone	
2 people	
3 people	
4 people	
5 people	
6 people	
7 people	
8 people	
....	

a) Most families have __________ people living in their homes.

b) The smallest number of people living in a home is __________

c) The number of families having 4 people is __________

3. What have your classmates brought for lunch today? Find out and note down.

Food item	*Number of students*

a) Food item brought for lunch by the biggest number of students __________

b) Food item brought by the smallest number of students __________

Getting Smart with Charts

Attendance Board			
Date 8/2/2007			
Class	*Number of students*	*Students present*	*Students absent*
Class I	27	25	2
Class II	23	22	1
Class III	24	21	3
Class IV	22	18	4
Class V	25	23	2
Total			

This board shows the number of students in each class. It also shows the number of students present and absent.

* How many children in all are there in the school? ________
* How many children in all are absent on that day? ________

Absent Students' Chart

Class	*Absent students*
Class I	☺ ☺
Class II	☺
Class III	☺ ☺ ☺
Class IV	☺ ☺ ☺ ☺
Class V	

This is a chart to show the number of absent students. Each absent student is shown by ☺ .

* In the chart show the absent students of Class V.

Now look at the chart and fill in the blanks:

a) The class with the highest number of absent students is ________.

b) The class with the least number of absent students is ________.

c) The class with 3 students absent is ________.

d) The number of students absent in Class IV and Class V are ________ and ________.

How Long is Your Hand?

* Make a group of 4 friends.
* Cut strips from waste paper. The strips should be of the same width.
* Measure the length of each student's hand with the paper strip. Cut the strip and write the name of the student.

Rohan, Jacob and Geeta also measured their hands. They stuck their strips as shown.

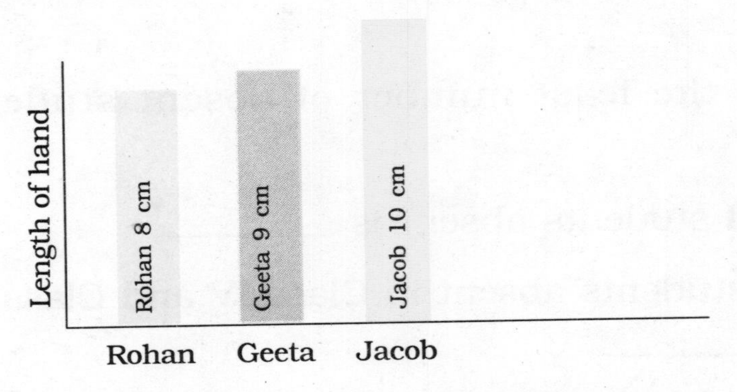

Look at the picture and fill in the blanks:

a) The length of Jacob's hand is ________ (more/less) than Geeta's hand.

b) The length of Geeta's hand is ________ (more/less) than Rohan's hand.

c) ________ has the longest hand.

d) ________ has the shortest hand.

In the chart below stick the strips of all the friends in your group. Keep some space between the strips.

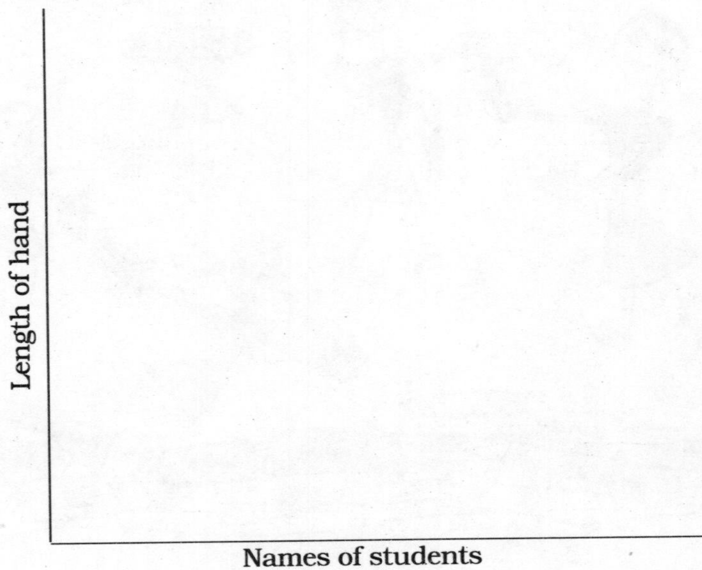

Children coming to School

Look at the picture and fill in the table.

Way of coming	Tractor				
Number of students	3				

3 students are coming by a tractor. We write 3 in the table. We also draw 3 faces on top of 'tractor' in the chart. Draw faces in the chart to show how many children come by bus, bicycle, etc.

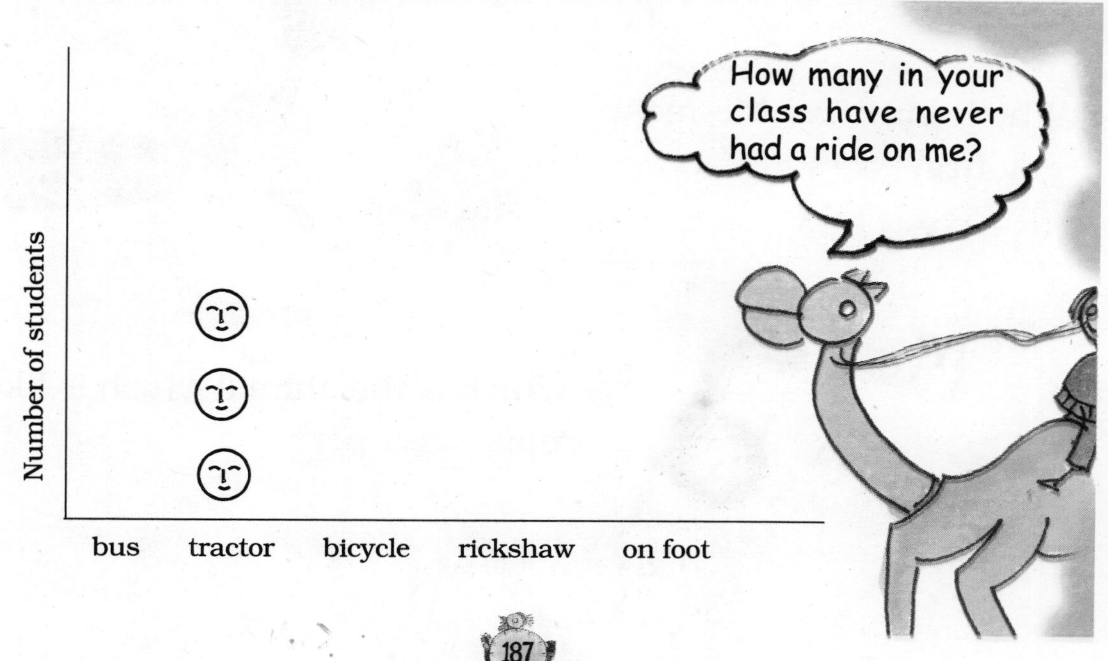

Fill in the blanks:

a) The most students come to school by ___________.

b) The number of students walking to school is ___________ (more/less) than the students coming on bicycle.

c) The least students come to school by ___________.

So, isn't this a smart chart! By simply looking at it we can know so much. Let us make more such charts.

Practice Time

Make your own smart charts about things around you.

Like —

* Which bird has the most colours?

* Which is the animal which is liked most as a pet?

A Vegetable You do not Like!

Which vegetable is most disliked? Ask your friends and complete the table.

Vegetable disliked	*Number of students*
________	________
________	________
________	________
________	________
________	________
________	________

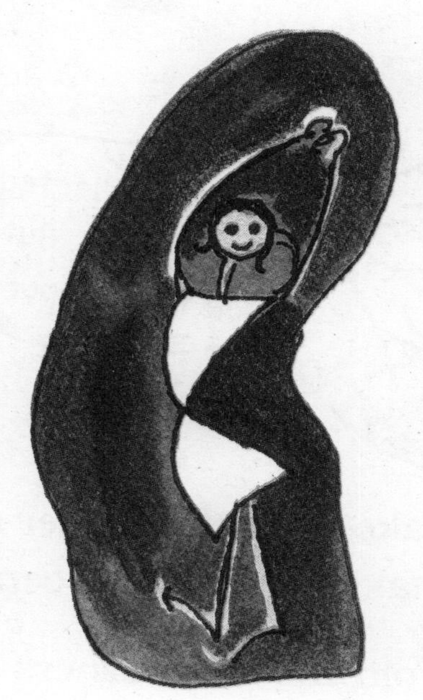

Use this table to draw faces in the chart below. Draw ☺ for each child on top of the vegetable disliked.

- The most disliked vegetable is ________.
- The vegetable disliked by very few children is ________.

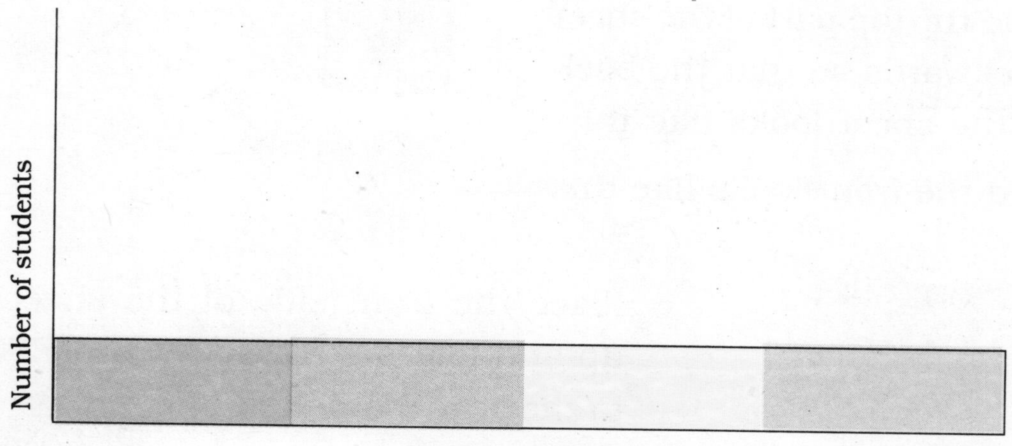

14 Rupees and Paise

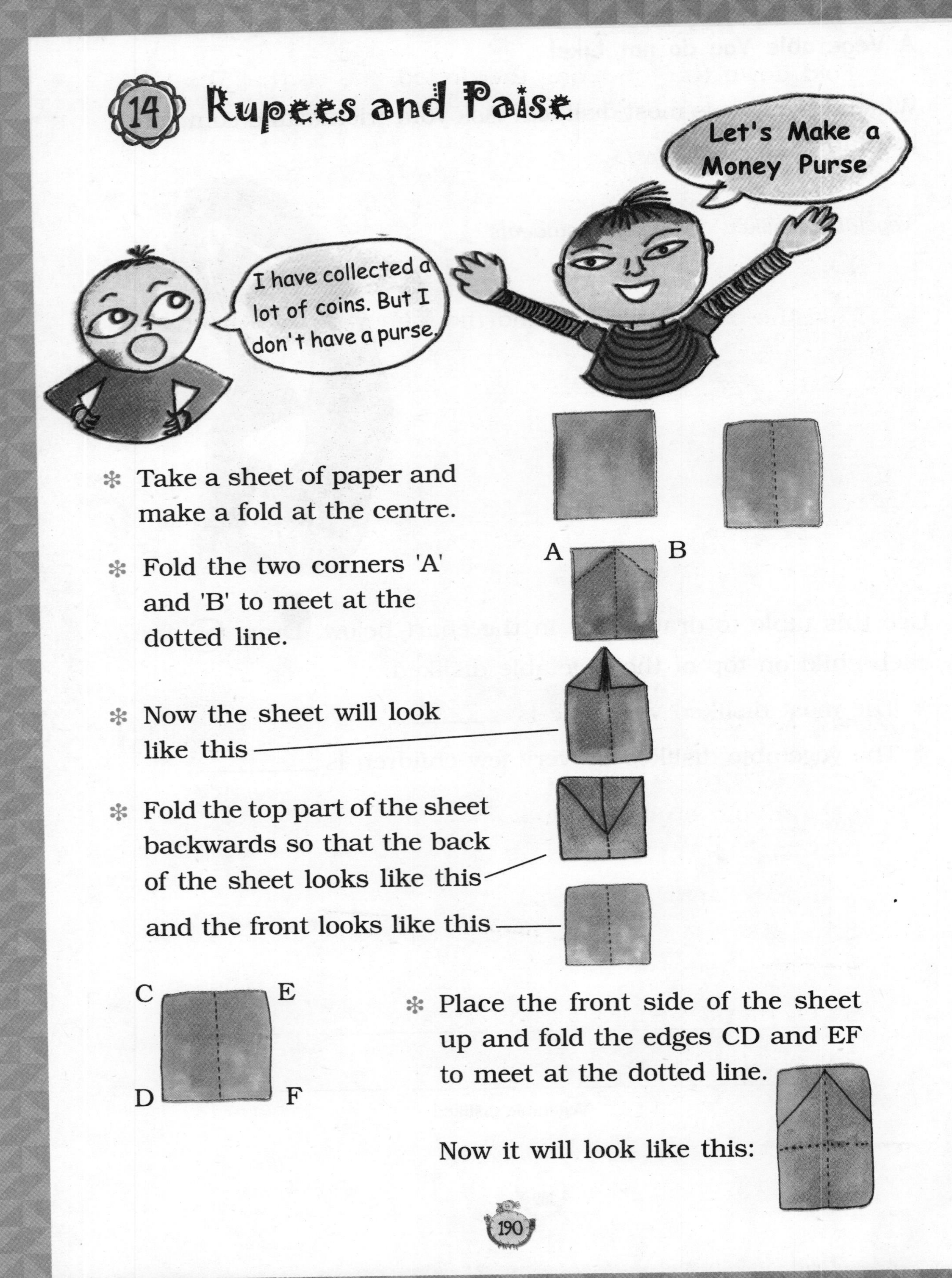

* Take a sheet of paper and make a fold at the centre.
* Fold the two corners 'A' and 'B' to meet at the dotted line.
* Now the sheet will look like this
* Fold the top part of the sheet backwards so that the back of the sheet looks like this

  and the front looks like this
* Place the front side of the sheet up and fold the edges CD and EF to meet at the dotted line.

  Now it will look like this:

* Fold down the top along the dotted line so that the figure now looks like this:

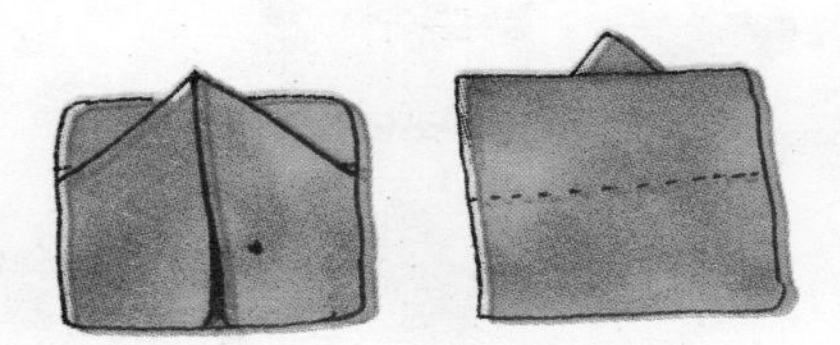

* Fold the back flap down and the money purse is ready!

Money for Our Purse

* Collect different coins.
* Keep a coin on a flat table. Place a thin paper on it.
* With one hand hold the paper tight. Rub the tip of the pencil over the paper softly to trace the coin.
* Slowly the face of the coin will appear.
* Cut out the traced coins and keep them in your purse.

Now make notes by cutting paper and writing the value of the note on each.

Money Game

★ Use notes and coins to show the following amounts of money (you can also keep some money in the purse you had made).

– Twenty-six rupees

– 4 rupees 75 paise

– 78 rupees

– 130 rupees

– 8 rupees 75 paise

– 53 rupees

Write the amounts of money shown by the notes and coins.

One hundred one rupees

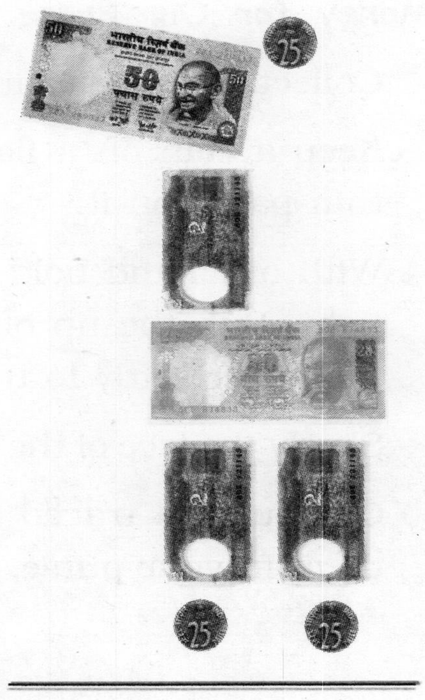

____

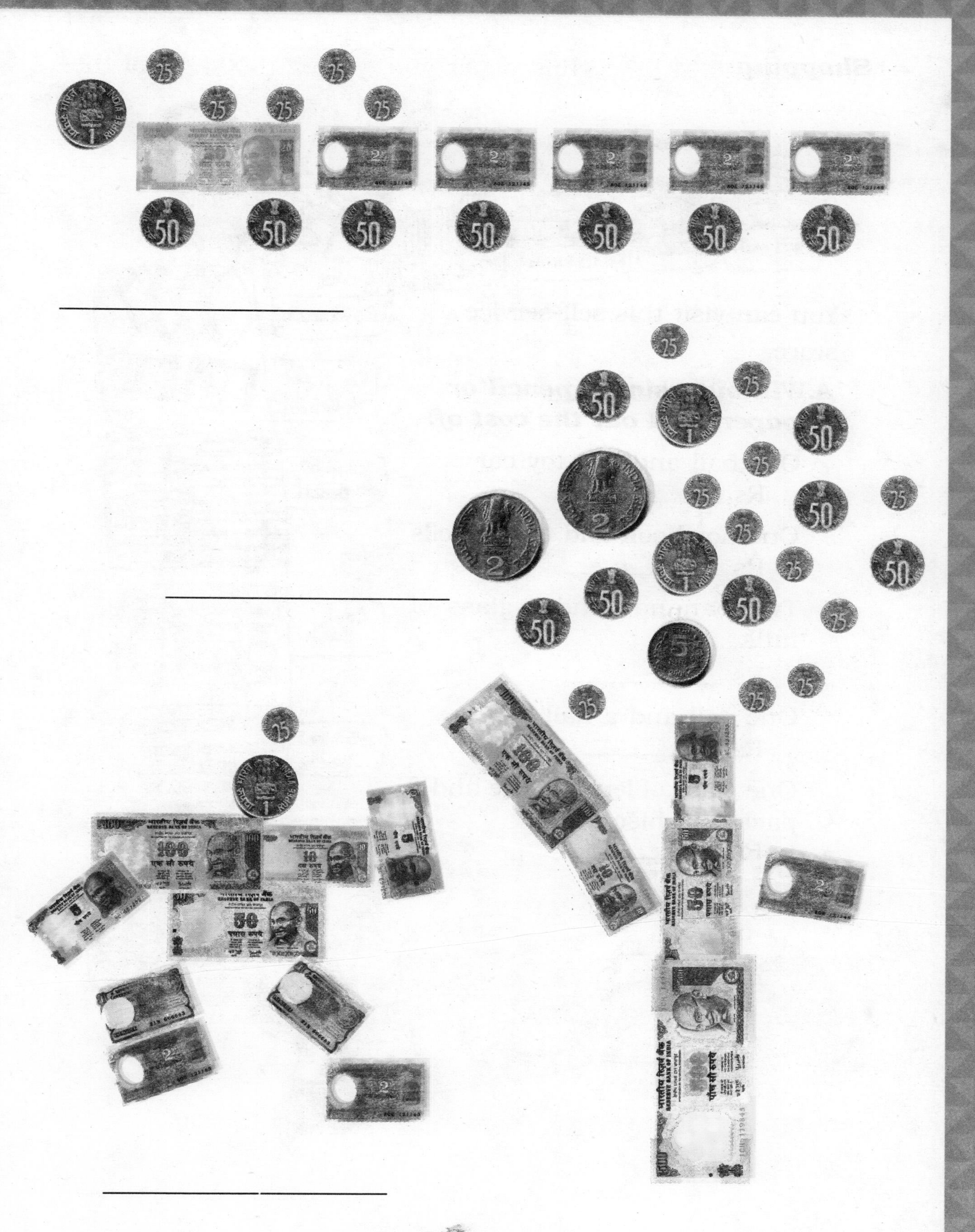

Shopping

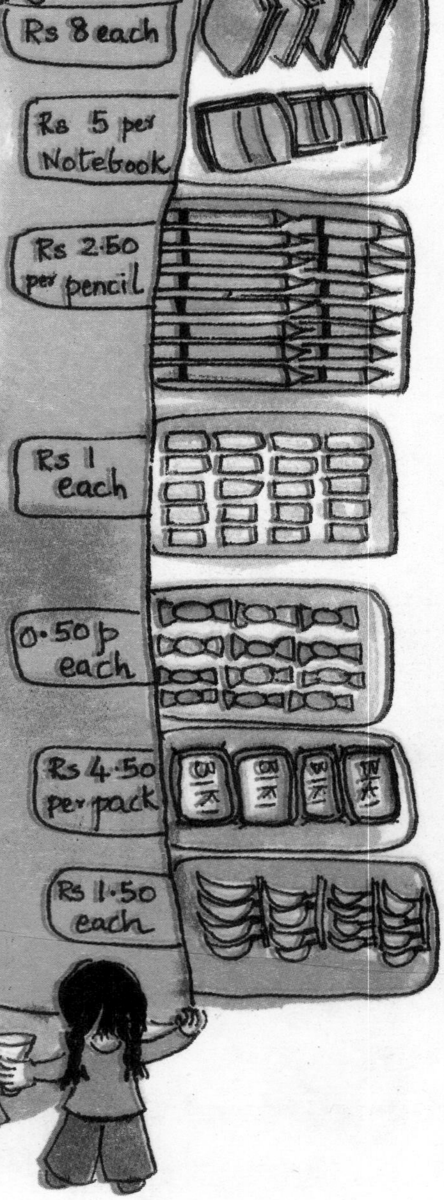

You can visit this self-service store.

A. Without using a pencil or paper, find out the cost of:

- One ball and one toy car
  Rs ___________
- One notebook and two pencils
  Rs ___________
- Two bananas and a glass of milk
  Rs ___________
- One doll and a ball
  Rs ___________
- One glass of lemon juice and a packet of biscuits
  Rs ___________

B. Find out the total cost of:

- One toy giraffe, one copy and a glass of lemon juice Rs ______
- One glass of milk, one packet of biscuits and a banana Rs ______
- One notebook, two pencils and two erasers ______
- Two tops, three toffees and two bananas ______

C. What can you buy if you have a twenty-rupee note?

- 1 toy car, 1 lemon juice, 1 banana
- ____________, ____________, ____________
- ____________, ____________, ____________
- ____________, ____________, ____________
- ____________, ____________, ____________

Cash Memo

Self Service Store

Item	Rate per Item	Rs	Paise
	Total		

D. You need to make a cash memo for the things you bought.

Before adding, first guess how much money will be needed. Then find the total and check your guess.

Monu prepared the following cash memos:

Check the cash memos and correct them if you find a mistake.

Cash Memo
Self Service Store

Item	Rate per Item	Rs	Paise
1 Ball	7	7	00
3 Pencils	2.50	7	50
5 Toffees		2	50
	Total	17	00

Cash Memo
Self Service Store

Item	Rate per Item	Rs	Paise
1 Toy car		15	00
3 Glass milk	3.50	10	00
4 Notebooks	5	20	50
	Total	45	00

Cash Memo
Self Service Store

Item	Rate per Item	Rs	Paise
1 Toy car	6.50	6	50
3 Pencils	2.50	7	50
7 Toffees	.50	3	50
1 Biscuit	4.50	4	50
	Total	21	50

* Add the following:

a) Rs 12.50
+ Rs 13.00

b) Rs 55.50
+ Rs 14.00

c) Rs 30.00
+ Rs 31.50

* Subtract the following:

a) Rs 25.50
– Rs 11.50

b) Rs 103.50
– Rs 62.00

c) Rs 19.50
– Rs 7.00

E. *You have 30 rupees with you. Find out how much money will be left after buying the following items:*

* One ball, one doll and one toy giraffe

Total cost ______. Money left ______.

* Two bananas, one pack of biscuits and two glasses of lemon juice.

Total cost ______. Money left ______.

* Three notebooks, two pencils and two erasers.

  Total cost ______. Money left ______.

Practice Time

A. Three friends wanted to buy a cricket bat and ball.

Bina had Rs 48.50, Raman had Rs 55.50 and Venu had Rs 38.00. How much money did they have in all?

B. Hari booked a railway ticket for Rs 62.50. He gave a 100-rupee note. How much money will he get back with the ticket?

C. Gita and her friends went shopping. She bought things for Rs 58, Rs 37 and Rs 22. Gita had a hundred-rupee note. How much money should she borrow from her friends to pay the bill?

D.

Mumbai News

Children Freed from Factory

10 young children working in a bangle factory were set free today. A news reporter and the police found them in a sad condition. The factory made the children work very hard. It paid them only Rs 20 a day.

The children are happy to go back to their homes in their village. They will go to a special school so that they can learn to study like other children their age. By making children work, the factory tries to save money. The police will now take action.

Let us see how much money the factory tries to save.

Money 1 older worker should get = Rs 85 a day

Money 1 child is paid = Rs 20 a day

On 1 person the factory saves Rs 85 – _____ = Rs 65 a day

On 10 persons the factory saves

Rs 65 × 10 = Rs _____ a day

Find Out

In your area are there shops or factories where young children are made to work?

Talk to some of these children.

How much are they paid there?

Understanding of 'money' need not only be about buying or selling. Teachers can talk about children's experiences of related issues, such as, wage and work etc.

Train Journey

This train goes from New Jalpaiguri to Guwahati. On its way, it stops at New Mal, Alipurduar and Goalpara stations.

The cost of a rail ticket to different stations is given in the table.

Distance from New Jalpaiguri (in km)	*Station*	*Fare (in Rs)*
57	New Mal	12.50
175	Alipurduar	28.00
366	Goalpara	49.50
495	Guwahati	62.50

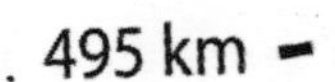

Find the distance:

a) From New Mal to Guwahati ____________

b) Between New Mal and Goalpara ____________

c) From Alipurduar to Guwahati ____________

d) Between New Mal and Alipurduar ____________

e) From Goalpara to Guwahati ____________

Find the cost of tickets:

a) Bhupen is going from New Jalpaiguri to Alipurduar. What is the cost of his ticket?

b) Indira has to go from New Jalpaiguri to Goalpara. How much does she pay for the ticket?

c) Debu, Shoma and Gobind are going from New Jalpaiguri to New Mal. What amount will they pay for three tickets?

They give a Rs 50 note for the tickets. How much money will they get back?

A Page to Cut Out

5-piece tangram (p 66)

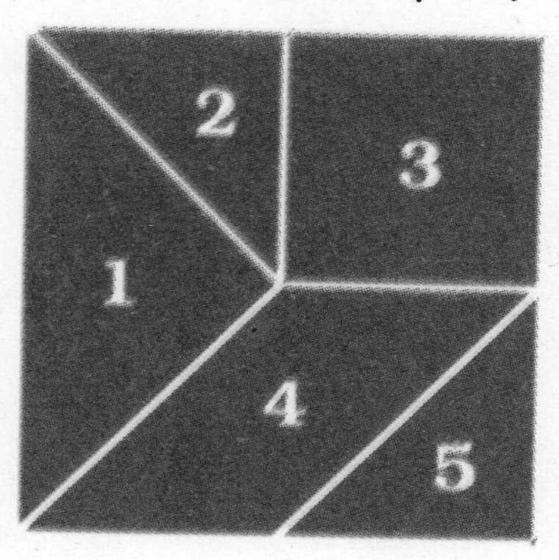

7-piece tangram (p 67)

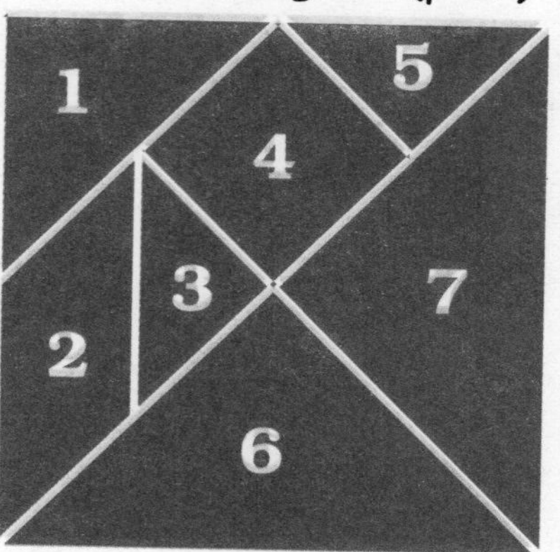

Cut these tiles and paste on a card. Make as many copies as you want and cover the floor.

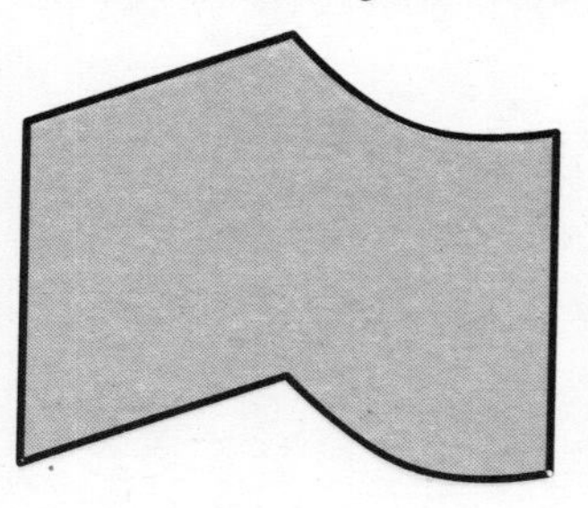

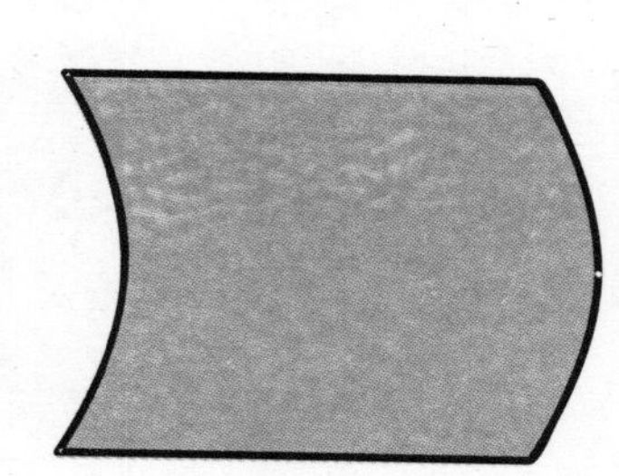

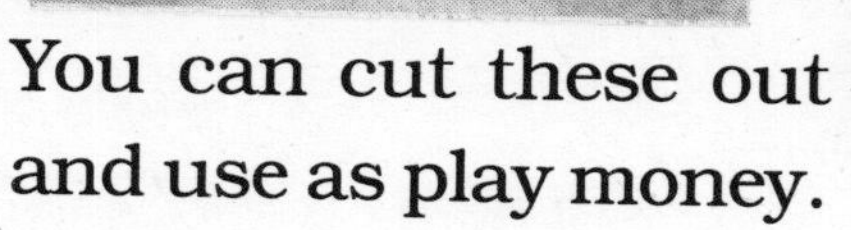

You can cut these out and use as play money.